Sports Performance Measurement and Analytics

The Science of Assessing Performance,

Predicting Future Outcomes,

Interpreting Statistical Models,

and Evaluating the Market Value of Athletes

LORENA MARTIN

Publisher: Paul Boger
Editor-in-Chief: Amy Neidlinger
Executive Editor: Jeanne Glasser Levine
Cover Designer: Alan Clements
Managing Editor: Kristy Hart
Project Editor: Andy Beaster
Manufacturing Buyer: Dan Uhrig
Consulting Editor: Thomas W. Miller

©2016 by Lorena Martin
Published by Pearson Education, Inc.
Old Tappan, New Jersey 07675

For information about buying this title in bulk quantities, or for special sales opportunities (which may include electronic versions; custom cover designs; and content particular to your business, training goals, marketing focus, or branding interests), please contact our corporate sales department at corpsales@pearsoned.com or (800) 382-3419.

For government sales inquiries, please contact governmentsales@pearsoned.com.

For questions about sales outside the U.S., please contact international@pearsoned.com.

Company and product names mentioned herein are the trademarks or registered trademarks of their respective owners.

Printed in the United States of America

First Printing February 2016

ISBN-10: 0-13-419330-X
ISBN-13: 978-0-13-419330-4

Pearson Education LTD.
Pearson Education Australia PTY, Limited.
Pearson Education Singapore, Pte. Ltd.
Pearson Education Asia, Ltd.
Pearson Education Canada, Ltd.
Pearson Educación de Mexico, S.A. de C.V.
Pearson Education—Japan
Pearson Education Malaysia, Pte. Ltd.
Library of Congress Control Number: 2015958702

Contents

Preface

"Impossible is just a big word thrown around by small men who find it easier to live in the world they've been given than to explore the power they have to change it. Impossible is not a fact. It's an opinion. Impossible is not a declaration. It's a dare. Impossible is potential. Impossible is temporary. Impossible is nothing."

—Muhammad Ali

I have played sports my entire life. I began playing the sport of tennis at the age of thirteen, too late in the eyes of many tennis experts to become a top professional tennis player. I trained six hours a day from the first day that I won a match against a boy at a neighborhood tennis court. In an instant, I was addicted to the sport.

I dreamed of becoming a professional tennis player. I spent countless hours on the court, skipping hangouts, holidays, and dates just to hit tennis balls. I went on to play high school and college tennis. I dropped out of college to play professional tennis. I worked for an airline so I could travel inexpensively to compete in professional tennis tournaments around the world. Tournaments were (and still are) scattered across the globe, giving a person of lower socioeconomic status a very slim chance of making it. Through my tennis training and competition, I reached a Florida state ranking of number three and a top 200 women's professional ranking in the USA.

As an undergraduate, I majored in psychology. I wanted to learn about the psychological and behavioral profiles of successful professional athletes. I went on to get a master's degree in psychology.

After studying psychology, I wanted to obtain a deeper understanding of the importance of physiology and physical fitness variables in sports, such as muscular strength, power, endurance, anaerobic power, cardiorespiratory endurance, and flexibility. I felt it was essential to learn as much as possible about the processes going on inside an elite athlete's mind and body. I earned a doctorate in exercise physiology from the University of Miami and was recruited to conduct postdoctoral research in behavioral medicine at the University of California, San Diego.

I have always been driven to learn about statistics, about what is and is not being said by the numbers. I wanted to see which variables could be used to predict sport performance and to answer a simple question: "What are the qualities a person must have to become a world class athlete?" This question and many more may be answered through research, measurement, statistics, and analytics.

I went on to teach research methods and statistical design at Florida International University. Later I joined Northwestern University, where I currently teach introduction to statistical analysis as well as sports performance analytics.

As a teacher of sports performance analytics, I tried to find a book that encompassed sports-relevant anatomy and physiology and described athletic performance measures. I wanted a book that included statistical analyses and models used in various individual and team sports, along with statistics adopted by the sports industry. But I found no such book.

I chose to write this book to give athletes, coaches, and managers a better understanding of measurement and analytics as they relate to sport performance. To develop accurate measures, we need to know what we want to measure and why. This book provides new insights into constructs and variables that have often been neglected in sports to this day. It also reviews fundamentals of sports anatomy and physiology, sport measurement, and performance analytics.

This book serves many readers. People involved with sports, including players, coaches, and trainers, will gain an appreciation for performance measures and analytics. People involved with analytics will gain new insights into sports performance and see what it takes to become a competitive athlete. And students eager to learn about sports analytics will have a practical introduction to the field. Data sets and programs in the book are available from the book's website `http://www.ftpress.com/martin/`.

Many thanks to Thomas W. Miller, my consulting editor, for making this book happen, as it would not have been possible to complete without him. And special thanks go to my editor, Jeanne Glasser Levine, and publisher, Pearson/FT Press, for giving me the opportunity to publish my first book. Of course, any writing issues, errors, or items of unfinished business are my responsibility alone.

I want to give a special thank you to my brother and professional tennis player, Juan J. Martin Jr., who constantly provides me with insightful information based on his experience in professional sports and exercise physiology. I would also like to thank the Dallas Cowboys' Director of Football Research, Tom Robinson, for his instrumental remarks and comments. Thanks to Roy Sanford, a lead faculty member in Northwestern University's Master's Program in Predictive Analytics, who provided constructive critiques on statistical methods. I want to thank my mother, Estela Martin, for being there day and night and offering continued support. *Tambien, gracias a mi padre,* Juan J. Martin Sr., for providing me with a sports-like motivation, impelling me to complete this book. In addition, I would like to mention my dogs, which are always there for me and brought a smile to my face while working on this book.

Most of all, I want to thank God for making this possible.

Lorena Martin
San Diego, California
December 2015

Figures

Tables

Exhibits

1

Anatomy and Physiology

"A muscle is like a car. If you want it to run well early in the morning, you have to warm it up."

—FLORENCE GRIFFITH JOYNER

Understanding the basics of anatomy and physiology is fundamental to obtaining a more comprehensive knowledge of what it means to be an athlete. Let us start by answering the question, "What is an athlete?" We can think of an athlete as a person who is skilled at a sport, trains, and possesses physical attributes such as muscular strength, power, endurance, speed, and agility, to name a few.

The physical attributes and variables of an athlete will be detailed and explained in chapter 2. This chapter focuses on the fundamental anatomy and physiology of an athlete. The objective of this chapter is to help the sports data analyst, as well as athletes themselves, understand the human body and how its machinery functions during athletic events in order to comprehend how performance is affected by physiology. This chapter will open your eyes to new ways of thinking about number crunching and sports analytics. Knowledge of the main physiological mechanisms will make you a more competitive and insightful sports data scientist.

Table 1.1. *Types of Bones*

Type of Bone	Example of Bone
Long bones	Femur, Humerus, Tibia
Short bones	Tarsals of the foot, Carpals of the hand and wrist
Flat bones	Scapula, Sternum, Cranium
Irregular bones	Vertebrae, Sacrum, Mandible
Sesamoid bones	Knee Cap, there are four sesamoid bones in the hand, there are two sesamoid bones in the foot

Let us review the basic bone structure and anatomical information you should be aware of. The human body is made up of 206 bones and more than 430 skeletal muscles. The topic of anatomy alone could take several books to do it justice. We will cover the part of human anatomy and physiology most relevant to sports performance.

The study of bones is called osteology. Osteologists dedicate their lives to understanding how bones function. Bones are responsible for providing constant renewal of red and white blood cells, and are vital not only to our organs, but to gaining a competitive edge in sports performance. There are several types of bones: long bones, short bones, flat bones, irregular bones, and sesamoid bones. Long bones are associated with greater movement due to the lever length, compared to short bones which have limited mobility, but are known to be stronger. Please refer to table 1.1 for examples of each type of bone.

The musculoskeletal system is integral to human movement, as it is comprised of ligaments that connect bone to bone and tendons that connect muscles to bone. Consequently, when the muscle pulls on the bone, motion occurs. Depending on the method of classification or grouping, estimates of the number of muscles in the body range between 430 to over 900. In fact, each skeletal muscle is considered an organ that contains muscle tissue, connective tissue, nerves, and blood vessels. Much of the debate is a matter of definition in terms of how the muscles are quantified.

Like bones, muscles may be classified by type: smooth muscle is found in the blood vessels and organs, cardiac muscle is found in the heart, and skeletal muscle is abundant throughout the human body and is responsible for our daily movement.

Upper body muscles and muscle groups to become familiar with include the latissimus dorsi, trapezius, deltoids, rotator cuff, pectorals, biceps, triceps, and brachioradialis. Midsection muscles involved in sports performance include the rectus abdominus, external and internal obliques, and the transversus abdominis. Lower body muscles vital for many sports include the quadriceps, hamstrings, gluteus (maximus, minimus, medius), gastrocnemius, and the soleus. Please refer to table 1.2 for the locations of these muscles and their function in sports.

Many of you have heard of fast twitch and slow twitch muscle fibers. Most people are only aware of two fiber types, fast and slow, or white and red. However, it is much more accurate to say that there are hybrid fiber types that lie within the spectrum of Type I and Type II muscle fibers. More recently, the scientific field revealed three distinct categories of muscle fibers. These are Type I, Type IIa, and Type IIx muscle fibers. Type I fibers are commonly referred to as slow-twitch while both Type IIa and Type IIx are recognized as fast-twitch muscle fibers.

To facilitate understanding, we will focus on the differences between Type I and Type II because they are inherently different as they relate to the following characteristics: ability to utilize oxygen and glycogen as determined by aerobic enzyme content, myoglobin content, capillary density, and mitochondria size and density.

Typically, slow-twitch muscle fibers tend to be high in all the criteria mentioned above. In comparison, fast-twitch muscle fibers tend to be low in these characteristics, while having greater nerve conduction velocity, speed of muscle contractility, anaerobic enzyme content, and power output. Fast twitch fibers are known to have high glycolytic activity, meaning they utilize glycogen (the storage form of glucose, which many call sugar) at high levels, whereas slow-twitch muscle fibers rely on their oxidative capacity. Please refer to table 1.3 for additional muscle fiber type characteristics.

Table 1.2. Muscles in Sport

Name of Muscle	Location of Muscle	Function in Sport
Upper Body Muscles		
Latissimus dorsi	located in the posterior part of the body, largest muscle group in the upper body, also called the back	involved in extension and adduction of the shoulder as well as pulling motions; relevant for all sports
Rhomboids	located in the upper back underneath the trapezius and consists of two muscles; rhomboid major and minor	involved in retraction of shoulder blades relevant for all sports
Trapezius	located above and superficial to rhomboids extends from shoulders to neck muscles	involved in distributing loads away from the neck and keeping the shoulders stabilized
Deltoids	commonly referred to as the shoulders	involved in throwing motions used extensively in overhead athletes
Rotator Cuff	located in the shoulder area deep under the deltoids, muscles that hold the shoulder in place	involved in throwing motions; quarterbacks, pitchers, and tennis players when serving
Pectorals	commonly referred to as the chest includes pectoralis major and minor	involved in chest press strength, and abduction of the shoulder and pushing movements
Biceps	located in anterior part of the arm and called biceps because of the two heads of the muscle	involved in swinging motion; tennis players forehand and baseball swings; also involved in bending of the elbow and for picking up motions
Triceps	located in posterior part of the arm and called triceps because of the three heads of the muscle	extension of elbow; used to straighten the elbow; used in stiff-arm movement in football players
Brachioradialis and Pronator Teres	forearm muscles	utilized in sports using the wrist
Core and Midsection Muscles		
Rectus Abdominus	located in the anterior part of the body under the abdomen	utilized for flexion of the spine and core stabilization; relevant for all sports
External Obliques	located above and superficial to the internal obliques on each side of the trunk	utilized for sideways bending and rotation of the torso; integral for tennis strokes
Internal Obliques	located underneath the external abdominal oblique on each side of the trunk	utilized for flexion of the spine, sideways bending, trunk rotation and compression of the abdomen; relevant for all sports
Transversus Abdominis	located in the deepest layer of abdominal muscles that wraps around the torso	utilized for respiration and core stabilization; relevant for all sports
Lower Body Muscles		
Quadriceps	located in anterior part of thigh consisting of four muscles	responsible for extension of the knee; major source of strength for soccer players; relevant for all sports
Hamstrings	located in posterior part of thigh consisting of three muscles	responsible for flexion and bending of the knee; relevant for all sports
Gluteus Maximus, Gluteus Medius, and Gluteus Minimus	located in the area usually called the buttocks	utilized in explosive first step movements; integral for lower body strength and power
Gastrocnemius	located in the lower leg area and typically referred to as part of the calf muscle	utilized in jumping and tip-toe motions including being on the ball of your feet
Soleus	located in the lower leg area and typically referred to as part of the calf muscle	utilized in jumping and tip-toe motions including being on the ball of your feet

Table 1.3. *Characteristics of Fiber Types*

Characteristics	Type I	Type IIa	Type IIx
Motor neuron size	Small	Large	Large
Nerve conduction velocity	Slow	Fast	Fast
Contraction speed	Slow	Fast	Fast
Relaxation speed	Slow	Fast	Fast
Fatigue resistance	High	Intermediate/Low	Low
Force production	Low	Intermediate	High
Power output	Low	Intermediate/High	High
Endurance	High	Intermediate/Low	Low
Aerobic enzyme content	High	Intermediate/Low	Low
Anaerobic enzyme content	Low	High	High
Capillary density	High	Intermediate	Low
Myoglobin content	High	Low	Low
Mitochondria size/density	High	Intermediate	Low
Fiber diameter	Small	Intermediate	Large
Color	Red	White/Red	White

Adapted from Baechle and Earle (2008).

Table 1.4. *Muscle Fiber Types and Sports*

Sport	Type I Contribution	Type II Contribution
100 meter sprint	Low	High
800 meter sprint	High	High
Marathon	High	Low
Soccer	High	High
American Football Wide Receiver and Linemen	Low	High
Basketball	Low	High
Baseball Pitcher	Low	High
Tennis	High	High

Adapted from Baechle and Earle (2008).

It is evident that anatomy and physiology play a major role in sports performance. A sprinter may benefit from a greater number of fast twitch muscle fibers, whereas a long-distance runner will benefit much more from having a greater distribution of slow twitch muscle fibers. Refer to table 1.4 for Type I and Type II muscle fiber contribution in a variety of sports.

In addition to the controversy over the number of muscle fiber types, there also remains the question of whether one can train and modify one's own fiber type through conditioning. Several animal studies have shown that enzymes that would otherwise be dormant are activated through physical training, implying that there is a possibility of changing the fiber type to a certain degree.

Now that we have the basics of the skeletal and muscular system, let us consider the physiology of sports performance. First, we must realize that human metabolism includes both anabolic and catabolic processes that are ongoing in our bodies. Anabolic processes involve the synthesis of larger molecules from smaller molecules. Conversely, catabolic processes involve the breakdown of larger molecules into smaller ones, and are associated with the release of energy. Energy released in a biological reaction is quantified by the amount of heat that is generated. The amount of heat required to raise one kilogram of water one degree Celsius is called a kilocalorie. This corresponds to the energy found in food that is broken down within our bodies and stored in the form of adenosine triphosphate (ATP).

In the body, energy systems are responsible for providing the ATP (energy) that is utilized under varying intensities and durations of sport performance. There are three main energy systems at play during sports performance. They are the phosphagen (ATP-PCr) system, the glycolytic system, and the oxidative phosphorylation system. All three systems are constantly at work and interacting with each other, functioning on some level as they are not "all or nothing" systems. The predominance of one system is largely determined by the intensity and duration of the sporting activity, as well as the substrate (food source) that the athlete has consumed. Substrate utilization is a fancy term for the food that is being consumed by the athlete. Correspondingly, these three energy systems are also sometimes referred to as bioenergetics systems.

The athlete's ability to perform is based on his or her muscles' capacity to function and depends on the oxygen or glucose (substrate) availability. What does this mean? Well, if an athlete is sprinting, muscles within the body do not necessarily have the time required to be able to utilize oxygen, as a body at rest does. This causes the body to shift into an anaerobic state in which it can extract energy in the form of ATP, without the use of oxygen. However, when the human machine is running at a slower pace, the standard metabolic processes that utilize oxygen are allowed to occur in the mitochondria (the engine of the cell). Some might say that the human body is inherently intelligent and can be compared to a computer, in that after the program is built and algorithm established, it knows what to do on its own.

To simplify, the three energy systems will be referred to as the phosphagen, glycolytic, and oxidative systems. These systems produce ATP and replenish ATP stores within the human body. The body naturally stores ATP sufficient for basic cellular functions, not the amount necessary for sports. The phosphagen system utilizes an enzyme, creatine kinase, to maintain ATP levels during intense, explosive movements of short duration, allowing for the release of one mole of ATP or the equivalent of 0.6 kilocalories. The phosphagen system is heavily involved in sports that consist of high intensity, short-term explosive movements. This system is used in all sports at the point of initiation of activity—at the shift from sedentary to active.

Table 1.5. *Rate/Capacity of Adenosine Triphosphate (ATP)*

Energy System	Rate of ATP production	Capacity of ATP production
Phosphagen	1	5
Fast Glycolysis	2	4
Slow Glycolysis	3	3
Oxidation of Carbohydrates	4	2
Oxidation of Fats and Proteins	5	1

Note: 1 = fastest/greatest; 5 = slowest/least

Adapted from Baechle and Earle (2008).

The glycolytic system is responsible for controlling glycolysis (breakdown of glycogen) for energy production, as well as the onset of lactate formation. Glycolysis is the term for the processes that break down glycogen stored in the muscles to glucose, ultimately yielding ATP. Remarkably, intensity and duration of the sport also dictates the type of glycolysis that occurs. There are two possible pathways: The shorter path, termed anaerobic (fast) glycolysis, consists of fewer steps that lead to lactate; the other path, aerobic (slow) glycolysis, has a longer trajectory and yields two to three moles of ATP or the equivalent of 1.2 to 1.8 kilocalories. Aerobic glycolysis is a slower process. It requires sufficient quantities of oxygen to operate, compared to anaerobic glycolysis which can function with limited amounts of oxygen.

Finally, the oxidative system is responsible for breaking down glycogen, fat, and protein. It is also responsible for producing ATP when the body is at rest or during long lasting, low intensity sporting activities. It is a commonly held belief that when training at low intensity, the body utilizes more fat than other sources (carbohydrates or protein) of energy. This concept is the result of a simplified interpretation of this third system.

The oxidative system's primary source of fuel is fat, since it initiates the release of triglycerides from fat cells. This leads to the roaming of free fatty acids in the blood, which are transported to the muscle fibers for oxidation (burned for energy). The breakdown of fat to glucose is called lipolysis and yields between thirty-six to forty moles of ATP or the equivalent of 21.6 to 24 kilocalories.

Additionally, this system is able to oxidize protein, however, protein is not its favored source of fuel. The mechanism of breaking down protein into energy is less than efficient. Proteolysis requires several steps to break down protein into amino acids, and eventually converts the products to glucose through another process called gluconeogenesis. A greater span of time is needed to synthesize ATP. Therefore, fat and carbohydrate are the preferred fuels for sport, because they yield energy at a much faster rate over longer periods. Please refer to table 1.5 for the rate and capacity of ATP production for each energy system.

The athlete's predominant energy system differs not only by sport, but also by player position or style of play within a particular sport. For instance, when a tennis player sprints to hit a forehand, a basketball player jumps explosively to slam dunk, a baseball player sprints to get on base, a quarterback throws the football, or a striker shoots to score a goal, their bodies are using the phosphagen system as the primary energy mechanism. If, on the other hand, a wide receiver is sprinting down the field for more than six seconds, his body has shifted from using the phosphagen system to a hybrid state consisting of both the phosphagen and glycolytic (anaerobic glycolysis) systems.

A soccer midfielder running non-stop, back and forth at a fast pace for the duration of one to two minutes is in a true state of anaerobic glycolysis. If the soccer player were to continue running for a longer period of time, ranging from two to three minutes, they are likely to be in a hybrid state of fast glycolysis and oxidative phosphorylation. Finally, a long distance runner who runs for prolonged periods of time at a slower rate is using the oxidative system as the primary mechanism for producing ATP. Refer to table 1.6 for the ranges of intensity and duration typical of each energy system.

In summary, the phosphagen energy system primarily supplies ATP for high-intensity activities of short duration. The glycolytic system is associated with moderate- to high-intensity activities of short to medium duration. And the oxidative system is the primary system at work during low-intensity activities of long duration.

Table 1.6. *Primary Energy System Duration and Intensity*

Duration	Intensity	Primary Energy System
0-6 seconds	Extremely High	Phosphagen
6-30 seconds	Very High	Phosphagen and Fast Glycolysis
30 seconds to 2 minutes	High	Fast Glycolysis
2-3 minutes	Moderate	Fast Glycolysis and Oxidative System
>3 minutes	Low	Oxidative System

Adapted from Baechle and Earle (2008).

Table 1.7. *Limiting Factors for Energy Systems*

Degree of Exercise	ATP and Creatine Phosphate	Muscle Glycogen	Liver Glycogen	Fat Stores	Lower pH
Light (Marathon)	1	5	4-5	2-3	1
Moderate (1,500 m run)	1-2	3	2	1-2	2-3
Heavy (400 m run)	3	3	1	1	4-5
Very intense (discus)	2-3	1	1	1	1
Very intense and Repetitive Motions	4-5	4-5	1-2	1-2	4-5

Note: 1 = Least Probable Limiting Factor; 5= Most Probable Limiting Factor

Adapted from Baechle and Earle (2008).

Table 1.7 describes the limiting factors of the bioenergetics systems. It shows how athletes, depending on the sport they play, involuntarily utilize bioenergetics systems. If we take a look at the discus thrower, it is important for their performance to have enough ATP and creatine phosphate in order to throw the discus in a powerful manner. On the other hand, if we take a look at marathon runners, they are much more limited by the amounts of glycogen (large amounts of glucose grouped together) stored in the muscles and liver because of its role in glycolysis and oxidative phosphorylation. Thereby, if they are limited in muscle or liver glycogen their performance will be hindered greatly.

Table 1.8 describes the primary system that will be utilized by percent maximum power and duration of exercise (sport). With this information we can learn to train our bodies to utilize different systems. For example, if you are an athlete that wants to improve utilization of the phosphagen system, then you would train one time (sprint) at 90 percent intensity for five seconds in

Table 1.8. *Athletic Training and Energy Systems*

Percent Maximum Power	Primary System Utilized	Typical Exercise Time	Range of Work-to-rest Period Ratios
90-100	Phosphagen	5-10 seconds	1:12 to 1:20
75-90	Fast Glycolysis	15-30 seconds	1:3 to 1:5
30-75	Fast Glycolysis and Oxidative	1-3 minutes	1:3 to 1:4
20-30	Oxidative	> 3 minutes	1:1 to 1:3

Adapted from Baechle and Earle (2008).

duration at a work to rest ratio of one to twenty, meaning you would rest (5 × 20) 100 seconds, or a minute forty. If however, you would want to improve your cardiorespiratory endurance, you would train at 20–30 percent for longer duration at a work to rest ratio of one to three at most.

Table 1.9 details physiological markers of performance outcomes. It is well documented in the literature that testosterone, growth hormone, and IGF-1 are strongly related to muscle mass development and maintenance as well as bone density. Lactate levels are commonly used to assess whether the athlete is fatigued. Training that requires high level of technique or skill should not be performed since coordination is significantly decreased and risk of injury is increased when high amounts of lactate are present in the blood. Additionally, the hormone cortisol is known to be extremely elevated when an athlete is overtraining causing inflammation and stress in the body, which chronically, may lead to injury.

More recently there has been extensive research on delaying aging. Telomeres are located at the end of our chromosomes within our DNA. You may ask, "Why is this relevant to sport?" Professional athletes are interested in prolonging their athletic careers and since telomeres have been shown to be strongly related to physical aging, this is a relevant marker of having an extended athletic career. Many studies have already shown that longer telomeres are associated with healthier and longer lifespans in both animal and human models. A newer method of assessing aging is Methylome analysis. It has been shown to have an even stronger correlation to physical aging than telomere length. It is now recognized as a measure of biological age and can have major implications for injury prevention and the extension of athletic careers.

Table 1.9. *Physiological Markers of Athletic Performance*

Physiological Performance Outcomes	Markers
Muscle mass development and maintenance	Testosterone, growth hormone, IGF-1
Bone density	Testosterone, estrogen
Fatigue	Lactate levels
Overtraining	Cortisol
Cellular aging	Telomere length and Methylome assessment
Heart function	Heart rate, stroke volume, heart rate variability, cardiac output, and blood pressure
Aerobic threshold	Aerobic enzyme content, VO_2 max
Anaerobic threshold	Respiratory rate

Heart function is important to athletic performance. The ability of the heart to distribute blood and oxygen to the muscles is fundamental for optimal performance. Heart rate is commonly used to assess intensity. For instance, many strength and conditioning experts utilize heart rate zones as indicators of exercise intensity (training). It is important to assess heart functionality by not only measuring heart rate, but also stroke volume, heart rate variability, and cardiac output.

Anaerobic and aerobic thresholds are also important to assess. Based on the sport, it is recommended that respiratory rate and VO_2 max be examined. Respiratory rate assessment is especially relevant for sprinters, whereas VO_2 max would be most appropriate for marathoners.

In order to obtain an accurate predictive model of sport performance, it is important to include cardiovascular physiological measures, such as heart rate, resting heart rate, heart rate variability, stoke volume, cardiac output, and blood pressure. It is also important to include measures of lactate threshold, insulin and glucose levels, a vision assessment, and markers of cellular aging. Physiological variables reflect the internal state of the body and yield a picture of the body's engine and how and why it runs the way it does.

Now you can begin to see the whole picture and conduct more relevant exploratory analyses. Knowledge of anatomy and physiology will make you a more marketable and competitive sports data analyst against those who only see the numbers, whether those numbers come from a laboratory setting, training facility, or wearable technology in the field. Wearable technology provides measurements related to anatomy and physiology, as well as physical measures discussed in chapter 2.

This chapter drew on various sources in anatomy and physiology, including *Essentials of Strength Training and Conditioning* (Baechle and Earle 2008) and the *Laboratory Manual for Exercise Physiology* (Haff and Dumke 2012). Those who want to pursue these subjects further may want to consult Tanner, Gore, et al. (2013) and Sherwood (2015) as well.

2

Assessing Physical Variables

"The five Ss of sports training are: stamina, speed, strength, skill, and spirit; but the greatest of these is spirit."

—KEN DOHERTY

As a sports performance analyst, you will serve your clients best if you are aware of the measurement methods for physical performance variables. This chapter focuses on physical variables: body composition, muscular strength, power and endurance, flexibility, balance, anaerobic power, aerobic power, reaction time, agility, and level of sport-specific skill.

Years ago physicality measures were associated with only five fundamentals of fitness: muscular strength, muscular endurance, flexibility, cardiorespiratory fitness, and body composition. These measures were used to assess fitness across the general population.

More recently, exercise physiologists and fitness experts have come to agree that other factors, such as muscular power, coordination, balance, and anaerobic power should be included, so that physicality is measured as accurately as possible. This is not a novel idea.

Table 2.1. *Physical Measures and Fitness Models*

Fundamental Five-Component Model	Expanded Model (Nicks and Fleishman 1960)
Muscular strength	Strength (explosive, dynamic, and static strength)
Muscular endurance	Coordination (multiple limb and gross body coordination)
Flexibility	Flexibility (extent and dynamic flexibility)
Cardiorespiratory endurance	Running speed
Body composition	Balance and agility

Adapted from American College of Sports Medicine (2013a).

Nicks and Fleishman (1960) sought to include muscular strength, muscular power, muscular endurance, static flexibility, dynamic flexibility, coordination, balance, anaerobic power, cardiorespiratory endurance, and agility. See table 2.1.

Body composition can be defined as the proportion of muscle, fat, bone, and other substances in the athlete's body. A superficial and quick method for assessing body composition is the body mass index (BMI). BMI is used to calculate an individual's fat content based on the relationship between his or her height and weight. BMI is calculated as the weight in kilograms (kg) divided by the height in meters squared (m^2):

$$\text{Formula for BMI:} \frac{\text{weight in kilograms}}{(\text{height in meters})^2}$$

For example, the BMI of a female athlete weighing 136 pounds who is five feet four inches tall is calculated by first converting the weight into kilograms (61.7) and height to meters (1.62). Second, determine the square of the height, which is $1.62 \times 1.62 = 2.62$ meters squared. Finally, divide the weight in kilograms by height in meters squared: $\frac{61.7}{2.62} = 23.55$.

Table 2.2. *Body Fat Percentage Categories*

Category	Men	Women
Essential fat	2-4%	10-12%
Athletes	6-13%	14-20%
Fitness	14-17%	21-24%
Acceptable	18-25%	25-31%
Obese	26% or >	32% or >

Adapted from American College of Sports Medicine (2013a) and Heyward, Wagner, et al. (2004).

BMI is used most often for clinical purposes, to assess patients who may not be as physically active or involved in sports as are athletes. Caution is emphasized when using BMI to assess the body composition of athletes. BMI is not accurate for assessing the athlete's body composition because their bodies are usually composed of a high proportion of muscle which is known to weigh more than fat. As a result, when BMI is used to assess an athlete's body composition, you will notice that the majority of the time the BMI falls in the overweight or obese categories because of an athlete's increased muscularity compared with other individuals. See tables 2.2 and 2.3 for a summary of categories.

Another method for examining body composition is by assessing the fat distribution in the athlete's body. A commonly used method to measure fat distribution is the waist-to-hip ratio method, in which the waist circumference is divided by the hip circumference. This is easily assessed by using a spring-loaded tape to measure the waist midway between the lowest rib and the iliac crest (a common reference point is the narrowest part of the waist near the navel). The hip circumference is measured at the level of the greater trochanters (and a commonly used place of reference is the widest part of the hips).

Table 2.3.   Body Mass Index (BMI) Categories

Classification		BMI
Underweight		<18.5
Normal		18.5-24.9
Overweight		25-29.9
Obese		
	Class I	30-34.9
	Class II	35-39.9
	Class III	40 and up

Adapted from American College of Sports Medicine (2013a).

More precise measures of body composition distinguish between fat and lean tissue. Lean tissue includes lean muscle, organs, and bones. It is important to remember that fat weighs less than muscle. I am sure you have heard the phrase "muscle weighs more than fat." But what does this actually mean? The saying derives from the fact that muscle is denser than fat and therefore weighs more per cubic centimeter.

A reliable measure of body density is underwater (hydrostatic) weighing, formally known as hydrodensitometry. Underwater weighting is based on the Archimedes principle, which states that a partially or fully submerged object will experience an upward buoyant force equal to the weight or the volume of fluid displaced by the object.

The protocol for underwater weighing includes the athlete stepping into a gigantic water bath in which he or she can be fully submerged. The amount of water that is displaced is noted and inserted into an equation, along with the density of water, which is a known parameter, one gram per centimeter cubed. For a detailed protocol on hydrostatic weighing and calculations, please refer to the *Laboratory Manual for Exercise Physiology* (Haff and Dumke 2012).

Table 2.4. *Body Density Equations Used to Calculate Body Fat Percentage*

Measurement Option	MEN	WOMEN
Option A: 3 site Men = chest, abdomen, and thigh Women = triceps, suprailiac, and thigh	Body Density (BD) = 1.10938 - 0.0008267 (multiply by the sum of three skinfolds) + 0.0000016 (sum of three skinfolds)2 - 0.0002574(age) [SEE = 0.008]	Body Density (BD) = 1.099421 - 0.0009929 (multiply by the sum of three skinfolds) + 0.0000023 (sum of three skinfolds)2 - 0.0001392(age) [SEE = 0.009]
Option B: 3 site Men = chest, triceps, and subscapular Women = triceps, suprailiac, and abdominal	Body Density (BD) = 1.1125025 - 0.0013125 (multiply by the sum of three skinfolds) + 0.0000055 (sum of three skinfolds)2 - 0.000244(age) [SEE = 0.008]	Body Density (BD) = 1.089733 - 0.0009245 (multiply by the sum of three skinfolds) + 0.0000025 (sum of three skinfolds)2 - 0.0000979(age) [SEE = 0.009]
Option C: 7 site Men = chest, midaxillary, triceps, subscapular, abdomen, suprailiac, and thigh Women = chest, midaxillary, triceps, subscapular, abdomen, suprailiac, and thigh	Body Density (BD) = 1.112 - 0.00043499 (multiply by the sum of seven skinfolds) + 0.00000055 (sum of seven skinfolds)2 - 0.00028826(age) [SEE = 0.008]	Body Density (BD) = 1.097 - 0.00046971 (multiply by the sum of seven skinfolds) + 0.00000056 (sum of seven skinfolds)2 - . 0.00012828(age) [SEE = 0.008]

Adapted from American College of Sports Medicine (2013a).

A simple, non-invasive method for determining body fat consists of using a bioelectrical impedance analysis machine. This machine works by sending multiple electrical currents through the body and assessing the degree of impedance. This analysis is based on the fact that tissues with high water content act as conductors of electrical current, whereas fat tissue impedes electrical conductivity.

Another method for assessing body fat is by skinfold body fat testing, using skinfold calipers. The protocol includes obtaining two consecutive sets of measurements made by the same investigator at three (two options) or seven designated sites on the right side of the body, as indicated in table 2.4. Measurements are recorded to the nearest millimeter (*mm*), with a rest interval of at least fifteen seconds between measurements. If the second measurement varies by more than two millimeters, a third measurement should be made to ensure accuracy. Several equations may be used to calculate body fat, depending on whether the fat was assessed in three (two options) or seven areas. It is also important to note that, when using these methods, the equations differ slightly between males and females. See table 2.4 and ACSM's *Guidelines for Exercise Testing and Prescription* for additional information about conducting a three-site (two options) or seven-site skinfold assessment (Heyward, Wagner, et al. 2004; American College of Sports Medicine 2013a).

Muscular strength is the maximum amount of force that can be generated by a particular muscle or muscle group during a contraction. The most accurate assessment used to assess upper and lower body strength is the one repetition maximum (1RM), which is the maximum amount of force that can be lifted in one repetition.

Standard muscular strength assessments should not be conducted on an elite athlete if he or she has had a previous injury or runs the risk of recurring injury to a vulnerable muscle. If there is a risk of injury or safety concern, it is better to obtain a submaximal assessment of muscular strength, using a four, six, or eight repetition maximum (4RM, 6RM, or 8RM). The amount of force (weight lifted) that is performed for four, six, or eight repetitions is then used to predict the 1RM of the athlete. See tables 2.5 and 2.6 for additional information on repetition maximum coefficients and predictive ability. For the 1RM, the athlete should complete a warm-up set for each muscle tested.

Here is a sample protocol for obtaining the 1RM, adapted from *Essentials of Strength Training and Conditioning* (Baechle and Earle 2008):

1. Determine whether the athlete is to perform the 1RM, or a submaximal lift of 4RM, 6RM, or 8RM with which to predict the 1RM. (This should be based on the view of the coaches or physical therapist with respect to the risk of injury, type of sport, and/or the muscle group of interest).

2. Have the athlete warm up by completing a number of submaximal repetitions at roughly fifty to seventy percent of the athlete's perceived capacity for the muscle, or muscle group, to be tested.

3. Have the athlete conduct four trials with three- to five-minute rest intervals between each trial.

4. If the athlete is to perform the 1RM, he or she should be instructed to rest for four minutes before the load is increased by ten to twenty pounds, or five to ten percent for upper body exercise, and by thirty to forty pounds, or ten to twenty percent, for lower body exercise until the 1RM is reached for the specified muscle or muscle group.

5. If the athlete fails to lift the weight, the load should be reduced by five to ten pounds or two-and-one-half to five percent for upper body exercise, and fifteen to twenty pounds, or five to ten percent, for lower body exercises.

For a more detailed protocol of the 1RM assessment please refer to the book, *Physiological Tests for Elite Athletes* (Tanner, Gore, et al. 2013).

Table 2.5. *Repetition Maximum Coefficients*

Number of Repetitions	Squat/Leg Press Coefficient	Bench/Chest Press Coefficient
1	1	1
2	1.05	1.04
3	1.13	1.08
4	1.16	1.12
5	1.2	1.15
6	1.24	1.18
7	1.28	1.22
8	1.33	1.26
9	1.37	1.29
10	1.41	1.33

Adapted from Baechle and Earle (2008).

Table 2.6. *Repetition Maximum Values*

Repetitions	% 1RM
1	100
2	95
3	93
4	90
5	87
6	85
7	83
8	80
9	77
10	75
11	70
12	67

Adapted from Baechle and Earle (2008).

Muscular power is the ability of the muscle to exert a certain amount of force per unit of time, also referred to as explosiveness. Muscular power is a factor that all athletes need at some point in their sport, whether to jump, sprint, or perform an explosive swing. In laboratories, isokinetic machines are used to capture and assess muscular power by quantifying several measures, including peak torque, time to peak torque, peak torque slope, and power (work done/time). However, a more practical way to assess muscular power (if access to an isokinetic machine is limited) is to use free weights, pneumatic machines, or standard resistance machines. This is done by using a low resistance weight that can be moved quickly through the entire range of motion of the exercise.

Muscular power assessment requires performing a warm-up similar to that of the muscular strength test, but rather than determining the maximum weight that can be lifted, the objective is to have the athlete perform three repetitions as quickly and explosively as possible at forty-five to sixty-five percent of the athlete's 1RM for that particular muscle or muscle group. The outcome is quantified on the basis of the time required to perform the three repetitions as quickly as possible. The idea behind this assessment is to examine the point in the force-velocity relationship that the athlete exhibits maximum power, so that it may later be applied in his or her sport (Martin et al. 2015).

Muscular endurance is the ability of a muscle, or muscle group, to perform muscle actions repeatedly over a period of time until fatigue has been reached. Measures exist of both absolute and relative muscular endurance. Absolute muscular endurance is quantified as the number of repetitions that can be performed at a designated percent repetition maximum for a given length of time. Relative muscular endurance is measured as a change in the athlete's muscular endurance over a period of time, such as occurs with training.

Muscular endurance is often captured by performing repeated muscular contractions until fatigue sets in, and can be tested for one minute to two full minutes. The athlete should perform as many repetitions as possible of an exercise for a particular muscle or group, at a low load, for example twenty-five to thirty-five percent of the athlete's 1RM.

A different method consists of the athlete performing as many repetitions as possible using their own bodyweight within a specified period of either one or two minutes. For abdominal muscle groups, the number of continuous crunches that an athlete can perform, without rest, is a good measure of abdominal muscular endurance (American College of Sports Medicine 2013a). See tables 2.7 and 2.8 for protocols to assess muscular strength, muscular power, and muscular endurance.

Flexibility is the ability to move a joint through a range of motion. Flexibility is important for activities of daily living as well as a crucial factor in athletic performance. Some sports such as gymnastics, basketball, and tennis require great flexibility. Positions in team sports vary in their need for flexibility. A soccer goalie, for example, requires greater flexibility than a soccer fullback.

There are several field tests that may be used to assess flexibility, such as the sit and reach test, back scratch test, and the functional reach test. The sit and reach test is commonly used to assess hamstring and lower back flexibility. Athletes should be instructed to remove their shoes and sit on the floor with legs fully extended and feet flat against the sit and reach box. Then the athlete should be instructed to place one hand on top of the other and reach forward, while keeping the back straight and the head up. This reach should be held steady without bouncing for approximately two seconds. Two practice trials are followed by a test trial, and typically used to obtain a reliable measure. The outcome is the length of the reach that is held for two seconds on the sit and reach box (Wells and Dillon 1952; American College of Sports Medicine 2013a).

The back scratch test is commonly used to assess shoulder flexibility. Athletes are instructed to place one hand over the shoulder, with the palm facing the back, and to reach as far down as possible, while simultaneously placing the other arm behind the back and reaching up as far as possible, in an attempt to touch or overlap their hands. This position must be held for at least two seconds. The test is then repeated for the other side by switching the positions of the arms. A ruler is used to record the reach distance. If the athlete is not able to touch his or her fingers, a negative score is given. If the athlete's hands touch, a zero is given. And if the athlete's fingers overlap he or she receives a positive score.

Table 2.7. *Body Muscle Group Testing for Athletes (Part 1)*

	Muscular Strength	Muscular Power	Muscular Endurance
Leg Press			
Have the athlete place the feet shoulder width apart on the footplate. Have him or her form a 90-degree angle between the hips and knees. Finally instruct the athlete to keep the gluteal muscles on the seat throughout the entire range of motion of this exercise. Measures quadriceps, gluteus, soleus, and gastrocnemius strength, power, and endurance. This is more of a muscle group assessment.	Use 1RM or submaximal loads; 4RM, 6RM, or 8RM	Perform 3 repetitions as explosive as possible (during contraction phase of exercise) between 45-65% of 1RM	Perform as many repetitions as possible until fatigue or up until 2 minutes using 20-35% of 1RM
Leg Extension			
Have the athlete sit with the seat adjusted so that the knees are in line with the machine's axis of rotation. Then instruct the athlete to perform the exercise by kicking out until the legs are almost fully extended and then return back to starting position. Another measure of quadriceps strength, power, and endurance. This is a more isolated muscle assessment than leg press.	Use 1RM or submaximal loads; 4RM, 6RM, or 8RM	Perform 3 repetitions as explosive as possible (during contraction phase of exercise) between 45-65% of 1RM	Perform as many repetitions as possible until fatigue or up until 2 minutes using 20-35% of 1RM
Leg Curl			
Have the athlete lie prone on the pad and align the knees with the pivot point of the machine. Next, the athlete should be instructed to begin the exercise by bringing the pad toward the buttocks, holding the movement, and then lowering the weight slowly without raising their body off the pad. This is a great assessment of the hamstring muscles and muscles in the gluteus region.	Use 1RM or submaximal loads; 4RM, 6RM, or 8RM	Perform 3 repetitions as explosive as possible (during contraction phase of exercise) between 45-65% of 1RM	Perform as many repetitions as possible until fatigue or up until 2 minutes using 20-35% of 1RM
Chest Press			
Have the athlete perform this exercise by pushing out on the handles until the arms are nearly straight and then return to starting position. Adjust the handles so that they are at chest level during the initial part of the movement. This is a great assessment for upper body muscle group including pectoralis major and minor for strength, power, and endurance.	Use 1RM or submaximal loads; 4RM, 6RM, or 8RM	Perform 3 repetitions as explosive as possible (during contraction phase of exercise) between 45-65% of 1RM	Perform as many repetitions as possible until fatigue or up until 2 minutes using 20-35% of 1RM
Back Row			
Have the athlete sit down on the bench for this machine with their back slightly arched, chest out, head aligned with the spine, and have the athlete extend his or her legs forward placing the feet on the foot plate while maintaining a slight bend of the knees. This is a great assessment for muscles groups located in the back, including the latissimus dorsi, rhomboids, and trapezius.	Use 1RM or submaximal loads; 4RM, 6RM, or 8RM	Perform 3 repetitions as explosive as possible (during contraction phase of exercise) between 45-65% of 1RM	Perform as many repetitions as possible until fatigue or up until 2 minutes using 20-35% of 1RM

Table 2.8. *Body Muscle Group Testing for Athletes (Part 2)*

	Muscular Strength	Muscular Power	Muscular Endurance
Shoulder Press			
Have the athlete push the handles overhead until the arms almost reach full extension, have them hold the position for a moment, and then return to the starting position. This is a great assessment for shoulder strength, power, and endurance.	Use 1RM or submaximal loads; 4RM, 6RM, or 8RM	Perform 3 repetitions as explosive as possible (during contraction phase of exercise) between 45-65% of 1RM	Perform as many repetitions as possible until fatigue or up until 2 minutes using 20-35% of 1RM
Lat Pull-Down			
Have the athlete grasp the bar with the palms facing forward at a width about 1.5 times wider than shoulder-width apart, lean back slightly, pull the bar down in front of the body toward the collarbone, and then slowly return the bar to the starting position. This is a great assessment for latissimus dorsi strength, power, and endurance.	Use 1RM or submaximal loads; 4RM, 6RM, or 8RM	Perform 3 repetitions as explosive as possible (during contraction phase of exercise) between 45-65% of 1RM	Perform as many repetitions as possible until fatigue or up until 2 minutes using 20-35% of 1RM
Biceps Curl			
If using the curl machine, have the athlete grab the curl bar with arms straight and palms facing away from the body. Instruct them to adjust the seat to the appropriate height, and sit up keeping the back straight. This can also be done using free weights, however, a different technique is required. This is a great assessment of strength, power, and endurance of the biceps.	Use 1RM or submaximal loads; 4RM, 6RM, or 8RM	Perform 3 repetitions as explosive as possible (during contraction phase of exercise) between 45-65% of 1RM	Perform as many repetitions as possible until fatigue or up until 2 minutes using 20-35% of 1RM
Triceps Dips			
Have the athlete extend both legs and place the heels of the hands on the bench next to each hip. Then instruct the athlete to bend the elbows, while lowering the body toward the floor, stop before the shoulders start to elevate, and finally have him or her push back up to the starting position so that the arms are almost fully extended while keeping the core stable throughout the movement.	Use 1RM or submaximal loads; 4RM, 6RM, or 8RM	Perform 3 repetitions as explosive as possible (during contraction phase of exercise) between 45-65% of 1RM	Perform as many repetitions as possible until fatigue or up until 2 minutes using 20-35% of 1RM
Squats			
Have the athlete stand with feet shoulder width apart or slightly wider than the width of the hips. Have the athlete keep the back straight. Have the athlete start to flex and bend his or her knees as if he or she were to sit on a chair. The athlete should not go below 90 degrees of knee flexion or where the hamstrings are parallel to the floor. When the athlete has reached this level, have him or her return to starting position.	Use 1RM or submaximal loads; 4RM, 6RM, or 8RM	Perform 3 repetitions as explosive as possible (during contraction phase of exercise) between 45-65% of 1RM	Perform as many repetitions as possible until fatigue or up until 2 minutes using 20-35% of 1RM

The functional reach test is an inexpensive method of assessing flexibility. Using a numbered scale mounted on a wall (the only equipment needed), the athlete should remove his or her shoes and stand with the right shoulder parallel to the scale on the wall, then fully extend the right arm horizontally with the hand closed into a fist. He or she must hold this position for two seconds so the standing reach may be recorded. Next, the athlete should be instructed to lean forward as far as possible without lifting either heel off the ground, otherwise the test is disqualified. Functional reach is then calculated by subtracting the standing reach from the leaning reach distance. For example, if an athlete's extended arm reach is thirteen inches when he or she stands with shoulders perpendicular to the wall, and thirty-four inches when leaning forward with feet flat on the floor, the reach distance is thirty-four minus thirteen, or eleven inches. The same procedure is repeated for the other side of the body.

If flexibility is assessed while an athlete is recovering from injury, it is recommended that range of motion of a joint be assessed using a goniometer and following the protocol by Rothstein and Company. Additional information is available in various sources (Palmer, Epler, and Epler 1998; Clarkson 2000; Stathokostas et al. 2012; and American College of Sports Medicine 2013a, 2013b). For select single-joint range of movement, see table 2.9.

Balance is another important factor that plays a role in sport performance. It is the ability to control equilibrium in the body. For more detailed information about balance refer to the book *Applied Biomechanics: Concepts and Connections* (McLester and Pierre 2007) or *Sports Injury: Prevention and Rehabilitation* (Shamus and Shamus 2001).

There are several methods which can be used to assess an athlete's balance: the single leg stand, Balance Error Scoring System (BESS), the Star Excursion Balance Test (SEBT), and the Proprio reactive balance test. The single leg stand test is a field test that is commonly used to assess balance. The athlete is instructed to stand with feet together and arms down at his or her sides. He or she is then asked to raise one foot six to eight inches from the ground by bending that leg at the knee while keeping both hands at his or her sides.

Table 2.9. Range of Motion of Select Single-Joint Movements in Degrees

Movement	Degrees
Shoulder Girdle Movement	
Flexion	90-120
Extension	20-60
Abduction	80-100
Horizontal abduction	30-45
Horizontal adduction	90-135
Medial rotation	70-90
Lateral rotation	70-90
Elbow Movement	
Flexion	135-160
Supination	75-90
Pronation	75-90
Trunk Movement	
Flexion	120-150
Extension	20-45
Lateral flexion	10-30
Rotation	20-40
Hip Movement	
Flexion	90-135
Extension	10-30
Abduction	30-50
Adduction	10-30
Medial rotation	30-45
Lateral rotation	45-60
Knee Movement	
Flexion	130-140
Extension	5-10
Ankle Movement	
Dorsiflexion	15-20
Plantarflexion	30-50
Inversion	10-30
Eversion	10-20

Adapted from American College of Sports Medicine (2013a).

Continuing with the single leg stand test, the athlete is informed that he or she should stand on one leg for as long as possible, keeping the standing leg straight, the other leg bent, and arms at his or her sides. Individuals administering the test should be trained to stop the test when the athlete's arms move away from his or her sides, the support foot moves across the floor, or the raised foot touches the floor. The outcome measured is the length of time the athlete remains balanced on each leg.

The Balance Error Scoring System is another relatively inexpensive field test used to quantify balance. The only equipment needed is a foam balance pad. This assessment is comprised of six positions consisting of three stances (double leg support, single leg support, and tandem) which are held by the athlete for twenty seconds on two different surfaces, a firm floor and foam pad. It is important to note that during this test the athlete's eyes should be closed and his or her hands on the hips. The athlete is to keep as steady as possible, and if the athlete loses his or her balance, he or she is to try to regain the initial position as quickly as possible. Athletes are deducted one point for any of the following errors: lifting the hands off the hips; opening the eyes; stepping, stumbling, or falling; and being out of position for five seconds or more. The score is a total of the number of errors for the six positions tested and is determined as follows: ten errors are allowed per position, and any incompletely held position (not held for at least five seconds) results in a score of ten for that position, with a lower score being representative of better balance (Bressel et al. 2007; Onate, Beck, and Van Lunen 2007; Finnoff et al. 2009; Bell et al. 2011).

The Star Excursion Balance Test is another relatively inexpensive and simple way to assess balance for athletes. All that is needed is athletic tape because the floor must be marked in a star pattern consisting of eight directions, forty-five degrees apart. The athlete should be instructed to place one foot in the middle of the star. Then he or she should be instructed to reach as far as possible sequentially (either clockwise or counter-clockwise) in all eight directions. The athlete is to tap the floor while maintaining his or her balance, and the distance from the center of the star to the place of the tap is measured.

The athlete is disqualified if any of the following errors occur: resting a foot on the ground, losing balance, making an impulsive and heavy touch to the floor, or being unable to return to the starting position with control. Scoring of this assessment is the average of three trials (Kinzey and Armstrong 1998; Plisky, Rauh, Kaminski, and Underwood 2006; Gribble and Hertel 2003).

The Proprio reactive balance system employs a more novel assessment of balance. This test is usually conducted in a laboratory setting using a dynamic motion analysis system that is capable of assessing the athlete's center of mass and movement. It can also quantify trunk movement in six degrees of freedom: lateral, up/down, anterior/posterior, rotation, flexion/extension, and lateral flexion. The machine is simply a platform that can tilt in various angles and at various rates. Platform movement options include predictable motion, random motion, variable speeds (twelve degrees/second to twelve and a half degrees/second), and adjustable degrees of tilt motion (two degrees to twenty-five degrees). Typically, a harness is attached to the frame of the unit and is used to help prevent any injury to the athlete. This is a great way of measuring and assessing different aspects of balance, however access to this method may be a limiting factor.

Anaerobic power is assessed via tests that stress the phosphagen (ATP-PC) system (see chapter 1). To measure values indicative of anaerobic power, tests are to be performed at very high intensities for very short durations, ranging from ten to thirty seconds.

The following tests may be used to assess anaerobic power: sprints, countermovement jump test, static squat jump test, Bosco sixty-second continuous jump test, and Wingate anaerobic cycle test (Margaria, Aghemo, and Rovelli 1966; Bosco, Luhtanen, and Komi 1983; Hoffman 2006).

Sprints are specifically used to assess horizontal power through the 30-yard dash, 40-yard dash (used in the NFL Combine), and 60-yard dash. The sprint is a simple field test in which the only equipment needed to quantify the athlete's sprint time is a stopwatch which has been shown to have a strong correlation with electronic timers ($r = .98$, $R^2 = .95$, $se = .24$). In order to be more precise you may use the following equation:

$$\text{Electronic time (seconds)} = \left(1.0113 \times \text{stopwatch time in seconds}\right) + 0.2252$$

The countermovement jump test is an assessment of the athlete's vertical power, and has been strongly correlated with sport performance. This particular jump test is dynamic in the sense that the athlete is instructed to start in a standing position with feet shoulder width apart, drop into a squat position, and jump as high as possible. In contrast to the countermovement jump, the static squat vertical jump eliminates the confounding factor of momentum. The static squat vertical jump differs in that it requires holding the squat position for at least three seconds prior to attempting to jump as high as possible.

The outcome scored for both the countermovement and the static squat jumps is the vertical displacement. The method for obtaining this value without the use of expensive equipment is to have the athlete reach as high as possible with his or her palm against a scale designated on a wall (or other area), and to mark the place that he or she initially reaches as the starting point. Then the athlete should be informed to perform either of the jump tests and reach for the highest point possible while jumping. The vertical jump displacement score is the difference between the standing reach height and the maximum height reached when the athlete jumps. Vertical displacement in centimeters (*cm*) = the jump height (*cm*) minus the reach height (*cm*). Vertical displacement can also be assessed in the laboratory with the athlete performing the vertical jump test on top of a force plate. Vertical displacement is then calculated using a formula that includes gravity and the amount of time the athlete is in the air.

The Bosco sixty-second continuous jump test is an assessment that is often used to assess anaerobic power. It is a good measure of anaerobic power endurance because it measures the ability to perform high power movements repeatedly. It can be designed to last anywhere between fifteen to sixty seconds. The athlete is instructed to jump as high and quickly as possible for the designated length of time. The outcome is the number of jumps completed and the sum of the flight times. As a predictor of sport performance, a fifteen-second continuous jump test may be more relevant for a sprinter, whereas a sixty-second test may more relevant for a running back. A quick note—this test is much easier to quantify if done on a force plate on which the flight time is easily captured. Refer to the *Laboratory Manual for Exercise Physiology* for the formulas and equations required to extrapolate power output from this test (Haff and Dumke 2012).

The Wingate anaerobic cycle test is a laboratory assessment used to quantify anaerobic power. It is usually conducted in the laboratory setting. It was originally performed for a thirty-second duration against 0.075 kilopounds (*kp*) per kilogram (*kg*) of body mass. Research shows that the first fifteen seconds of the test exhaust the ATP-PC system (see chapter 1) and that the glycolytic system is used for the remainder of the test. The cycle is connected to a software system that yields peak anaerobic output; the point at which the highest power is generated usually occurs within the first five seconds of the test. This is a face-valid test for cyclists. For non-cyclists, it is recommended as a point of reference since it is not sport-specific.

Aerobic power is also referred to as aerobic capacity, cardiovascular endurance, and cardiorespiratory fitness (CRF). Aerobic power is the ability to perform moderate-to-vigorous intensity exercise for prolonged periods of time and is a reflection of the functioning of three systems: the cardiovascular, pulmonary, and muscular systems. The determinants thought to represent these functions are expired gases. This results in a measurement of maximal oxygen consumption, derived either from arterial-venous oxygen difference (which is an indicator of oxygen utilization) or inferred from cardiac output (a function of heart rate and stroke volume), which is indicative of oxygen delivery.

Maximal oxygen consumption is commonly referred to as VO_2 max and is defined as the highest rate of oxygen transport achieved by the athlete at maximal physical exertion. Theoretically, the more oxygen that an athlete can use during moderate-to-vigorous exercise, the more energy (ATP) he or she produces, resulting in greater cardiovascular endurance. There are several laboratory and field tests that may be used to measure VO_2 max. Maximal tests, which can be very strenuous and costly, include the direct measurement of expired gases and ventilation. Other methods for obtaining VO_2 max are the graded exercise test, the cycle ergometer VO_2 cycle test, and the Cooper 1.5 mile run/walk test.

The graded exercise test is a laboratory assessment of VO_2 max. The equipment needed for this test is a treadmill, metabolic cart which can collect $\frac{VO_2 \, max}{VCO_2}$ data, a mouthpiece, heart rate monitor, stopwatch, and a rate of perceived exertion scale (used to monitor the athlete).

The protocol for VO_2 max consists of having the athlete walk on the treadmill while gradually increasing workload through stages ranging from one to three minutes in duration, until fatigue. The objective is to have the athlete continue as long as possible (usually eight to fifteen minutes) in order to capture the VO_2 max. For information about the protocol, refer to the *Laboratory Manual for Exercise Physiology* (Haff and Dumke 2012) or *ACSM's Guidelines for Exercise Testing and Prescription* (American College of Sports Medicine 2013a).

The cycle ergometer VO_2 max test is another laboratory assessment of VO_2 max. The equipment needed for this assessment includes a cycle ergometer, metabolic cart, mouthpiece, heart rate monitor, stopwatch, and the rate of perceived exertion scale. There are several variations of this protocol, including the Astrand and McArdle approach (Coyle et al. 1991).

The Cooper 1.5 mile run/walk test is commonly used in a field setting to estimate VO_2 max. Although walking is allowed during the test, the goal is to complete 1.5 miles as quickly as possible. The faster the athlete can complete 1.5 miles, the higher his or her estimated VO_2 max. The VO_2 max may be calculated for a male or female athlete using regression equations. The athlete should be assessed for his or her height and weight, as these variables are needed for the formulas. The athlete should be allowed to warm up for approximately ten minutes. The athlete should then be instructed to run or walk the 1.5 miles as fast as he or she can. The only equipment needed for this test is a stopwatch. The observed outcome for assessment is the time it takes the athlete to complete 1.5 miles. After this time has been obtained, the value is inserted into the appropriate equation. The formulas have been shown to have a high correlation ($r = .90$) with maximal testing and a low standard error of the estimate. For details about the protocol and equations, please refer to the *Laboratory Manual for Exercise Physiology* (Haff and Dumke 2012) or *ACSM's Guidelines for Exercise Testing and Prescription* (American College of Sports Medicine 2013a).

The theory behind aerobic power tests is that the better the CRF, the better the heart recovery response. These assessments are excellent measures of maximal aerobic power or the rate at which oxygen is utilized and transported to working muscles during exercise. For a more detailed description of each of the aerobic power tests please refer to the *Laboratory Manual for Exercise Physiology* (Haff and Dumke 2012).

Another factor that plays a role in sport performance is reaction time. Consider how reaction time can make the difference between winning and losing in various sports—the reaction time of a quarterback in throwing the ball before being tackled, a baseball player trying to steal a base, a basketball player getting a rebound, a tennis player hitting a volley, or a soccer goalie blocking a goal can ultimately make the difference between winning and losing.

Reaction time is quantified as the interval between the appearance of a stimulus and the athlete's time to respond to the stimulus. Several reaction time assessments have been developed. A few methods of measuring reaction time are being used in professional sports: the reaction time ruler test, light board reaction timer assessment, the SVT reaction test, and the BATAK light board reaction test. See Topend Sports (2015) for procedures and adaptations of these tests.

The reaction time ruler test is relatively simple. The only equipment needed is a ruler one meter in length and a timer. The test uses the property of gravity and determines the length of time it takes an athlete to respond to the dropping of an object by measuring the distance the object travels before it is caught. It is important to note that this is a good test for assessing eye-hand coordination and may be particularly relevant in tennis. For specifics on the procedure and adaptations of the test, as well as products such as reaction stick timers that have been developed to more accurately assess reaction time, see Topend Sports (2015).

The light board reaction timer assessment can also be used to quantify reaction time. This test has been used in boxing for many years as part of the SPARQ (speed, power, agility, reaction time and quickness) rating system. The equipment that is needed are a Bosu ball and a light board. Although Bosu balls are quite inexpensive, lightboards are typically very costly. The protocol includes having the athlete stand on top of the Bosu while trying to touch as many lighted areas on the light board as possible. The outcome is the number of lights touched out of a total of ninety. For more information about this test, refer to SPARQ rating system and Topend Sports (2015).

The BATAK light board reaction test is similar to the light board reaction timer test, although no Bosu ball is involved. The test seems to have evolved from the basic concept of the light board. It consists of randomly lit targeted areas in which the athlete's goal is to touch as many of the lighted areas within a specified time of either thirty or sixty seconds. The outcome is the number of lights touched within the specified time. For adaptations of the BATAK test, refer to Topend Sports (2015).

The SVT reaction test was developed by engineers to assess reaction time and eye-hand coordination among Australian football players. It consists of a grid with four rows of eight lights each, or a total of thirty-two lights. Similar to other reaction tests, the athlete is instructed to touch as many randomly lighted areas on the grid as possible within thirty seconds. The outcome is the number of grids touched within the half-minute time limit. Again, Topend Sports (2015) is a good resource for measurement procedures.

Agility is the ability to change directions as quickly as possible. There are several measures that can be used to assess as well as train this important factor. Currently the National Basketball Association (NBA) quantifies speed, agility, and anaerobic power through the following five drills: the lane agility drill, shuttle run, the 0.75-court sprint, the standing vertical leap, and the maximum vertical leap. In the speed and agility battery, several factors are assessed. And we can guess what they are:

1. Lane agility drill: agility
2. Shuttle run: anaerobic power and speed
3. 0.75-court sprint: anaerobic power and speed
4. Standing vertical leap: anaerobic power
5. Max vertical leap: anaerobic and muscular power

A major assessment of agility used in professional football is the 5-10-5 agility test, which is also called the 20-yard shuttle. The only equipment needed is a stopwatch and several cones. The protocol includes having the athlete start with his or her hand touching the ground at the five yard line mark. The athlete should turn ninety degrees to his or her right and sprint to the ten yard line (a total of five yards) as fast as possible, touch the line, turn back, sprint ten yards in the opposite direction, and finally turn back and sprint the final five yards to the starting point. Starting sides should be alternated when testing. The time to completion is the measure for this test of agility (Little and Williams 2005; Young and Farrow 2006; Young, McDowell, and Scarlett 2001).

Speed and coordination are variables that are considered to play a role in sport performance, but these have been difficult to assess accurately. Speed is usually assessed through sprinting as a measure of anaerobic power, while coordination is sometimes included in assessments of reaction time (Vescovi and Mcguigan 2008; Nimphius, McGuigan, and Newton 2010). For a list of sports ranked by coordination, see table 2.10.

Researchers are investigating constructs that may be useful in assessing level of coordination and reaction time. There are various confounding factors, including depth perception (Howard-Dolman apparatus) or how well an athlete's eyes become fixated on an object and how quickly the eyes accommodate to distances (Saladin near point balance card), as well as the way in which timing is affected by visual coordination, or lack thereof. Further research and development are needed in the field to improve measures and identify confounding factors.

Traditional physical measures and fitness models build on earlier work done by Nicks and Fleishman (1960), Fleishman and Kremer (1961), Fleishman and Ellison (1962), Scott (1964), Heyward (2006), and Brown (2001). For additional details on assessments typically used in sports, please refer to the *Laboratory Manual for Exercise Physiology* or ACSM's *Guidelines for Exercise Testing and Prescription* (American College of Sports Medicine 2013a).

Sport-specific skills are crucial to athletic performance. Martin and Miller's (2016) measurement model for sports describes how levels of sport-specific skills are to be included for a more accurate assessment and prediction of sport performance. Simply put, an individual may be completely fit, but unable to compete at the highest levels because of the lack of skill required to be successful in a particular sport.

Usain Bolt, a track athlete known as the fastest man in the world, cannot be expected to play baseball at a professional level. He would not be able to pitch, bat, or catch a baseball at a professional level. This is not to say that speed or anaerobic power is unimportant. Rather, without sport-specific skills, speed may be irrelevant to that sport.

Table 2.10. ESPN's List of Ranking Sports by Coordination

Rank	Sport	Rating
1	Baseball/Softball	9.25
2	Table Tennis	8.88
3	Tennis	8.38
4	Racquetball/Squash	8.38
5	Auto Racing	8.00
6	Team Handball	7.88
7	Ice Hockey	7.50
8	Basketball	7.50
9	Volleyball	7.25
10	Fencing	7.25
11	Badminton	7.25
12	Lacrosse	7.13
13	Boxing	7.00
14	Shooting	6.75
15	Field Hockey	6.63
16	Archery	6.63
17	Soccer	6.50
18	Rodeo: Calf Roping	6.38
19	Water Polo	6.25
20	Martial Arts	6.00

Source. http://sports.espn.go.com/espn/page2/sportSkills?sort=handEye.

Of course, coaches may seek people with athletic prowess with the idea of spending time, possibly 10,000 hours or more, to help athletes master sport-specific skills. Table 2.11 provides a summary of skills commonly associated with the five sports reviewed in chapters 5 through 9 of this book.

In order to obtain an accurate predictive model of sport performance, it is important to include certain physical measures such as muscular strength, power, and endurance. Measures of aerobic and anaerobic capacity, flexibility, and balance are also fundamental to sports performance. Wearables provide convenient access to many relevant measures.

Other physical measures are currently being assessed through what is now known as wearable technology. At the present time, we have seen the only tip of the iceberg in terms of wearable technology. Among the many companies pioneering the way are the likes of Catapult, Zebra, Adidas, Vert, SportsVU, Babolat, PlaySight, and others. Advances in technology, such as sensor-filled helmets and skin tattoos, are being tested for effectiveness and approval prior to marketing. Consumer and market researchers forecast financial growth in wearable devices for sports, with estimated revenues of $19 billion by 2018.

A very popular technology in the NFL is Catapult. It consists of a device that weighs three and a half ounces and is worn under the shoulder pads. It collects and parses more than one thousand data points per second, and tracks over one hundred metrics including speed, acceleration, distance, and heart rate.

Another very well-endorsed technology in professional football is Zebra, which utilizes chip sensors that are placed under each shoulder pad to capture data. This device has been called the NFL game-changer, and receivers have been installed in several stadiums to track acceleration, deceleration, and distance.

A popular wearable technology among soccer players is the Adidas miCoach. It consists of a battery cell that is inserted into a pack. It is worn by many soccer players, capturing data while training, as well as when scrimmaging. It can record speed, power, acceleration, and heart rate, among other measures.

Another wearable device, Vert, comes in the form of a lightweight sensor that is placed on the waistband of shorts. This technology is used to measure jump height and anaerobic power. The camera device known as SportVU, although not quite wearable, is a common technology in the NBA. Not only does it capture speed and distance traveled by players, it includes algorithms that allow for positional analysis of players (Lapinski, Berkson, Gill, Reinold, Paradiso, et al. 2009; Chi 2008; Panait and Cojocaru 2013; Cervone, D'Amour, Bornn, and Goldsberry 2014; Dellaserra, Gao, and Ransdell 2014; Safir 2015).

Table 2.11. *Sport-Specific Skills*

Sport	Sport-Specific Skills
Football	Quarterback position sport-specific skills include: decision-making, eye-hand coordination, vision, and throwing the ball with precision and accuracy. Adaptations for other player positions are recommended.
Basketball	Precision, accuracy, and consistency of shooting free throws, three pointers, and passing the ball precisely to teammates. Adaptations for other player positions are recommended.
Baseball	Batter requires excellent eye-hand coordination and reaction time. Precision, accuracy, and consistency of ball throwing from outfielders, pitchers, and catchers is suggested. Adaptations for other player positions are recommended.
Soccer	Precision, accuracy, and consistency of ball placement by kicking, eye-foot coordination, and the ability to pass the ball precisely to teammates. Adaptations for other player positions are recommended.
Tennis	Precision, accuracy, and consistency of ball placement should be measured for each of the major tennis strokes: serve, forehand, backhand, volley, slice.

The field of tennis has developed several new technologies. A state-of-the-art racquet, Babolat Play, has sensors installed within the grip handle of the racquet to quantify measures specific to tennis players. It records the frequency of strokes, type of spin used by a player, and racquet speed among other measures. Additionally, a SmartCourt is the latest development by PlaySight. It customizes the tennis court with a permanent kiosk system and six high-definition cameras, which capture lengths of rallies, speed of the ball, spin of the ball, player movement, and consistency. It offers the capability of live streaming as well as video replay (Pluim 2014).

Also available are compression shirts, sleeves, and shorts, which track movements using accelerometers. The Motus Sleeve is popular among baseball pitchers, as it senses throwing motion. The Motus even has the capability to send data to a smartphone via Bluetooth. It also has an app with an algorithm to calculate elbow torque, arm speed, maximum shoulder rotation, and elbow height at ball release.

Compression shorts are somewhat more expensive. They have sensors embedded in the trousers that measure leg imbalances. Currently several NBA teams and professional boxers utilize these shorts, which are called Myontec Mbody Pro. Then there is a lower leg compression sleeve termed BSX Insight. It is supposed to assess the level and intensity of lactic acid accumulation, in order to signal the point where performance begins to deteriorate. This compression sleeve functions differently than other compression sleeves. It utilizes near infrared spectroscopy instead of accelerometers. Then, we have the OptimEye S5, which is embedded in the garment and worn on the upper back of the athlete. It uses magnetometers, gyroscopes, and accelerometers to capture values of anaerobic power, agility, acceleration, deceleration, and other biometrics. A more comprehensive wearable technology is Athos, a smart clothing line consisting of shirts, shorts, and core sensors that track heart rate, respiratory rate, and muscle activation. Then there is a device called ShotTracker used by several NBA players. It consists of a wrist sensor that is worn by the player, and a net sensor that can track the number of shots attempted, missed, and made. Finally, there is a state of the art wearable wristband called the Readiband that can be used to predict fatigue. It is based on a model developed in the army, SAFTE (Sleep, Activity, Fatigue, Task, and Effectiveness).

Player salaries in sports are determined by performance. As such, a major area of concern for athletes is the data constantly being collected by wearable technology. This newest form of equipment is causing quite an upheaval among professional athletes and their labor unions. In fact, many players refuse to sign the informed consent to wear these devices during training, fearing that the information may be used against them during salary negotiations. Some players believe that the data collected reveal too much information and violate their privacy (Chi 2008; Dellaserra, Gao, and Ransdell 2014).

Wearable technology in the field of sports analytics is improving the ways we collect data, interpret it, and utilize it to predict future outcomes. Improved technology can also be used to monitor the health of players, hopefully leading to a reduced number of injuries. Such innovations in science and technology will help athletes prolong their careers longer than ever before. Additionally, data obtained from wearable technology will increase objectivity in terms of deciding who is faster or stronger, makes better plays, handles pressure better during clutch moments, and other determinants that have been thought to be subjective.

This chapter drew on Nicks and Fleishman (1960), the *Laboratory Manual for Exercise Physiology* (Haff and Dumke 2012), *ACSM's Guidelines for Exercise Testing and Prescription* (American College of Sports Medicine 2013a), and *Physiological Tests for Elite Athletes* (Tanner, Gore, et al. 2013). For those who want to pursue the subject further, there are many excellent resources to consider (Lapinski et al. 2009; Chi 2008; Panait and Cojocaru 2013; Dellaserra, Gao, and Ransdell 2014; Safir 2015).

3

Sport Psychological Measures

"Mental toughness is to physical as four is to one."

—BOB KNIGHT

As a data scientist or sport performance analyst you may have heard the phrase "get to know your data." This is rightfully so, because knowing the data is fundamental to understanding the factors that can play a role in the athlete's or team's performance, whether physical or psychological. This poses questions such as the following: "How much do we know about psychological variables in sport? How do we, as sports data scientists, examine psychological data? And how much variance in sport performance is due to individual and environmental moderators of psychological factors?"

Sport psychology is the scientific study of an athlete's thoughts and behavior as they pertain to sport. It is important to include psychological variables in sports performance predictive models. In this chapter we cover the fundamental psychological constructs previously linked with sport performance, the measures available to quantify these intangible variables, as well as theories and psychological models of sport performance. Psychological constructs are described in detail and, more importantly, the most recent scales of measurement for these constructs are identified.

Let us look at psychological variables that have been shown to affect sport performance. Motivation, confidence, anxiety, depression, aggressiveness, self-esteem, self-efficacy, and concentration are some of the most studied and researched psychological variables in sport literature.

A well-established factor known to affect sport performance is motivation, regardless of whether it derives from the coach or the athlete. Research shows the importance of motivation to sport performance (Vallerand 1999, 2004). Deterioration in performance is often attributed to a lack of motivation, just as surely as overcoming adversity or winning against a superior opponent is attributed to strong motivation. Although different forms of motivation exist, most types fall within two major subcategories: intrinsic and extrinsic motivation. Intrinsic motivation involves performing an activity or sport solely for satisfaction or, as I like to say, "enjoying the journey." Extrinsic motivation, on the other hand, relies on external rewards, what I refer to as "just focusing on the result." The Sport Motivation Scale, developed in France (Pelletier et al. 1995), measures both intrinsic and extrinsic motivation. Because factorial validity of the original scale was questioned, a six-factor, twenty-four-item scale was later developed and named the SMS-6 (Mallett et al. 2007). An assessment of motivation commonly used to determine situation-specific motivation is the Situational Motivation Scale (SIMS) (Guay, Vallerand, and Blanchard 2000).

Confidence is a major psychological construct often discussed in sports. What is confidence? Sport confidence is defined as the belief an individual possesses about his or her ability to be successful in a sport. A fine line exists between self-efficacy and confidence. Self-efficacy differs from confidence and refers to an athlete's belief in his or her capability to produce and achieve results in a particular situation. For example, in the 2015 NBA final championships, as games progressed and injuries occurred, the odds of the Cleveland Cavaliers winning decreased significantly. LeBron James (arguably the best basketball player in the world) was part of the Cleveland Cavaliers, but it takes a team effort, not a one-man show, to win a championship. Although LeBron is known to be very confident (well-deserved), it was evident during the last two games in the NBA finals that his self-efficacy of winning the championship may have waned due to a lack of production from his teammates. It must be noted that LeBron played outstandingly, amassed unbelievable statistics, and came close to having a triple-double during the finals.

The most commonly used general assessment of sports confidence is the Sport Orientation Questionnaire (SOQ). Confidence can be classified as trait and state sport confidence. The Trait Sport Confidence Inventory (TSCI) is used to assess trait sports confidence. Then we have the State Sport Confidence Inventory (SSCI), which measures an athlete's sports confidence just prior to an event and indicates his or her pre-competitive feeling of confidence for that event.

Narcissism is another interesting variable that is less often examined but may be particularly relevant to sport performance analysis. Although this construct carries a negative connotation, it seems that many superstar athletes have exhibited the characteristics and signs of narcissism, such as feelings of grandiosity, preoccupation with power, a strong need for admiration and attention, and exaggerated feelings of self-importance. Some famous athletes that have displayed narcissistic traits publicly include Muhammad Ali, Lance Armstrong, Floyd Mayweather, and Tiger Woods, to name just a few.

Intrigued by the notion that some of the world's greatest athletes seem to exhibit traits of narcissism, I conducted a pilot study on male professional tennis players to examine relationships between narcissism, match outcomes, and rankings. The findings showed a strong positive correlation between narcissism, match outcomes, and player rankings. The Narcissistic Personality Inventory (NPI) was used to assess narcissism (Raskin and Hall 1979; Corry et al. 2008). This was a small, single study, and further research is warranted. It will be interesting to see if these findings hold true across genders and for various sports.

Another method that can be used to assess narcissism is the projective Thematic Apperception Test (TAT), which asks athletes to complete sentences using their own subjective experiences. There is also the Minnesota Multiphasic Personality Inventory (MMPI), with various scales designed to assess various personality traits, one of which is narcissism. Currently, the NPI and the MMPI are widely accepted measures of narcissism, as defined in the *Diagnostic and Statistical Manual of Mental Disorders* (DSM-IV-TR).

When opposing athletes are equal in skill level and physical characteristics, a deciding factor between winning and losing is mental or psychological toughness. Many of us have seen players who may not be as talented as others but who are mentally tough and come through in clutch moments, such as Rafael Nadal and Tom Brady. We also know of players who are very talented and yet crumble when the pressure is on, and as a result face difficulty in recovering from the psychological failure (trauma). Such feelings can hinder an athlete from performing at the same level he or she once did prior to the psychological failure. Take, for instance, the Women's Tennis Association (WTA) professional tennis player Jana Novotná who, though up 4–1 in the third set of the 1993 Wimbledon finals, ended up losing to Steffi Graf. Novotná's tennis career fell into what seemed an interminable slump. It is nice to know that she was able to recover after a few years and redeem herself, first by reaching the 1997 Wimbledon finals, and finally winning it in 1998.

A great deal of credit and blame for either rising to the occasion or crumbling under pressure has been attributed to anxiety. This raises questions: "What exactly is anxiety? And why is it so deleterious to the athlete's performance?"

Before delving into the various anxiety-performance theories, let us discuss what anxiety really is and how it can be measured. Anxiety is a state of physiological arousal that is accompanied by worry and uncertainty. Researchers distinguish between somatic and cognitive anxiety. Somatic anxiety refers to the physiological changes that occur as a result of activation of the sympathetic nervous system when an athlete is apprehensive. Some physiological changes that occur include an increased heart rate, sweaty palms, muscle tension, and shallow breathing. Cognitive anxiety, on the other hand, refers to the mental changes an athlete undergoes when preoccupied with the uncertainty of the desired outcome.

An assessment that distinguishes between cognitive and somatic anxiety is the State Trait Anxiety Index (STAI). The STAI includes twenty items that refer to state anxiety and another twenty items that are allocated to trait anxiety.

There are several general anxiety assessments that do not distinguish between cognitive and somatic anxiety, but assess overall sport performance anxiety, such as the Competitive State Anxiety Inventory-2 Revised (CSAI-2R), the Sport Anxiety Scale-2 (SAS-2), the Sport Competition Anxiety Test (SCAT), and the Beck Anxiety Inventory (BAI).

Many anxiety-performance theories exist, including the inverted-U hypothesis, the drive theory, the catastrophe model, the multidimensional anxiety theory, and the individual zones of optimal functioning theory (IZOF). These theories evolved from the observation of a strong relationship between anxiety and sport performance. Researchers have found that athletes who interpret their anxiety as preparatory and facilitative (in a "now I am ready to play" manner) perform much better than athletes who interpret their anxiety as debilitative. The latter perform poorly. Let us take a closer look at these theories.

The inverted-U hypothesis holds that there exists an optimal level of anxiety, and that if the athlete has little or no anxiety he or she will be easily bored and insufficiently challenged to perform at his or her best. The theory also states that if an athlete feels overwhelmed by very high levels of anxiety, he or she will also perform poorly.

The drive theory states that the more anxiety an athlete feels, the better. This theory seems to have faded in importance, for obvious reasons. A controversial theory is the catastrophe model, which focuses on the interaction between physiological arousal and cognitive anxiety, as well as the athlete's interpretation of anxiety. It is based on the hypothesis that beyond a certain level of anxiety that is positively associated with physiological arousal and performance, additional anxiety leads to deterioration of performance.

Many experts agree with the logic of this theory, although theories that developed later, such as the multidimensional anxiety theory and the IZOF, appear to be more accurate in terms of depicting the way anxiety affects sport performance. Interestingly, the multidimensional anxiety theory hypothesizes a negative linear relationship between anxiety and performance, and a positive linear relationship between self-confidence and sport performance. It combines the constructs of confidence and anxiety. The IZOF model accounts for an additional factor not included in other theories: the concept that each individual athlete has a personal level of anxiety at which he or she performs optimally.

The state of mind in which many athletes achieve optimal performance has been called the "zone" or "flow" (Csikszentmihalyi 1991). To add to the complexity of assessing intangible psychological factors, this particular variable consists of intricate components not yet too clearly defined or understood by researchers, athletes, or coaches. The concept of flow emerged from observing creative processes. Csikszentmihalyi (1991) noticed that when an artist was immersed in painting, all other bodily necessities, such as hunger, fatigue, and discomfort, seemed to be ignored. The artist was engulfed in the process and detached from the end product. During flow, athletes experience intense focus and concentration, distortion of time, intrinsic satisfaction, and loss of reflective self-consciousness, yet all with a sense of control and mastery.

Instruments used to assess flow include the Flow Questionnaire and the Flow State Scale (Jackson et al. 2001). These instruments are designed to ascertain the level of challenge facing the athlete relative to his or her level of skill. Research suggests that in order for an athlete to be in a state of flow, his or her skill level and challenge level, or opposition, must be similarly matched. But if the athlete's skill level is very low compared with the opposition, he or she will experience too much anxiety, which is not conducive to being in a state of flow. Likewise, if the athlete's skill level is high and the opposition challenge level is low, the athlete will feel bored and may win, but not perform optimally.

Over the years, experts in the field of sport psychology have attempted to characterize the psychological profiles of elite athletes. Morgan (1980) declared that successful athletes possessed a particular psychological profile, which he called "the iceberg profile." His assessment included the following psychological constructs: tension, depression, anger, fatigue, confusion, and vigor. Studies showed that, although levels of anger did not differ, successful athletes displayed lower levels of fatigue and confusion, and higher levels of tension, depression, and vigor when compared to their less successful counterparts.

Although the finding of higher tension and depression may seem counterintuitive, there is a logical explanation for this. The more successful an athlete, the more pressure he or she may feel to succeed, thereby leading to greater levels of tension. If and when such an individual fails, he or she may exhibit greater levels of depression compared to his or her counterparts.

Although there are many theories and measures of personality, a common instrument used to examine personality traits in athletes is Cattell's Sixteen Personality Factor Questionnaire (16PF). Using factor analysis, Cattell identified sixteen factors with primary traits including introversion and extraversion, tough-mindedness and receptivity, low anxiety and high anxiety, independence and accommodation, and self-control or the lack thereof (Cattell, Eber, and Tatsuoka 1970). Cattell's model is currently used to help athletes learn more about themselves and to understand their own personalities, with the objective of obtaining improved self-regulation.

Many psychological constructs encompass subcategories. For instance, confidence is divided into state and trait confidence, as is anxiety into state and trait anxiety. Aggression is a psychological construct that researchers have also subdivided into two types: instrumental and reactive aggression. Instrumental aggression is a type of healthy aggression through which athletes strategically devise a plan to hinder their opponent's performance. In contrast, reactive aggression consists of intentionally harming the opponent. This can lead to the perception that athletes are aggressive individuals, when in fact it may signify a higher level of passion for the sport.

Assessments used to measure aggression and anger are the twelve-item Competitive Aggressiveness and Anger Scale (CAAS) (Maxwell and Moores 2007) and the Anger Rumination Scale (ARS). Note that anger is considered an emotional state, while aggression is a behavior manifested during competition. Aggression also varies from sport to sport as well as by gender. It is a variable to be considered not only in performance, but also during the debilitating process that occurs when an athlete is injured. When it comes to injury and recovery, we know that physical factors can nurture an athlete back to health. But psychological factors such as aggression, depression, and self-esteem, although often overlooked, can also affect the speed of recovery.

Many athletes display aggression or some form of anger when unable to play due to injury. An obstacle that is beyond the athlete's control, such as an injury standing in the way of his or her goal, can be frustrating.

Not surprisingly, studies have shown that injured athletes exhibit higher levels of anxiety and depression compared to injury-free athletes. Depression symptoms include low self-esteem and loss of enjoyment in usually pleasurable activities. The Beck Depression Inventory (BDI) is a clinical assessment that is used to diagnose the severity of depression (Appaneal et al. 2009; Didehbani et al. 2013).

Self-esteem or the feeling that one is valuable is a major contributing factor in both injury prevention and injury recovery. Often an athlete's self-worth is tied to his or her athletic persona. When unable to play, an athlete may experience a lowered sense of self-worth. The most widely accepted measure of self-esteem is the Rosenberg Self-Esteem Scale, a self-report in the form of a Likert scale (Rosenberg 1965; Gray-Little, Williams, and Hancock 1997; Gotwals, Dunn, and Wayment 2003).

For team sports, additional psychological variables should be considered. Variables such as team cohesion, social facilitation, and social support have been shown to affect team performance. As Michael Jordan says, "Talent wins games, but teamwork and intelligence win championships." This is in line with findings from evidence-based research. Researchers in the field of sports psychology have long considered team cohesion to have a significant role in performance. A group of athletes who interact with one another for the purpose of reaching a shared objective is considered a team, while cohesion refers to the ability of individual players within a team to "stick together."

A meta-analysis of forty-six studies found a moderate to strong correlation between cohesion and team performance. The instrument used in the study was the Group Environment Questionnaire (GEQ).

The GEQ consists of factors that evaluate attraction to a group and group integration based on task and social cohesion. Carron, Widmeyer, and Brawley (1985) and Carron (2002) provide details about team cohesion variables falling under these main factors: sense of belonging, membership, interaction with the team, teamwork, closeness, and interdependency. Other environmental variables known to affect sport performance are the social support of family and teammates, and the coach-player relationship (Smoll et al. 1978; Dawson, Dobson, and Gerrard 2000; Jowett and Cockerill 2003).

Most of the current measures of psychological variables are assessed by self-report or observation. A major limitation of self-report assessments is that they are prone to social desirability bias. An athlete may not want to report a true weakness for fear of being released by a team, losing his or her position on that team, or having his or her salary reduced.

There are alternatives to self-report questionnaires. Difficult-to-measure constructs, such as self-esteem, confidence, and anxiety, are sometimes assessed with reaction time tests, including the Dot-Probe Task and the Implicit Association Test (IAT). Additional study is needed to validate reaction time tests of psychological constructs, to ensure that they measure the constructs they are intended to measure and not other factors such as selective attention (McFarland and Crouch 2002).

It is hard to quantify a psychological construct, and even harder to demonstrate construct validity. Technology experts and sport scientists have been collaborating to develop objective assessments of the psychological variables that affect sport performance. There remains a great need for improvement in the area of psychological assessment of sport performance.

A decade or so ago, it was considered taboo for an athlete to see a sport psychologist, much less to have one on a team. Nowadays, this is expected by professional athletes competing in both individual and team sports. It is astonishing that measurement and assessment of psychological variables have been neglected for so long in predictive models of sport performance. There is now at least enough literature to show that the mental or psychological aspect of sport is as important, if not more so, than physical measures.

Table 3.1 provides an overview of psychological measures relevant to sport. The first three chapters of this book have focused on measurements relevant to predicting sport performance. Chapter 4 discusses statistical analysis of measures. And chapters 5 through 9 apply statistics to measures from five sports: football, basketball, baseball, soccer, and tennis. Whether working with physiological, physical, psychological, behavioral, environmental, or performance outcome measures, we look for measurements that have certain desirable attributes, as listed in table 3.2.

Table 3.1. *Sport Psychological Measures and Factors*

Name of Measure	Abbreviation of Measure	Factor Assessed
Anger Rumination Scale	ARS	Anger and rumination
Autonomic Perception Questionnaire	APQ	Anxiety
Beck Anxiety Inventory	BAI	Anxiety
Beck Depression Inventory	BDI	Depression
Competitive Aggressiveness and Anger Scale	CAAS	Anger
Competitive State Anxiety inventory	CSAI-2R	Anxiety and confidence
Dot-Probe Task	DPT	Implicit associations and reaction time
Exercise Self-Efficacy	ESE	Self-efficacy
Flow Questionnaire	FQ	Ability to enter into flow state
Flow State Scale	FSS	Flow state experiences
Group Environment Questionnaire	GPQ	Team cohesion
Implicit Association Test	IAT	Implicit associations and underlying beliefs
Minnesota Multiphasic Personality Inventory Scales	MMPI	Aggressiveness, psychoticism, constraint, neuroticism, extraversion/intraversion
Morgan's Iceberg Profile	Iceberg Profile	Vigor, depression, tension, anger, fatigue, confusion
Narcissistic Personality Inventory	NPI	Narcissism
Rosenberg Self-Esteem Scale	RSES	Self-esteem
Sixteen Personality Factor Questionnaire	16PF	Multiple personality traits
Situational Motivation Scale	SIMS	Situation-specific motivation
Sport Competition Anxiety Test	SCAT	Anxiety
Sport Motivation Scale	SMS	Motivation
Sport Orientation Questionnaire	SOQ	Confidence
Sports Anxiety Scale	SAS	Anxiety
State Sport Confidence Inventory	SSCI	State confidence
State Trait Anxiety Index	STAI	Anxiety
Thematic Apperception Test	TAT	Underlying motives
Trait Sport Confidence Inventory	TSCI	Trait confidence
Wechsler Adult Intelligence Scale-III	WAIS-III	Intelligence
Wonderlic Cognitive Ability Test	Wonderlic	Intelligence and decision making ability

Table 3.2.   *Desirable Attributes of Measurements*

Attribute	Description
Reliable	A measure should be trustworthy and repeatable.
Valid	A measure should measure the attribute it is said to measure
Explicit	Procedures should be unambiguous and defined in detail, so that each research worker obtains the same values when using the measurement procedure.
Accessible	A measure should come from data that are easily obtained.
Tractable	A measure should be easy to work with and easy to utilize in methods and models.
Comprehensible	A measure should be simple and straightforward, so it is easily understood and interpreted.
Transparent	The method of measurement should be documented fully, so research workers can share results with one another in a spirit of open and honest scientific inquiry. There should be no trade secrets in science.

Source. Miller (2016).

Table 3.3. *A Measurement Model for Sports Performance*

Physiological	Physical	Psychological	Behavioral	Environmental
Blood Pressure	Agility	Anxiety	Nutrition	Built Environment
Glucose and Insulin	Anaerobic Power	Competitiveness	Sleep	Social Support Groups (Coaches, Parents, Peers)
Heart Rate Variability	Balance	Confidence	Substance Use	Socioeconomic Status
Lactate Threshold	Body Composition	Depression		
Methylome	Cardiorespiratory Endurance	Impulsiveness		
Previous Injuries	Coordination Ability	Intellect of Sport		
Respiratory Rate	Flexibility	Motivation		
Resting Heart Rate	Muscular Endurance	Narcissism		
Telomere Length	Muscular Power	Perfectionism		
Vision	Muscular Strength	Resiliency		
VO$_2$ max	Reaction Time	Self-Efficacy		
	Sport-Specific Skills	Self-Esteem		
		Vigor		

Source. Martin and Miller (2016).

To obtain predictive models of sport performance, Nicks and Fleishman (1960) considered basic measures of physicality, including muscular power, muscular strength, muscular endurance, static flexibility, dynamic flexibility, coordination, balance, anaerobic power, cardiorespiratory endurance, and agility—all important factors to consider. But a comprehensive measurement model for predicting sport performance would consider psychosocial, behavioral, and environmental variables as well as physical and physiological variables (Martin and Miller 2016). Table 3.3 provides a summary.

Sports psychology is a broad area of study. To pursue the subject further, students may want to examine selected measures, such as the Sixteen Personality Factor Questionnaire (Cattell, Eber, and Tatsuoka 1970) or the Rosenberg Self-Esteem Scale (Rosenberg 1965; Gray-Little, Williams, and Hancock 1997; Gotwals, Dunn, and Wayment 2003). And motivation is a key construct in this domain worthy of additional study (Vallerand 2004).

4

Selecting Statistical Models

"Statistics are like a bikini. What they reveal is suggestive, but what they conceal is vital."

—Aaron Levenstein

As a data scientist, not only are you required to understand the sport, the players, and the performance data, but also how to convey this information to decision makers such as management and operations personnel. A crucial step which lies between understanding the performance data and the decision-making process is the selection of statistical and predictive models for optimal analysis.

Aside from generating hypothesis- or data-driven analyses, it is up to you to present the results in a meaningful metric to management. For instance, although we may be excited about p-values, standard errors, and beta coefficients, management and decision-makers do not need this information. They want the bottom line result. They want to answer questions such as, "What does all this mean?" and "How can I apply this information?" For this reason, this chapter is designed to guide you through some basic principles of statistical models and help provide a rationale for choosing models based on the types of variables being examined and the research questions you are interested in answering. This chapter provides a template for classical statistical models which can be used to better present your data to players, coaches, and team management.

There are several terms you should become well acquainted with as a sports data scientist. The first important concept to understand is that there are different types of variables. Incidentally, variables were categorized in 1946 by S. S. Stevens, who declared that all measurement in science is performed using one of four scales: nominal, ordinal, interval, and ratio. Below are examples of each variable for the five sports covered in this book.

In tennis, for example, a nominal (categorical) variable might be the type of tennis court surface. There are different surfaces such as red clay, hard court, grass court, and carpet. Since the order does not matter, it can be considered a nominal variable. An example of an ordinal variable is that of the level of a tennis player. For instance, if a data set were supplied with the categories as follows—top five professional tennis players, top five Division I tennis players, top five Division II tennis players, and top five Division III tennis players—you would have a data set consisting of an ordinal variable. The set has a hierarchy, which brands it an ordinal variable. An example of an interval variable that can be applied to all sports is temperature (Fahrenheit or Celsius). However, interval variables are hard to find in the sports world, since most measures in sports have a meaningful zero point and are ratio variables. For this reason, temperature will be utilized as the example of an interval variable for the five sports mentioned in this book. Examples of ratio variables in tennis are the weight of a tennis racquet as well as the speed of the serve because they have a meaningful metric and a zero point as well.

In football an example of a nominal variable is the two conferences, the American Football Conference and National Football Conference. Another example of a nominal variable in football is found in the different divisions within each conference (east, south, west, and north). Tier levels in football ordered from most to least skilled are considered an example of an ordinal variable. For instance, the National Football League (NFL), the American Football Association (AFA), National Collegiate Athletic Association (NCAA) Division I, NCAA Division II, and NCAA Division III, as a whole can be considered an ordinal variable because of their hierarchal nature. An example of a ratio variable in football, as in other sports, is the score because it has a starting point of zero and scores have meaningful magnitude.

In basketball, examples of nominal variables include team divisions and player positions (center, point guard, small forward, power forward, and shooting guard). An example of an ordinal variable is level of the league at which basketball is played, such as the NBA, FIBA, and the D-League. An example of a ratio variable in basketball is the flight time of a player slam dunking a ball.

In baseball, the nine player positions can serve as a nominal variable. The major league and minor league can be examined as an ordinal variable, and the speed of a baseball pitch can be considered a ratio variable.

In soccer, an example of a nominal variable is player position. Examples of ordinal variables in soccer include team rankings and league divisions, such as Real Madrid and Real Madrid B-team, which have a hierarchy and specified order to them. An example of a ratio variable in soccer is the distance players run throughout an entire soccer match.

Having introduced types of variables, we turn to the analysis of data, beginning with data exploration. What does it mean to explore data? One way to begin exploring data is to plot them, construct frequency distributions, and examine descriptive statistics. Statistics such as means, medians, standard deviations, and correlation coefficients may guide us in developing interesting questions to be examined with inferential statistics and more advanced models. Table 4.1 provides an overview of statistical methods for sport performance.

Let us begin by taking a look at correlational analysis. Pearson product-moment correlation quantifies the strength and direction of a linear relationship between two variables. The strength of the relationship is determined by how close or far the correlation values are to zero or one. The closer the numbers are to one, the stronger and more positive the relationship between two variables. The closer the numbers are to zero, the weaker the relationship, and if close to negative one, then the association may be strong, but inversely correlated. It is important to recognize that, although a correlation between two variables may exist, it does not necessarily mean that one variable caused the other. It is strongly recommended that you get to know your data, as there are no specified units of measurement displayed in the output from statistical analyses.

Table 4.1. *Overview of Statistical Methods*

Method or Model	Definition or Usage
Indices of Central Tendency and Variability	
Mode	The most common value
Mean	The mathematical average
Median	The center value
Variance	The spread of the distribution
Standard Deviation	How much the values deviate from the mean
Inferential Statistics Used to Examine Group Differences	
Chi-square	Compare observed frequencies with expected frequencies
t-test	Examine differences between two groups on variable of interest
ANOVA	Examine differences between two or more groups
ANCOVA	Control for another variable that may influence the dependent variable
MANOVA	Examine group differences on multiple dependent variables
MANCOVA	Control for another variable that may influence the dependent variables
Statistics and Models Used to Examine Relationships or Predict Outcomes	
Correlation	Examine the association among two variables
Simple Linear Regression	Predict outcome with a single predictor variable
Multiple Linear Regression	Predict outcome with multiple predictors
Logistic Regression	Estimate the probability of the dependent variable class as the values of independent variables change

Pearson's product-moment correlation is intended for two normally distributed variables, otherwise a non-parametric test should be used. Spearman's rho and Kendall's tau may be used because they are not restricted in this manner—they are distribution free.

Note that many use the terms "correlation" and "association" interchangeably, and this should not be the case. In the field of data science, the term correlation is specific to the intensity and direction of the linear relationship between variables; the term association is used in a more casual manner, and does not imply direct inference from your analyses.

The first thing to do is understand the research question and objective of the study, then determine the types of variables you will be analyzing and calculate the appropriate summary statistics. For interval and ratio variables, check histograms and look for normality. Additionally, it is important to examine your data for outliers. This is important because if the sample chosen is biased or contains extreme outliers, the results of your analyses may contradict the actual values of the norm. As an example, I ran a "hypothetical model" utilizing outliers only for demonstration purposes. Examining height (twenty of the shortest and tallest) of former NBA basketball players on field goal percentage and points per game made. Results showed that neither field goal percentage nor points per game differed by height. These findings are not practical as they are based on an aberrant sample. Conversely, results from running an analysis on a normally distributed sample of current NBA basketball players show that there is a significant difference in field goal percentage and points per game by height. Specifically, taller players have a higher field goal percentage compared to shorter players, while shorter players score significantly more points per game. This example exemplifies the importance of understanding both the sport of interest and the ability to run the appropriate statistical models.

After determining whether your sample is normally distributed and distinguishing which types of variables make up your data set, it is time to choose a model and check assumptions. The assumptions that must be met in order to use a parametric test include normally distributed data, homogeneity of variance, and independence of observations. If, however, your data do not meet the assumptions for parametric tests, then non-parametric counterparts should be used.

When examining associations between ordinal variables, rather than using Pearson's product-moment correlation, it is recommended to use Spearman's rho, a non-parametric statistic that is a function of ranking the data prior to applying Pearson's equation to it. Spearman's rho is typically used when you explore the data and observe a large sample data set for which a non-parametric test should be used. For a relatively small data set, Kendall's tau is preferred over Spearman's rho. Sports performance analysts often become accustomed to analyzing their data in a particular manner, and this is not a good idea as there are a number of different assumptions that need to be met for each type of statistical analysis.

Researchers in various disciplines utilize the Student's *t*-test, a simple statistical test used to compare means and determine statistical significance. However, it should be noted that there are several types of *t*-tests: the one-sample *t*-test, independent means *t*-test (two-sample *t*-test), and the matched pair *t*-test (dependent means *t*-test). A *one-sample t-test* should be used when comparing the mean of the group of interest to the mean of a population for which the parameters are already known.

If a tennis coach wanted to know whether the speed of students' serves exceeded the speed of serves for the world's top twenty tennis professionals, the coach could use an independent means *t*-test. This test would look at the mean or average of speed of his students' serves, which he would compare against the average speed of the population of interest, in this case the speed of serves of the world's top twenty tennis professionals. In summary, the group of interest is the group of tennis players the coach is training, the dependent variable is the speed of serve, and the *t*-test will yield a *p*-value resulting in either significant or non-significant findings compared to a known parameter, the speed of serves of the world's top twenty professional tennis players.

The first assumption that should be met for an *independent t-test* is that the dependent variable, outcome variable, or response variable (used interchangeably; some terms may be preferred more in certain fields than in others) lies on a continuous scale. Examples of continuous variables are distance run on the football field, time spent training on the tennis court, or duration of tennis match or baseball game.

The second assumption to be met for the independent *t*-test is that the independent, explanatory, or predictor variable consists of two independent groups that are categorical. For instance, we could examine differences between two sports such as baseball and football, with baseball and football representing levels of the categorical variable sport and with the study observations being independent of each other.

The third assumption is that of independence of observations which is designed to ensure that every athlete in a group be examined only in that group, and not in more than one group. Independence of observations is a critical assumption of many statistical models and test.

The fourth assumption of the *t*-test is that there are no extreme outliers. Including extreme outliers in your data set might tarnish your independent *t*-test results. If you find something interesting and would like to include the extreme outlier, you may want to use a different analysis that is more robust. Remember, you want to use the best model for the type of data you have. The fifth assumption is that your dependent variable is normally distributed for each of the independent variable groups (such as baseball and football). Tests of normality such as the Shapiro-Wilk test and the Kolmogorov-Smirnov test can be used to check that this assumption is met. Finally, the sixth assumption pertains to the criterion of homogeneity of variances, or that the variances should be equal among the groups. Levene's test is specific to assessing homogeneity of variances.

When you are interested in comparing two means that are related by either time or group, the appropriate model is a paired *t*-test. The additional assumption of having no extreme outliers must be met in order to satisfy the criteria for running a paired samples *t*-test. An example of when to use this type of *t*-test is if you want to answer a sport performance question such as, "Did our soccer players' speed improve from the first day of preseason conditioning compared to the last day of preseason conditioning?" Two time points are assumed in this question. Thus, you will have values for the soccer players' speed at baseline and after conditioning. The paired *t*-test will yield a result that indicates whether the improvement in speed was significant over those two time points. However, caution is advised, especially when using too many *t*-tests. They may yield false positives and increase the likelihood of a Type I error.

When you have multiple *t*-tests to run, you are probably better off using an analysis of variance (ANOVA) model. ANOVA is the statistical model of choice when the research question consists of examining the effect of an intervention on two or more groups and if the goal is to determine whether there are group mean differences in the dependent variable. This is a great model to use when you want to determine if differences between player positions or teams affect a particular performance variable. For instance, if we were interested in examining the differences between player positions in basketball on three-point percentage, this model would be appropriate. Our research question would be, "Are there differences between centers, small forwards, and shooting guards on three-point percentage?"

It is important to understand that the ANOVA model can determine significant differences between player positions on the three-point percentage, but it does not tell us between which player positions the significant differences are located. Thus, further investigation is needed, and post hoc analyses should be performed to determine which group pairings are statistically different from one another. Prior to deciding ANOVA is the model you want to run, you must make sure to check that six assumptions are met. The first assumption is that the dependent variable be continuous. The second assumption is that your independent variable or variable of interest consists of two or more groups or categories.

The third assumption of ANOVA is that there is independence of observations, meaning that no relationship between the independent variables exists. For instance, if interested in examining differences between basketball teams, this last assumption is met when we verify that players on the Miami Heat are only in that group and do not belong to any other group or team, such as the Oklahoma City Thunder. If we were trying to compare shooting percentage across player positions, for example, the assumption would be violated if an athlete played multiple positions, such as point guard and shooting guard. If we want to use ANOVA, we must ensure that the players in each position are designated, and playing only a single position. Otherwise, another statistical model may be a better choice.

The fourth assumption of ANOVA that should be met is that there are no extreme outliers. Typically, the rule of thumb is, if the value lies outside two standard deviations, it is considered an outlier. The fifth assumption for

ANOVA is that of a normal distribution. ANOVA tends to be robust against the violation of normality, however, if the data are obviously skewed, you might be better off transforming your data or opting for a non-parametric test, such as the Kruskal-Wallis model. The sixth, and final assumption that needs to be met to run an ANOVA model is homogeneity of variance, which can be verified by running Levene's test. If the assumption for homogeneity of variance is not met, there are two alternate models that can be used: Welch's test, and the Brown and Forsythe test. If all six assumptions are met, you are free to run the ANOVA model. Remember, after running the ANOVA model, if you had more than two groups, you will need to run post hoc analyses. Post hoc analyses typically used are the Games-Howell and Tukey's tests.

SPSS, SAS, R, or other statistical software may be used to perform statistical analyses. The R output displayed after running an ANOVA model includes the sum of squares, degrees of freedom, mean square, *F*-value, and the *p*-value denoted under a header titled, *Sig*, which is an indicator of the statistical significance.

Moving to a more complex model, analysis of covariance (ANCOVA) is recommended when the independent variables are categorical and the dependent variable is a continuous variable, but you want to control for a possible confounding variable. A confounding variable is a factor that may be contributing variance to the independent variable. Therefore, to obtain a true measure of the variance accounted for by the independent variable on the dependent variable, you should control for this third variable. For example, if you wanted to examine the differences between basketball teams' training regimens and performance, it is important to control for the budgets invested in player training (covariate). This is of interest because the amount of money invested in training and equipment can make a difference in coaching, equipment, physical therapy, and strength and conditioning of the players, all of which indirectly influence training regimen and performance. Again, if we are interested in how basketball teams differ in performance based upon training regimen, and the influence of financial resources is controlled for, we can obtain a glimpse into which team is getting more "bang for their buck" training-wise.

To run the ANCOVA model, the six assumptions for an ANOVA model are to be satisfied. Additionally, the following three assumptions also have to be met: The covariate (third variable) should be linearly related to the outcome for each independent variable group, the assumption of homoscedasticity, and the assumption of homogeneity of regression slopes.

What does all this actually mean? What are we checking for? The assumption of the covariate being linearly associated with the dependent variable can be verified with a simple scatter plot. If you find that the relationship is nonlinear, ANCOVA is not the optimal choice to analyze your data. The assumption of homoscedasticity checks that the error term in the relationship between the independent variable and the dependent variable is equal across all levels of the independent variables. Finally, the assumption of homogeneity of regression slopes is meant to determine whether the slopes, although they differ, run parallel to each other. There is no evidence of interaction between the covariate and the independent variable if slopes run parallel to each other. This is a great model for comparing differences across groups such as teams or player positions on a particular outcome, while simultaneously controlling for an intervening variable.

Multivariate models are specifically designed to assess multiple dependent variables and correlated outcomes. For instance, suppose you are now interested in examining differences among three positions in football (quarterback, running back, and defensive lineman) on the 40-yard dash, shuttle run, and 5-10-5 agility drill. A multivariate analysis is preferred because the dependent variables are all somewhat correlated in this example; they are measures of anaerobic power. In this case a multivariate analysis of variance (MANOVA) is the optimal choice. On the other hand, suppose you wanted to analyze the differences in these same player positions on the 40-yard dash, 225 pound bench press, and the Wonderlic cognitive ability test. The MANOVA is not the correct model to use. Why is this? Because the dependent variables are not correlated. The 40-yard dash is a measure of anaerobic power and speed, while the 225 pound bench press is an assessment of upper body muscular strength, and the Wonderlic test is an assessment of a completely unrelated aptitude. Again, results obtained using this model will tell you that there are significant differences between groups, but not exactly between which pairs of groups the differences lie.

Additional analyses are required to determine more specific information. If you decide that the MANOVA model is appropriate, based on the type of data and the number of dependent variables, a total of nine assumptions must be met. The independence of observations assumption is standard. So is the fact that the ANOVA, ANCOVA, MANOVA, and multivariate analysis of covariances (MANCOVA) require the independent variables to be categorical. However, for MANOVAs and MANCOVAs there is an additional criterion of multiple dependent variables. Large sample sizes are preferred. Using MANOVA or MANCOVA requires that there be more subjects in each independent variable group than the total number of dependent variables.

Another assumption is that there are no univariate or multivariate outliers. "Univariate outliers" is a term used interchangeably with "outliers," because it is indicative of outliers within each group of the independent variables, compared to multivariate outliers which refers to those in the dependent variables. You should assess for outliers (univariate) using boxplots, and assess for multivariate outliers using Mahalanobis distance. Another assumption is that of multivariate normality, which is checked using the Shapiro-Wilk test of normality. Additionally, MANOVA requires the assumption of a linear relationship among the dependent variables for all independent variables, which usually can be verified by a simple scatterplot matrix. Further, there is the assumption of homogeneity of variance-covariance matrices that is checked using Box's *M* test of equality of covariance. The final assumption necessary to run these types of multivariate analyses necessitates an absence of multicollinearity, meaning that there should not be too strong of a correlation between the dependent variables. It may sound counterintuitive, but in order to run MANOVAs or MANCOVAs you should have multiple dependent variables which are moderately correlated. If the correlation is too low, it is better to assess the dependent variables individually using ANOVA. And if the correlation is too strong, multicollinearity may be an issue.

MANOVAs can also be used to assess a particular variable at several different time points. This model is called a repeated measures MANOVA. An example of when it is appropriate to use this model is when assessing muscular power pre-season, during season, and post season, because there are at least two or more time points.

When using a repeated measures MANOVA, it is important to refer to Wilks' Lambda and the significance of the overall multivariate tests. If you don't find significance, your analysis is done. However, if you find significance, you should follow up using univariate ANOVAs and determine if the tests of between-subjects effects (across the independent variables) is significant. It is protocol to run a Bonferroni correction after finding significance in the multivariate and between-subjects tests, to correct for the number of ANOVAs conducted.

An additional test that is similar to correlations is the chi-square test of independence, also termed Pearson's chi-square. The chi-square test differs from the well-known Pearson's product-moment correlation in that it is used to examine the relationships between two categorical (not continuous) variables. This test requires that only two assumptions be met: both variables are categorical, and there are at least two independent groups. Suppose you wanted to explore the relationship between the two soccer teams Real Madrid and Barcelona (considered one categorical variable consisting of two groups) on penalty shots made versus penalty shots missed during a season. The chi-square test is appropriate for exploring this type of data, especially because the dependent variable is of a dichotomous (penalty shots made/penalty shots missed) nature. Typically your output, depending on the software being used to analyze the data, will yield a crosstabs section and the chi-square test results. An easy way to present your exploratory analysis of the data is with a histogram or bar graph, which are efficient at displaying frequency counts for categorical groups.

When the goal in question is to predict performance, you are better off choosing a regression model. This model functions to examine the variance accounted for in the dependent variable (outcome) by a predictor variable (Keith 2014). The interesting thing about regression is that the predictor variable (independent variable) can be either continuous or categorical, unlike in the ANOVA and MANOVA models. Regression models can be used when either one (simple linear regression) or several predictor variables (multiple linear regression) exist. Like all other models mentioned in this chapter, regression has assumptions that need to be met prior to being utilized. Most often, regression is used because of the nature of the independent variable (continuous), or if you are interested in predictive modeling.

The first assumption for regression is that the variables to be analyzed are either interval or ratio variables. Additionally, the variables must have a linear relationship. If this second assumption is not met, another model such as a non-linear regression, or a non-linear mixed-effects model would be more appropriate. The third assumption is that there are no significant outliers such that there is a large residual, which indicates that the value is far from the predicted line. The assumptions of independence and homoscedasticity also apply to this model.

There is another assumption that must be met in order to run a regression model, and that is that the residual errors be normally distributed. This final assumption can be verified by simple visualization with a histogram. When you run a regression model, an output containing R and R^2 values is displayed. Although in correlational analysis we are interested in R, in regression we are interested in R^2, which is representative of the output variable variance accounted for by the regression model. As an example, suppose we regressed performance (outcome) on hours of training (predictor variable), and the R^2 was 0.79. This is interpreted as seventy-nine percent of the variance in performance is accounted by hours of training. Additionally, the omnibus results will yield an F-value and a p-value, indicative of significance or non-significance. The output of a regression analysis describes how good the model is at predicting the outcome.

When running regressions, it is imperative to examine the output, specifically, the beta coefficients. The big B represents the unstandardized coefficient, typically used when the variables in your model are in transferrable units of measure. If you were testing athletes in both the max vertical leap and the static squat jump as predictors of their ability to slam dunk, the primary outcome of interest is the height reached quantified in inches.

The key point is that both predictors are measured in the same units (inches) and thus unstandardized coefficients are preferred. Unstandardized coefficients represent how much variance in the dependent variable is accounted for by a particular predictor variable, while controlling for other variables. But if you wanted to compare the importance of the max vertical jump (inches) versus the 40-yard dash (seconds), you would first convert to a common unit of measure and then look at the relative values of the Beta regression coefficients. These would be standardized coefficients.

Regression provides an overall fit of the variance accounted for by each predictor variable on the total variance as explained by multiple predictors. For multiple regression there are a total of eight assumptions that must be met. The first assumption is that the dependent variable is continuous. The next assumption is that there are at least two or more independent variables; in this case they can be continuous, categorical, or a combination of both. The third assumption is that there is independence of observation, as is standard with the majority of models. The fourth assumption is similar to that of simple linear regression: a linear relationship between the dependent variable for each level of the predictor variables.

There is also the assumption of homoscedasticity, as explained earlier. Similar to the MANOVA, the sixth assumption for multiple linear regression is that the data must be free of multicollinearity. The seventh assumption ensures there are no significant outliers, and finally, the eighth assumption is that the residuals be normally distributed. This last assumption can be verified using a Q-Q plot. After these assumptions are met, and you choose to run a multiple linear regression, you will obtain an R value, an R^2 value, and an adjusted R^2 value. Remember, similar to simple linear regression, the multiple correlation coefficient (R) and the coefficient of determination (R^2) will be in your output.

The multiple linear regression model differs from the simple linear regression model in that there is a new item in the output, the adjusted R^2 value. Because there is more than one predictor variable, we need to understand the variance accounted for in the dependent variable by each of the predictors. This is represented in the output by the adjusted R^2 value, and answers the question, "How much variance in the dependent variable is accounted for by the inclusion of an additional predictor variable in the model?" To examine whether your chosen predictor variables produced a good fit, refer to the F-ratio as well as the p-value.

Another model to use when both the independent variables and dependent variables are categorical in nature is the logistic regression model, also referred to as a logit model. This model uses a linear combination of the predictor variables to determine the log of odds of the outcome. It is typically used to predict the odds of winning or losing for different teams.

If you are interested in trajectories over time, several of these models may be used, but more advanced models such as linear mixed effects models, longitudinal growth curve models, and non-linear mixed effects models function much better to capture trends over time. For more specific details on these advanced models, please refer to Singer and Willett (2003) and articles by Bauer and Curran (2003), Curran, Bauer, and Willoughby (2004), Pinheiro, Bates, DebRoy, Sarkar, et al. (2007), and Duncan, Duncan, and Strycker (2013).

Nonparametric methods represent an alternative to parametric methods (Sprent and Smeeton 2007; Neuhauser 2011; Kloke and McKean 2014). And Bayesian methods provide an alternative to classical inference (Robert 2007). Contemporary modeling may also utilize machine learning as well as statistical models (Izenman 2008; Hastie, Tibshirani, and Friedman 2009; Murphy 2012).

Table 4.2 reviews the statistical tests and models covered in this chapter. Additional terms are defined in the statistics glossary (page 187). We will see applications of statistical tests and models in the chapters to follow.

This review of statistical models has focused on traditional parametric methods and classical inference, which are frequently used within sports performance measurement and analytics. Additional coverage of traditional statistics is provided by Snedecor and Cochran (1989), Black (2011), Wasserman (2010), and Triola (2014). Growth curve (Duncan, Duncan, and Strycker 2013), longitudinal data analysis (Singer and Willett 2003), and mixed models (Pinheiro, Bates, DebRoy, Sarkar, et al. 2007) are especially useful in working with athletic performance data over time.

Table 4.2. *Review of Statistical Tests and Models*

Statistical Model	Data and Variables	Questions Answered by the Statistical Model
Chi-square	One or more categorical variables	Are basketball players more susceptible to injuries than baseball players? (Are two categorical variables related?)
t-test	Dichotomous independent variable for groups, one continuous dependent variable variable	Are there differences between the New England Patriots and the Miami Dolphins on touchdowns scored? (Do differences exist between two groups on a dependent variable?)
ANOVA	One or more categorical independent variables, one continuous dependent variable	Are there differences between the sports of basketball, tennis, and soccer on athletes' salaries? (Do differences exist between two or more groups on one continuous dependent variable?)
ANCOVA	One or more categorical independent variables, one continuous dependent variable, and one or more control variables	Are there differences between the sports of basketball, tennis, and soccer on athletes' salaries after controlling for ticket sales? (Do differences exist between two or more groups after controlling for a covariate on one dependent variable?)
MANOVA	One or more categorical independent variables, two or more continuous dependent variables	Are there differences between basketball player positions; center, point guard, and power forward on field goals, rebounds, and assists? (Do differences exist between two or more groups on multiple dependent variables?)
MANOVA with Repeated Measures	One or more categorical independent variables, two or more continuous dependent variables, with the dependent variables being repeated measures of the same attribute	Are there differences between basketball player positions; center, point guard, and power forward on field goals, rebounds, and assists at at pre season, during the season, and post season? (Do differences exist between two or more groups on multiple dependent variables over different time points?)
MANCOVA	One or more categorical independent variables, two or more continuous dependent variables, and one or more control variables	Are there differences between basketball player positions; center, point guard, and power forward on field goals, rebounds, and assists after controlling for minutes played? (Do differences exist between two or more groups after controlling for a covariate on multiple dependent variables?)
Correlation	Two continuous variables for a single correlation, linear relationship	Is there a relationship between socioeconomic status and playing tennis professionally? (Is there a relationship between these variables and in what direction?)
Simple Linear Regression	One dichotomous or continuous independent variable and one continuous dependent variable	How much variance in home runs is accounted for by upper body muscular strength in baseball players? (How much variance in the dependent variable is accounted for by the independent variable? Also, how strongly related to the dependent variables is the coefficient to the independent variable?)
Multiple Linear Regression	Two or more dichotomous or continuous independent variables (one or more being control variables) and one continuous dependent variable	How much variance in home runs is accounted for by upper body muscular strength, core strength, lower body muscular strength, and anaerobic power in baseball players? (How much variance in the dependent variable is accounted for by the linear combination of the independent variables? Also, how strongly related to the dependent variables is the coefficient to the independent variable?)
Logistic Regression	Two or more dichotomous or continuous independent variables and one dichotomous dependent variable	What are the odds that a particular team will win based on previous performance? (What are the odds probability of the dependent variable occuring as the values of the independent variables' change?)

5

Touchdown Analytics

"The true competitors are the ones who always play to win."

—TOM BRADY

Football is not only a beautifully complex game, full of strategy and intricacy, it is the quintessential sport of the United States. In fact, playbooks specific for offensive and defensive plays have been carefully designed to train players in the different strategies that can be used against opponents. The game of football is rumored to have evolved from games which involve kicking, possibly *futbol* and rugby.

Legend has it that an individual who was playing futbol suddenly became tired midgame of kicking the ball around, so he picked it up with his bare hands and began to run with it, and a new game was formed. As the game grew popular, football leagues began to develop across the country, and in 1922 the American Professional Football Association changed its name to the National Football League (NFL).

The first NFL playoff game was held in Chicago in 1932. The NFL's inaugural player was Jim Thorpe, who later became the president of the NFL. During the 1940s, football was characterized by the restructuring of teams, the inclusion of black players into the league, and the war.

The 1950s were known for the development of the Eastern and Western divisions and the addition of championship games. In 1959 the American Football League (AFL) was founded, but it was not until the late 1960s that the first AFL-NFL Super Bowl took place and was won by the Green Bay Packers. In the 1970s, the Miami Dolphins won Super Bowl VII with the significant record of a perfect winning season. During this period the AFL joined the NFL and, as a result, two subdivision conferences emerged: the National Football Conference (NFC) and the American Football Conference (AFC). Both the NFC and the AFC are comprised of sixteen teams each and have their own playoffs. The victors of each conference then meet at the Super Bowl where the winner is crowned the NFL champion.

The 1980s are remembered for the strike initiated by the NFL Players Association, while the 1990s seemed to be a time of change for teams, particularly in the State of California. Both the Los Angeles Rams and the Raiders were relocated within a two month period—the Rams to St. Louis and the Raiders to Oakland. At the time of the writing of this book, teams are competing with each other for the right to leave their current cities and return NFL football to Los Angeles. Those teams include the San Diego Chargers who would be moving just up the coastline, and both the Oakland Raiders and St. Louis Rams who would be making a return to the area. Some think there may be a team in Los Angeles in the near future, possibly as soon as the 2016 season.

The latter part of 2014 and early 2015 was a period during which football was better known worldwide for the "Deflategate" controversy than for its players. On a positive note, the 2015 salary cap was increased to $143.28 million, reaching an all-time high. Rules for the sport of football were adopted in 1869 based on those of the London Football Association. Universal league rules were written in 1904 and major modifications took place in 1933. An existing rule was amended in 1938, in which a fifteen-yard penalty for roughing the passer was implemented. Finally, in the 1970s several regulations were added to the rule book, and included the decision of the league to place the players' names on the backs of their jerseys, instituting the scoreboard clock as the official timer of the game, and establishing that the point scored after a touchdown is worth one point.

Fundamental rule changes were implemented in 1974. The rules were modified and the game made more exciting with the introduction of sudden death in overtime, goal posts were relocated to the end lines, and the place for the starting kickoff was changed from the forty-five to the thirty-yard line. More recently, safety rules have been in the spotlight due to growing evidence of the deleterious effects of concussions. Research findings have led to innovation in equipment, such as additional padding and sensors in helmets and shoulder pads.

The football uniform consists of a helmet, which nowadays is specifically designed to attenuate the effects of being tackled and reduce the potential harm from concussions. Shoulder pads and kneecaps are mandatory, along with a mouth guard, cleats, same-colored socks, and a number identifying the player on the jersey. The sport of football technically requires only a ball of conical shape, typically brown in color and of leather material with seams and a weight of four hundred grams. Although the game can be played anywhere, in a park or an empty street, the official playing field is one hundred yards long and fifty-three and one-third yards wide and has end zones and goal posts at both ends, where touchdowns and field goals are scored. Throughout the field are yard markers which look like dashes on the field and are placed there to help the players, fans, and officials keep track of the ball as well as the yardage covered by players.

The yard markers that are located in the center of the field are known as hash marks and are designed to set the boundaries for where a play can begin. Each play begins with the ball placed at the exact spot on the field where the previous play ended, unless the play finished outside the hash marks (away from the middle of the field). If a play finishes outside the hash marks the next play begins with the ball placed on the hashmark closest to where the play ended. Football is quantified and played within four quarters. Each quarter consists of fifteen minutes, with a twelve-minute half-time break occurring between the second and third quarters. The teams alternate sides and play on different sides of the fields each quarter. The team that possesses the ball at the end of the first and third quarters continues to have possession at the start of the following quarter. However, this rule does not apply before or after halftime because the second half is begun with a kickoff.

In the NFL, each team must play sixteen games during the regular season, a requisite being that each team play every other team within its division twice. There are four teams per division, thus within one's own division a total of six games are played. In addition, both AFC and NFC teams must play all teams from one other division within their conference, adding another four games. Further, each team plays all the teams in one division from the opposite conference, racking up another four games. Lastly, two final games are played against two teams within their own conference that they have not played previously.

A football team is composed of eleven players. The team in possession of the football is called the offense—their objective is to score a touchdown. On the other hand, the eleven-man team which does not have possession of the ball is called the defense. The defense's objective is to prevent the offensive team from scoring, as well as to get possession of the ball as quickly as possible (by intercepting). However, if the offensive team scores, roles are automatically switched, as is possession of the ball. This manner of play continues until time runs out.

A football game begins with the "kickoff" when the ball is kicked from the defensive team's thirty-five yard line by the "placekicker," who's job is to kick the ball as far as he can into the opponent's territory. The opposing team will try to counter by catching the ball and running it down the field as far as they can before being tackled.

For deep kicks that travel into the end zone, the opposing team may elect to not return the kick and instead opt for a "touchback" which automatically gives the team possession at their own ten yard line. Kickoffs that travel at least ten yards are known as a "live-ball" and can be recovered for a possession by both the kicking and receiving team. Teams usually prefer to kick the ball deep into their opponent's territory to make the opposing offense drive the length of the field, but at times teams alter their strategy and attempt an onside kick (short kickoff) in hopes of recovering the kick before the opponent has an opportunity to do so.

Another form of initiation is the well-known "snap," a cue that is traditionally used to start each play. The center "snaps" the ball under his legs to the quarterback, who is typically recognized by "calling plays" in code. The quarterback then decides within seconds what to do with the ball, whether to throw it to a teammate or run it down the field.

As mentioned previously, football is a very elegant game. Ironically, the game is more commonly admired for its displays of brutality rather than the complex plays and elaborate formation. Each eleven-man team consists of three different sections which, oddly enough, are also called teams: the offensive team, the defensive team, and the special teams. The offense is the part of the team which has possession of the ball and whose objective is to score a touchdown. Conversely, the defense is the section of the team whose main objective is to stop the other team's offense. The special teams unit consists of players used in kicking situations such as kickoffs, punts, field goals, and point-after-touchdown attempts.

Within each team are several positions that encompass very different physical and psychological attributes. Arguably, the most important position is the quarterback, which requires the ability to make decisions quickly under pressure. The quarterback leads the offensive team and informs his teammates playing offense of the plays they will be executing. Ultimately, the quarterback is the orchestrator of the offensive team.

There are only two ways for the offense to advance the ball, by running or passing the ball. There are several ways to score points. The most common ways include the touchdown which scores six points, the extra point which yields a single point, the two-point conversion for two points, safety also for two points, and a field goal which is three points. Some less common methods of scoring points include the defensive two-point conversion in which the defense returns a failed point-after-touchdown attempt by the offense, a one point safety which can also be earned on point-after-touchdown attempts, and the fair-catch kick which scores three points and happens when a team elects to attempt an uncontested field goal in lieu of running a normal play from scrimmage.

A fundamental concept in football is that of "downs." Basically, the offense has four attempts in which to gain a total of ten yards. If the team is successful in its first attempt, it earns a first down and another set of four downs as well as the opportunity to gain another ten yards. Play typically ends if the player is tackled to the ground, one or both knees touch the ground, or if he runs, or is forced, out of bounds.

A turnover, such as a fumble or interception, can be a game changer. A fumble occurs when a player drops the ball or loses possession when he was considered to have possession of the ball. Alternately, an interception occurs when a defensive player from the opposing team catches a ball that was not intended for him, causing a shift in the momentum of the game. See the football glossary (page 193) for additional definitions of football terms.

An understanding of how to play the game answers the question, "What are the things you have to do to play the game?" As sports and data scientists we are led to ask, "What are the things you need to do well to win, or be the best at this sport?" Logically, this leads us to discuss assessment and measurement of variables affecting football performance.

The NFL has established its own battery of physical measures for rookies and players new to the NFL, called the NFL Scouting Combine. It consists of the following physical tests: forty-yard dash, bench press, vertical jump, broad jump, three-cone agility drill, and the 20-yard shuttle (5-10-5 agility test). These assessments are conducted once every year as part of the NFL Combine. Factors such as speed, anaerobic power, agility, muscular strength and power are assessed. Currently, the NFL is in the process of restructuring the NFL Combine performance tests and variables measured in order to improve the prediction of player performance (McGee and Burkett 2003).

There are clear differences in the physical and psychological makeup among player positions. The position of quarterback requires the ability to perform a variety of tasks in comparison to positions such as linebacker and defensive end. With this in mind, it is suggested to refer back to chapter 2, as specific measures are recommended for physical factors most important to each player position. This is not to say that the measures currently used in the NFL Combine are not important for all positions. Measures differ in importance from position to position.

The position of quarterback requires quick reaction time, decision-making skills, anaerobic power, and flexibility, among other factors. Psychological assessment can provide insight into the quarterback's mindset and capabilities. The quarterback requires a high "football IQ," so a test of cognitive ability or intelligence is highly recommended. Currently, the Wonderlic is used in professional football. Additionally, it is recommended that reaction time as well as confidence be assessed for players in this position, especially because the ability to play under pressure is key. The Wonderlic, IAT, and CSAI-2R should be utilized when assessing a quarterback.

Conversely, the players attacking the quarterback should be assessed differently. Emphasis should be placed on measures that quantify first-step explosiveness (anaerobic power), muscular strength, and muscular power. All of these physical measures should be considered in addition to video playback, tape study, and game-time performance. Psychological assessments recommended for this player position include the 16PF and the CAAS mentioned in chapter 3.

The defensive tackle position should be assessed quite differently. There is also a difference between a nose tackle and a pass-rushing three-tech defender. The typical stats of a nose tackle include a mean height of six feet and mean weight of 300 pounds. Nose tackles are known to run the forty-yard dash in under five and a half seconds and bench press more than thirty repetitions with a resistance load of 225 pounds. Although similar to the nose tackle, a typical defensive tackle averages a mean height of six feet three inches, and a mean weight of 280 pounds. Players in this position are known to be quicker, running the forty-yard dash in under five seconds, yet they have a good deal of muscular endurance (although slightly less than the nose tackle) and are able to do an average of twenty-five repetitions with a resistance load of 225 pounds on the bench press. The descriptive statistics mentioned above describe how players in similar positions may differ physically, thus emphasizing the need for individualized performance assessments.

Assessment of players for the running back position should include measures of vision and speed because the position requires excellent eye-hand coordination and the ability to find openings in a fast-paced, high-pressured game situation. Speed is important, but only if a player has the ability to retain possession of the ball and change direction quickly. A running back benefits by having an explosive first step. Other assessments relevant to this position include physical measures of agility and lower body muscular power such as the 20-yard shuttle and the maximal vertical jump. Additionally, psychological assessments recommended include the IAT and the Wonderlic.

The position of wide receiver is founded on speed and the ability to change direction quickly. The wide receiver's objective is to catch the ball and gain as many yards as possible toward the end zone in order to score a touchdown. Thus, this position requires excellent eye-hand coordination in order to catch the ball under the constant pressure that is applied by defenders from the opposite team. Assessment measures recommended for this position include speed, anaerobic power, agility and balance. Psychological assessments recommended for the position of a wide receiver include the SOQ, the IAT, and the CSAI-2R.

Defensive ends are typically characterized by being big, fast, and strong. Throughout the years, athletes in this position seem to be getting bigger, faster, and stronger. Aside from physical attributes, these athletes must also have the ability to make split-second decisions, particularly, whether to target the quarterback or the running back. Erroneously in the past, scouting teams relied heavily on categorizing athletic ability simply by assessing a player's performance in the forty-yard dash. However, muscular strength is crucial for defensive ends as it is a fundamental requirement for tackling ball carriers, stopping forward momentum on runs, and taking on double teams by the offense. The typical height and weight of defensive ends participating in the combine range between six feet and six feet seven inches, with a mean height of six feet three inches and weight between 235 to 352 pounds. Physical measures recommended for this position include upper and lower body muscular strength and power using the bench and leg press (or squat).

It is important to examine appropriate variables for each position played. For instance, if a defensive lineman has a slow first step, intuitively it may seem to be due to lack of speed or anaerobic power. In fact, the slow first step may stem from his inability to concentrate or focus. Thus, it is important to examine both physical and psychological variables. Psychological assessments recommended include the IAT and the CAAS.

Another important set of attributes for all football players includes reaction time and anticipatory skills. The ability of defensive players to read and react effectively against players on the offense is crucial to their success. The same is true for offensive players facing opposing defenders. Measures of agility and anaerobic power such as the three-cone agility drill, the

20-yard shuttle, an explosive first step assessment, and the maximal vertical jump test are recommended. The ability to cut and change directions is extremely relevant to the majority of positions on a football team. Upper body strength and endurance using the bench press is strongly recommended for offensive and defensive linemen, especially for those players who play in the middle of the line. That would include offensive guards, offensive centers, and defensive tackles. In addition, a test of leg strength and power is recommended. Squats or leg presses can be used to assess muscular leg strength, power, and endurance. Additionally, both the vertical jump and broad jump can be used to ascertain the explosive power a player has available in his lower body. Underestimated by many, the legs (when used appropriately) are responsible for power and strength being transferred up through the core to the upper body.

In summary, there are many physical and psychological factors that contribute to a football player's performance. The proper use of relevant measures and assessments for each player position is crucial in order for data scientists to develop more accurate sports performance models and to make meaningful recommendations to trainers and coaches. Regarding football player performance on the field, there are a number of key measures to consider, as documented in table 5.1. Those wanting to learn more about football may consult sources such as Sullivan (1985), Waddington and Roderick (1996), Winston (2009), Swain and Harvey (2012), and Van Pelt (2014).

Exhibit 5.1 (page 82) shows the R program code and listing for analyzing data from the NFL Combine. Figure 5.1 shows agility quantified using the three-cone agility drill by player position. Figure 5.2 shows anaerobic power, speed, and agility quantified using the 20-yard shuttle by player position. Figure 5.3 shows anaerobic power quantified using the vertical jump by player position. Figure 5.4 shows anaerobic power quantified using the 40-yard dash speed assessment by player position. Figure 5.5 shows anaerobic power quantified using the broad jump by player position during the NFL scouting combine. And figure 5.6 shows muscular strength and endurance quantified using the bench press test with a load of 225 pounds by player position.

Exhibit 5.2 (page 92) shows an additional R program and listing. This program provides an analysis of NFL game time performance data.

Table 5.1. *Football Performance Measures*

Performance Measure	Abbreviation
Assisted tackles	AST
Attempts (third and fourth down, passing, rushing, kickoff and punt return)	ATT
Average (yards per reception, gross punts, kickoff, and punt returns)	AVG
Blocked punts	BP
Completion percentage (third and fourth down, field goals and extra point made)	PCT
Conversions (third and fourth down)	MADE
Extra point attempts	XPA
Extra points made	XPM
Fair catches	FC
Field goals attempts	FGA
Field goals made	FGM
Total (first downs, penalties, and tackles)	TOTAL
Forced fumbles	FF
Fumbles (rushing and receiving)	FUM
Fumbles lost (rushing and receiving)	FUML
Fumbles recovered	REC
Interceptions	INT
Longest (kickoff and punt returns, field goals made and punts)	LNG
Longest (pass, rush, reception, and interception return)	LONG
Net yards (passing, rushing, penalty, receiving, kickoff return, punting, and intercepted returned)	YDS
Net passing, rushing, receiving yards per game	YDS/G
Net punting average	NET
Pass defended	PD
Passer rating	RATE
Passing first downs	PASS
Penalty first downs	PEN
Punts inside the 20 yard line	IN20
Punts returned	RET
Receptions	REC
Rushing first downs	RUSH
Sack yards lost	YDSL
Sacks	SACKS
Total punts	PUNTS
Touchbacks	TB
Touchdowns (passing, rushing, receiving, kickoff and punt returns, fumbles returned)	TD
Unassisted tackles	SOLO
Yards per pass or rush attempt	YDS/A
Yards returned on punts	RETY
Completions	COMP

Figure 5.1. *Three-Cone Agility Drill by Player Position (NFL Combine)*

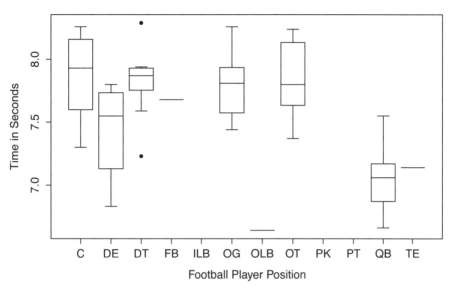

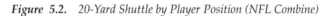

Figure 5.2. *20-Yard Shuttle by Player Position (NFL Combine)*

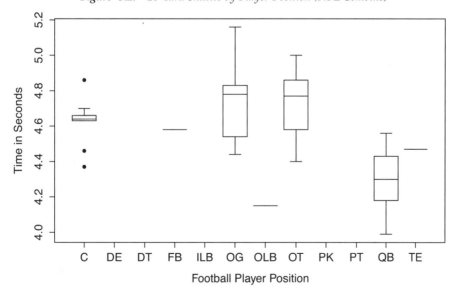

Figure 5.3. *Vertical Jump by Player Position (NFL Combine)*

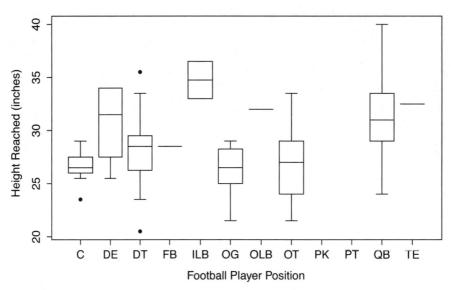

Figure 5.4. *40-Yard Dash by Player Position (NFL Combine)*

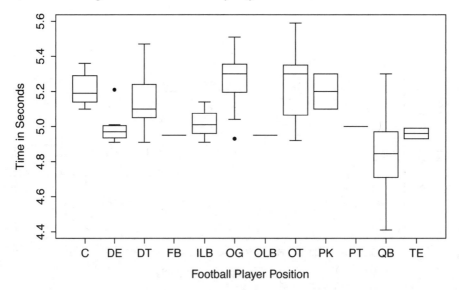

Figure 5.5. Broad Jump by Player Position (NFL Combine)

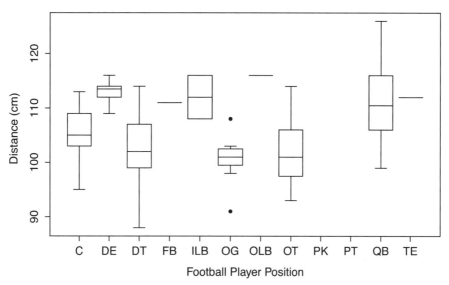

Figure 5.6. Bench Press by Player Position (NFL Combine)

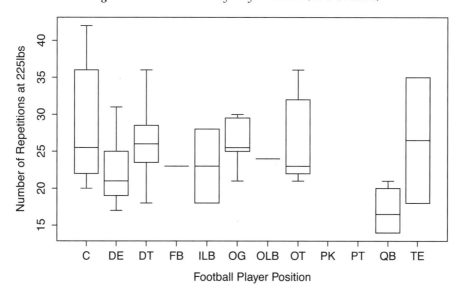

Exhibit 5.1. *Analyzing NFL Combine Measures (R)*

```
# Analyzing NFL Combine Measures (R)

##########################################
##       Touchdown Analytics R code      ##
##########################################


NFLcombine<-read.csv(file.choose())

#######################################################
##    NFL Combine Performance and Player Positions   ##
#######################################################


summary(NFLcombine)
# NAME      Year...4..2014      POS        X
# Aaron Corp      : 1   Min.   :0.00   QB     :75   Mode:logical
# Aaron Murray    : 1   1st Qu.:2.00   DT     :26   NA's:166
# Andrew Luck     : 1   Median :4.00   OT     :19
# Andy Dalton     : 1   Mean   :2.97   OG     :15
# Anthony Johnson : 1   3rd Qu.:4.00   C      :12
# Anthony Steen   : 1   Max.   :4.00   DE     : 7
# (Other)       :160                 (Other):12


#   X40.SPEED        X3CONE         SHUTTLE         VERTICAL
# Min.   :4.410   Min.   :6.640   Min.   :3.990   Min.   :20.50
# 1st Qu.:4.900   1st Qu.:7.043   1st Qu.:4.280   1st Qu.:27.00
# Median :5.010   Median :7.335   Median :4.440   Median :29.00
# Mean   :5.021   Mean   :7.406   Mean   :4.458   Mean   :29.59
# 3rd Qu.:5.190   3rd Qu.:7.800   3rd Qu.:4.620   3rd Qu.:32.50
# Max.   :5.590   Max.   :8.290   Max.   :5.160   Max.   :40.00
# NA's   :1       NA's   :52      NA's   :71      NA's   :34


#   BROAD          BENCH
# Min.   : 88.0   Min.   :14.00
# 1st Qu.:102.0   1st Qu.:21.00
# Median :108.0   Median :25.00
# Mean   :107.7   Mean   :25.23
# 3rd Qu.:113.0   3rd Qu.:28.00
# Max.   :126.0   Max.   :42.00
# NA's   :33      NA's   :87


# Let us examine shuttle speed by different player positions
# We will use ANOVA as the independent variable is categorical
# and the dependent variable is continuous

SHUTTLEbyPOSANOVAModel<-aov(NFLcombine$SHUTTLE~NFLcombine$POS)
summary(SHUTTLEbyPOSANOVAModel)
#                 Df Sum Sq Mean Sq F value  Pr(>F)
# NFLcombine$POS   6  3.418  0.5697   21.36 2.52e-15 ***
# Residuals       88  2.347  0.0267
# Signif. codes:  0 *** 0.001 ** 0.01 * 0.05 . 0.1   1
```

```
# After running an ANOVA if there are differences between groups
# as was evident from our p value
# It is customary to run post hoc analyses
# Tukey and Games Howell are preferred
TukeyHSD(SHUTTLEbyPOSANOVAModel)

# Here is the output of comparisons obtained from the post hoc
# Tukey multiple comparisons of means
# 95% family-wise confidence level

# Fit: aov(formula = NFLcombine$SHUTTLE ~ NFLcombine$POS)

# $'NFLcombine$POS'
#              diff           lwr         upr      p adj
# FB-C    -0.0422222222 -0.56170510  0.47726065 0.9999809
# OG-C     0.1032323232 -0.11827592  0.32474057 0.7970296
# OLB-C   -0.4722222222 -0.99170510  0.04726065 0.0997784
# OT-C     0.1037777778 -0.10401537  0.31157093 0.7398832
# QB-C    -0.3094152047 -0.48618407 -0.13264634 0.0000186
# TE-C    -0.1522222222 -0.67170510  0.36726065 0.9740431
# OG-FB    0.1454545455 -0.36928409  0.66019318 0.9783760
# OLB-FB  -0.4300000000 -1.12695941  0.26695941 0.5108420
# OT-FB    0.1460000000 -0.36298719  0.65498719 0.9766767
# QB-FB   -0.2671929825 -0.76432194  0.22993597 0.6686972
# TE-FB   -0.1100000000 -0.80695941  0.58695941 0.9990874
# OLB-OG  -0.5754545455 -1.09019318 -0.06071591 0.0183342
# OT-OG    0.0005454545 -0.19508533  0.19617624 1.0000000
# QB-OG   -0.4126475279 -0.57494553 -0.25034953 0.0000000
# TE-OG   -0.2554545455 -0.77019318  0.25928409 0.7455144
# OT-OLB   0.5760000000  0.06701281  1.08498719 0.0161997
# QB-OLB   0.1628070175 -0.33432194  0.65993597 0.9553029
# TE-OLB   0.3200000000 -0.37695941  1.01695941 0.8080715
# QB-OT   -0.4131929825 -0.55620604 -0.27017993 0.0000000
# TE-OT   -0.2560000000 -0.76498719  0.25298719 0.7335129
# TE-QB    0.1571929825 -0.33993597  0.65432194 0.9622422


# Let us run a regression model to examine if our results would differ
# from the ANOVA model
SHUTTLEregressionmodel<-lm(SHUTTLE~POS, data=NFLcombine)
summary(SHUTTLEregressionmodel)

# Call:
# lm(formula = SHUTTLE ~ POS, data = NFLcombine)

# Residuals:
#   Min       1Q    Median      3Q       Max
# -0.32600 -0.13281  0.00778  0.10927  0.43455

# Coefficients:
#             Estimate Std. Error t value Pr(>|t|)
# (Intercept)  4.62222    0.05444  84.907  < 2e-16 ***
```

```
# POSFB      -0.04222    0.17215  -0.245  0.80682
# POSOG       0.10323    0.07340   1.406  0.16314
# POSOLB     -0.47222    0.17215  -2.743  0.00737 **
# POSOT       0.10378    0.06886   1.507  0.13537
# POSQB      -0.30942    0.05858  -5.282 9.15e-07 ***
# POSTE      -0.15222    0.17215  -0.884  0.37898


# Signif. codes:  0 *** 0.001 ** 0.01 * 0.05 . 0.1   1


# Residual standard error: 0.1633 on 88 degrees of freedom
# Multiple R-squared:  0.5929,  Adjusted R-squared:  0.5651
# F-statistic: 21.36 on 6 and 88 DF,  p-value: 2.516e-15
# The results reveal significant differences as did the ANOVA model
# Differences between the models include the number of comparisons
# As well as the values that are obtained from the output
# If interested in examining group mean differences go with ANOVA
# If interested in examining slopes and intercepts regression is a better model


# Run analyses to examine differences by player position on vertical jump

VERTICALregressionmodel<-lm(VERTICAL~POS, data=NFLcombine)
summary(VERTICALregressionmodel)


# Call:
# lm(formula = VERTICAL ~ POS, data = NFLcombine)


# Residuals:
#    Min     1Q Median     3Q    Max
# -7.6500 -1.9841  0.0159  1.8165  8.5159


# Coefficients:
#             Estimate Std. Error t value Pr(>|t|)
# (Intercept) 26.6500     1.0037  26.553  < 2e-16 ***
# POSDE        4.0167     1.6390   2.451  0.01567 *
# POSDT        1.5000     1.2292   1.220  0.22471
# POSFB        1.8500     3.3287   0.556  0.57939
# POSILB       8.1000     2.4584   3.295  0.00129 **
# POSOG       -0.3167     1.3590  -0.233  0.81613
# POSOLB       5.3500     3.3287   1.607  0.11059
# POSOT        0.2250     1.2794   0.176  0.86069
# POSQB        4.8341     1.0804   4.474 1.73e-05 ***
# POSTE        5.8500     3.3287   1.757  0.08135 .


# Signif. codes:  0 *** 0.001 ** 0.01 * 0.05 . 0.1   1


# Residual standard error: 3.174 on 122 degrees of freedom
# Multiple R-squared:  0.3545,  Adjusted R-squared:  0.3068
# F-statistic: 7.443 on 9 and 122 DF,  p-value: 1.294e-08


# Run an ANOVA model on vertical jump by player position
VERTICALANOVAmodel<-aov(VERTICAL ~ POS, data = NFLcombine)
```

```
# Get the summary of the ANOVA model
summary(VERTICALANOVAmodel)

# Df Sum Sq Mean Sq F value   Pr(>F)
# POS          9  674.8   74.98   7.443 1.29e-08 ***
# Residuals  122 1228.9   10.07


# Signif. codes:  0 *** 0.001 ** 0.01 * 0.05 . 0.1   1

# Conduct post hoc analyses to examine which player positions
# differ on vertical jump
TukeyHSD(VERTICALANOVAmodel)

# Tukey multiple comparisons of means
# 95% family-wise confidence level

# Fit: aov(formula = VERTICAL ~ POS, data = NFLcombine)

# $POS
# diff          lwr         upr        p adj
# DE-C    4.0166667  -1.2658413   9.2991746 0.3059528
# DT-C    1.5000000  -2.4618809   5.4618809 0.9677442
# FB-C    1.8500000  -8.8788243  12.5788243 0.9999217
# ILB-C   8.1000000   0.1762381  16.0237619 0.0407549
# OG-C   -0.3166667  -4.6966908   4.0633575 1.0000000
# OLB-C   5.3500000  -5.3788243  16.0788243 0.8422035
# OT-C    0.2250000  -3.8986564   4.3486564 1.0000000
# QB-C    4.8341270   1.3519812   8.3162727 0.0007077
# TE-C    5.8500000  -4.8788243  16.5788243 0.7600416
# DT-DE  -2.5166667  -7.2782550   2.2449216 0.7914253
# FB-DE  -2.1666667 -13.2158247   8.8824914 0.9997712
# ILB-DE  4.0833333  -4.2690451  12.4357117 0.8571960
# OG-DE  -4.3333333  -9.4480996   0.7814330 0.1733884
# OLB-DE  1.3333333  -9.7158247  12.3824914 0.9999963
# OT-DE  -3.7916667  -8.6886826   1.1053492 0.2814152
# QB-DE   0.8174603  -3.5530730   5.1879936 0.9998454
# TE-DE   1.8333333  -9.2158247  12.8824914 0.9999434
# FB-DT   0.3500000 -10.1321517  10.8321517 1.0000000
# ILB-DT  6.6000000  -0.9864244  14.1864244 0.1468270
# OG-DT  -1.8166667  -5.5519638   1.9186305 0.8609423
# OLB-DT  3.8500000  -6.6321517  14.3321517 0.9735410
# OT-DT  -1.2750000  -4.7060895   2.1560895 0.9714333
# QB-DT   3.3341270   0.7086418   5.9596121 0.0029812
# TE-DT   4.3500000  -6.1321517  14.8321517 0.9427739
# ILB-FB  6.2500000  -6.2785676  18.7785676 0.8418830
# OG-FB  -2.1666667 -12.8139018   8.4805684 0.9996896
# OLB-FB  3.5000000 -10.9667437  17.9667437 0.9987506
# OT-FB  -1.6250000 -12.1693609   8.9193609 0.9999698
# QB-FB   2.9841270  -7.3262728  13.2945267 0.9950577
# TE-FB   4.0000000 -10.4667437  18.4667437 0.9964925
# OG-ILB -8.4166667 -16.2296012  -0.6037321 0.0240101
# OLB-ILB -2.7500000 -15.2785676   9.7785676 0.9994254
```

```
# OT-ILB  -7.8750000 -15.5471495  -0.2028505 0.0391878
# QB-ILB  -3.2658730 -10.6131633   4.0814172 0.9144899
# TE-ILB  -2.2500000 -14.7785676  10.2785676 0.9998898
# OLB-OG   5.6666667  -4.9805684  16.3139018 0.7846814
# OT-OG    0.5416667  -3.3648006   4.4481340 0.9999878
# QB-OG    5.1507937   1.9287937   8.3727936 0.0000431
# TE-OG    6.1666667  -4.4805684  16.8139018 0.6911095
# OT-OLB  -5.1250000 -15.6693609   5.4193609 0.8613964
# QB-OLB  -0.5158730 -10.8262728   9.7945267 1.0000000
# TE-OLB   0.5000000 -13.9667437  14.9667437 1.0000000
# QB-OT    4.6091270   1.7453508   7.4729032 0.0000371
# TE-OT    5.6250000  -4.9193609  16.1693609 0.7823877
# TE-QB    1.0158730  -9.2945267  11.3262728 0.9999994


# Let us run a predictive model of regression on speed
# as measured by the 40-yard dash
# with player position as the predictor variable
X40.SPEEDregressionmodel<-lm(X40.SPEED~POS, data=NFLcombine)

# Get a summary of the data
summary(X40.SPEEDregressionmodel)

# Call:
# lm(formula = X40.SPEED ~ POS, data = NFLcombine)

# Residuals:
# Min      1Q Median      3Q     Max
# -0.4332 -0.1000  0.0000  0.1090  0.4568

# Coefficients:
#              Estimate Std.Error t value Pr(>|t|)
# (Intercept)  5.21417    0.04881 106.830  < 2e-16  ***
# POSDE       -0.21845    0.08041  -2.717  0.00735  **
# POSDT       -0.07378    0.05901  -1.250  0.21306
# POSFB       -0.26417    0.17598  -1.501  0.13538
# POSILB      -0.19417    0.10914  -1.779  0.07721  .
# POSOG        0.06717    0.06548   1.026  0.30664
# POSOLB      -0.26417    0.17598  -1.501  0.13538
# POSOT        0.01689    0.06234   0.271  0.78687
# POSPK       -0.01417    0.12913  -0.110  0.91279
# POSPT       -0.21417    0.10914  -1.962  0.05154  .
# POSQB       -0.37092    0.05262  -7.050  5.77e-11 ***
# POSTE       -0.25417    0.12913  -1.968  0.05085  .

# Signif. codes:  0 *** 0.001 ** 0.01 * 0.05 . 0.1   1

# Residual standard error: 0.1691 on 153 degrees of freedom
# Multiple R-squared:  0.5383,  Adjusted R-squared:  0.5051
# F-statistic: 16.22 on 11 and 153 DF,  p-value: < 2.2e-16

# The output from the regression yields the
# Estimate, standard error, t value and the p value
# To examine how a regression model differs from the ANOVA model
```

```
# Let us run an ANOVA model on speed using the 40-yard dash by player positions
X40.SPEEDANOVAmodel<-aov(X40.SPEED~POS, data=NFLcombine)
summary(X40.SPEEDANOVAmodel)

# Df Sum Sq Mean Sq F value Pr(>F)
# POS          11  5.099  0.4635   16.21 <2e-16 ***
# Residuals   153  4.374  0.0286

# Signif. codes:  0 *** 0.001 ** 0.01 * 0.05 . 0.1   1

# The results of ANOVA model indicate that there are significant differences
# on 40-yard dash speed by player positions
# however additional analyses will need to be run to determine the location
# Let us run Tukey post hoc analyses

TukeyHSD(X40.SPEEDANOVAmodel)
# Tukey multiple comparisons of means
# 95% family-wise confidence level

# Fit: aov(formula = X40.SPEED ~ POS, data = NFLcombine)

# $POS
# diff           lwr          upr          p adj
# DE-C   -2.184524e-01 -0.48536657  0.04846181 0.2283696
# DT-C   -7.378205e-02 -0.26964352  0.12207942 0.9837284
# FB-C   -2.641667e-01 -0.84830480  0.31997147 0.9382295
# ILB-C  -1.941667e-01 -0.55643376  0.16810043 0.8267502
# OG-C    6.716667e-02 -0.15019359  0.28452692 0.9968830
# OLB-C  -2.641667e-01 -0.84830480  0.31997147 0.9382295
# OT-C    1.688596e-02 -0.19005570  0.22382763 1.0000000
# PK-C   -1.416667e-02 -0.44280687  0.41447354 1.0000000
# PT-C   -2.141667e-01 -0.57643376  0.14810043 0.7177360
# QB-C   -3.709234e-01 -0.54557691 -0.19626994 0.0000000
# TE-C   -2.541667e-01 -0.68280687  0.17447354 0.7138677
# DT-DE   1.446703e-15 -0.09430649  0.38364715 0.6863498
# FB-DE  -4.571429e-02 -0.64568559  0.55425702 1.0000000
# ILB-DE  2.428571e-02 -0.36299410  0.41156553 1.0000000
# OG-DE   2.856190e-01  0.02872668  0.54251141 0.0157542
# OLB-DE -4.571429e-02 -0.64568559  0.55425702 1.0000000
# OT-DE   2.353383e-01 -0.01280084  0.48347754 0.0807664
# PK-DE   2.042857e-01 -0.24569277  0.65426419 0.9366058
# PT-DE   4.285714e-03 -0.38299410  0.39156553 1.0000000
# QB-DE  -1.524710e-01 -0.37439906  0.06945698 0.4949289
# TE-DE  -3.571429e-02 -0.48569277  0.41426419 1.0000000
# FB-DT  -1.903846e-01 -0.76229728  0.38152805 0.9940736
# ILB-DT -1.203846e-01 -0.46258950  0.22182027 0.9906072
# OG-DT   1.409487e-01 -0.04101891  0.32291635 0.3055013
# OLB-DT -1.903846e-01 -0.76229728  0.38152805 0.9940736
# OT-DT   9.066802e-02 -0.07871790  0.26005393 0.8279721
# PK-DT   5.961538e-02 -0.35220880  0.47143957 0.9999982
# PT-DT  -1.403846e-01 -0.48258950  0.20182027 0.9688814
# QB-DT  -2.971414e-01 -0.42508892 -0.16919382 0.0000000
```

```
# TE-DT     -1.803846e-01 -0.59220880  0.23143957 0.9503173
# ILB-FB     7.000000e-02 -0.57804308  0.71804308 0.9999999
# OG-FB      3.313333e-01 -0.24829402  0.91096068 0.7590050
# OLB-FB     2.664535e-15 -0.79368744  0.79368744 1.0000000
# OT-FB      2.810526e-01 -0.29474875  0.85685402 0.8990875
# PK-FB      2.500000e-01 -0.43735348  0.93735348 0.9876871
# PT-FB      5.000000e-02 -0.59804308  0.69804308 1.0000000
# QB-FB     -1.067568e-01 -0.67175784  0.45824432 0.9999716
# TE-FB      1.000000e-02 -0.67735348  0.69735348 1.0000000
# OG-ILB     2.613333e-01 -0.09361448  0.61628114 0.3836142
# OLB-ILB   -7.000000e-02 -0.71804308  0.57804308 0.9999999
# OT-ILB     2.110526e-01 -0.13761242  0.55971768 0.6864794
# PK-ILB     1.800000e-01 -0.33232304  0.69232304 0.9907054
# PT-ILB    -2.000000e-02 -0.47823565  0.43823565 1.0000000
# QB-ILB    -1.767568e-01 -0.50728105  0.15376753 0.8288365
# TE-ILB    -6.000000e-02 -0.57232304  0.45232304 0.9999998
# OLB-OG    -3.313333e-01 -0.91096068  0.24829402 0.7590050
# OT-OG     -5.028070e-02 -0.24412433  0.14356293 0.9993674
# PK-OG     -8.133333e-02 -0.50380573  0.34113907 0.9999657
# PT-OG     -2.813333e-01 -0.63628114  0.07361448 0.2721156
# QB-OG     -4.380901e-01 -0.59700624 -0.27917395 0.0000000
# TE-OG     -3.213333e-01 -0.74380573  0.10113907 0.3329300
# OT-OLB     2.810526e-01 -0.29474875  0.85685402 0.8990875
# PK-OLB     2.500000e-01 -0.43735348  0.93735348 0.9876871
# PT-OLB     5.000000e-02 -0.59804308  0.69804308 1.0000000
# QB-OLB    -1.067568e-01 -0.67175784  0.45824432 0.9999716
# TE-OLB     1.000000e-02 -0.67735348  0.69735348 1.0000000
# PK-OT     -3.105263e-02 -0.44826037  0.38615511 1.0000000
# PT-OT     -2.310526e-01 -0.57971768  0.11761242 0.5524969
# QB-OT     -3.878094e-01 -0.53214827 -0.24347051 0.0000000
# TE-OT     -2.710526e-01 -0.68826037  0.14615511 0.5833597
# PT-PK     -2.000000e-01 -0.71232304  0.31232304 0.9785507
# QB-PK     -3.567568e-01 -0.75892747  0.04541396 0.1361280
# TE-PK     -2.400000e-01 -0.80122177  0.32122177 0.9579981
# QB-PT     -1.567568e-01 -0.48728105  0.17376753 0.9157033
# TE-PT     -4.000000e-02 -0.55232304  0.47232304 1.0000000
# TE-QB      1.167568e-01 -0.28541396  0.51892747 0.9982125


# Tukey post hoc analyses conducts multiple comparisons

# Now let us generate simple boxplots to get a picture of the
# different physical measures by football player position
attach(mtcars)

pdf('Agility by Player Position.pdf',
    height = 4, width = 4 * (1 + sqrt(5)) / 2)
plot(NFLcombine$POS, NFLcombine$X3CONE,
     main="Three-Cone Agility by Player Position",
     xlab="Football Player Position", ylab="Time in Seconds", pch=16,)
dev.off()
pdf('ShuttleSpeedbyPlayerPosition.pdf',
    height = 4, width = 4 * (1 + sqrt(5)) / 2)
```

```
plot(NFLcombine$POS, NFLcombine$SHUTTLE,
    main="20-Yard Shuttle by Player Position",
    xlab="Football Player Position", ylab="Time in Seconds", pch=16)
dev.off()


pdf('MuscularStrengthandEndurancebyPlayerPosition',
    height = 4, width = 4 * (1 + sqrt(5)) / 2)
plot(NFLcombine$POS, NFLcombine$BENCH,
    main="Bench Press by Player Position",
    xlab="Football Player Position", ylab="Number of Repetitions at 225lbs",
    pch=16)
dev.off()


pdf('AnaerobicPowerusingBroadJumpbyPlayerPosition',
    height = 4, width = 4 * (1 + sqrt(5)) / 2)
plot(NFLcombine$POS, NFLcombine$BROAD,
    main="Broad Jump by Player Position",
    xlab="Football Player Position", ylab="Distance (cm)", pch=16)
dev.off()


pdf('AnaerobicPowerusingVerticalJumpbyPlayerPosition',
    height = 4, width = 4 * (1 + sqrt(5)) / 2)
plot(NFLcombine$POS, NFLcombine$VERTICAL,
    main="Vertical Jump by Player Position",
    xlab="Football Player Position", ylab="Height Reached (inches)", pch=16)
dev.off()


pdf('Speed40yarddashbyPlayerPosition',
    height = 4, width = 4 * (1 + sqrt(5)) / 2)
plot(NFLcombine$POS, NFLcombine$X40.SPEED,
    main="40-Yard Dash by Player Position",
    xlab="Football Player Position", ylab="Time in Seconds", pch=16)
dev.off()




# As you can see different player positions perform better
# than others in different physical measures.
# Right off the bat you can see that there are differences in anaerobic power
# values when using two different tests: the broad jump versus the vertical jump.
# There are also noticeable differences by player position on the
# two different assessments of speed: 40-yard dash and the shuttle.
# Very noticeable is also the low number of repetitions
# a quarterback performs compared to a tightend on the bench press
# assessment. Measures along with analytics can help us better ascertain
# which assessments are more relevant to each position.
```

```
#################################
##      NFL Team Analyses      ##
#################################


NFLteam<-read.csv(file.choose())
summary(NFLteam)
# ID         Group.AFC.0.vs.NFC.1            Team.Name
# Min.   : 1.00  Min.    :0.0       Atlanta Falcons     : 1


# 1st Qu.: 8.75  1st Qu.:0.0        Buffalo Bills       : 1
# Median :16.50  Median :0.5        Chicago Bears       : 1
# Mean   :16.50  Mean    :0.5       Cleveland Browns    : 1
# 3rd Qu.:24.25  3rd Qu.:1.0        Houston Texans      : 1
# Max.   :32.00  Max.    :1.0       Jacksonville Jaguars: 1
# (Other)              :26


# Wins          Loss            Tied            PCT
# Min.   : 2.000  Min.    : 4.000  Min.   :0.0000  Min.    :125.0
# 1st Qu.: 6.000  1st Qu.: 5.000  1st Qu.:0.0000  1st Qu.:375.0
# Median : 8.500  Median : 7.500  Median :0.0000  Median :531.0
# Mean   : 7.969  Mean    : 7.969  Mean   :0.0625  Mean    :500.1
# 3rd Qu.:11.000  3rd Qu.:10.000  3rd Qu.:0.0000  3rd Qu.:688.0
# Max.   :12.000  Max.    :14.000  Max.   :1.0000  Max.    :750.0


# PF             PA              PFG             PPG
# Min.   :249.0  Min.    :254.0  Min.   :15.56  Min.    :15.88
# 1st Qu.:309.0  1st Qu.:331.0  1st Qu.:19.31  1st Qu.:20.69
# Median :350.5  Median :354.0  Median :21.91  Median :22.12
# Mean   :361.4  Mean    :361.4  Mean   :22.59  Mean    :22.59
# 3rd Qu.:403.0  3rd Qu.:403.2  3rd Qu.:25.19  3rd Qu.:25.20
# Max.   :486.0  Max.    :452.0  Max.   :30.38  Max.    :28.25


# Difference     DPG        X10Wins
# -       : 1    -      : 1   Min.    :0.0000
# -118    : 1    -1.125 : 1   1st Qu.:0.0000
# -123    : 1    -1.25  : 1   Median :0.0000
# -133    : 1    -1.4375: 1   Mean    :0.4062
# -137    : 1    -1.875 : 1   3rd Qu.:1.0000
# -163    : 1    -10.1875: 1  Max.    :1.0000
# (Other):26    (Other) :26


# To examine binary data we can use a chi-square test with the code below
chisq.test(NFLteam$Group.AFC.0.vs.NFC.1, NFLteam$X10Wins)

Pearson's Chi-squared test with Yates' continuity correction
data:  NFLteam$Group.AFC.0.vs.NFC.1 and NFLteam$X10Wins
X-squared = 0, df = 1, p-value = 1


# A chi-square was used to explore the dataset
# on which teams had 10 or more wins
# To further examine if there are significant differences
# with these types of variables
```

```
# Conduct a logistic regression
NFLteamwins<-glm(formula = X10Wins ~ Group.AFC.0.vs.NFC.1,
                 family = binomial, data = NFLteam)
summary(NFLteamwins)
# Call:
# glm(formula = X10Wins ~ Group.AFC.0.vs.NFC.1, family = binomial,
#     data = NFLteam)
# Deviance Residuals:
# Min       1Q    Median      3Q       Max
# -1.0727  -1.0727  -0.9695   1.2858   1.4006


# Coefficients:
# Estimate Std. Error z value Pr(>|z|)
# (Intercept)           -0.2513    0.5040  -0.499    0.618
# Group.AFC.0.vs.NFC.1  -0.2595    0.7216  -0.360    0.719


# The results of the logistic regression did not yield significance
# Let us run a t-test on total number of wins by AFC versus NFC conference
t.test(NFLteam$Group.AFC.0.vs.NFC.1, NFLteam$Wins)

# The results significantly differed by conference on number wins
# Welch Two Sample t-test

# data:  NFLteam$Group.AFC.0.vs.NFC.1 and NFLteam$Wins
# t = -13.1713, df = 32.594, p-value = 1.333e-14
# alternative hypothesis: true difference in means is not equal to 0
# 95 percent confidence interval:
# -8.62296 -6.31454
# sample estimates:
# mean of x mean of y
# 0.50000   7.96875


# These are examples of various analyses of NFL Combine data.
# As we can see from the box plots, there are times when
# only one player from a particular position is tested using
# a measure. This explains the existence of horizontal lines
# for box plots with no surrounding boxes.


# Expertise in performance measures and statistical models
# allows the data scientist to explore many aspects of physical
# performance measures such as those from the NFL Combine
# and NFL performance data.
```

Exhibit 5.2. *Analyzing NFL Game Time Performance Data (R)*

```
# Analyzing NFL Game Time Performance Data (R)

#########################################
##   NFL Gametime Performance R code   ##
#########################################


NFLafcnfc<-read.csv(file.choose())
summary(NFLafcnfc)
# Team                W                L
# :12   Min.  : 3.000   Min.   : 0.000
# * -Carolina Panthers   : 1   1st Qu.: 5.000   1st Qu.: 5.000
# * -New England Patriots: 1   Median : 6.000   Median : 8.000
# AFC=0 NFC=1            : 1   Mean   : 6.969   Mean   : 6.969
# Atlanta Falcons       : 1   3rd Qu.: 9.000   3rd Qu.: 9.000
# Baltimore Ravens      : 1   Max.   :14.000   Max.   :11.000
# (Other)               :28   NA's   :13       NA's   :13


# PCT            PF             PA             Conference
# Min.   :0.2140   Min.  :202.0   Min.  :243.0   Min.   :0.0
# 1st Qu.:0.3570   1st Qu.:279.5   1st Qu.:272.0   1st Qu.:0.0
# Median :0.4290   Median :313.5   Median :334.0   Median :0.5
# Mean   :0.4994   Mean   :319.9   Mean   :319.9   Mean   :0.5
# 3rd Qu.:0.6430   3rd Qu.:351.5   3rd Qu.:358.2   3rd Qu.:1.0
# Max.   :1.0000   Max.  :449.0   Max.  :397.0   Max.   :1.0
3 NA's   :13       NA's   :13     NA's   :13     NA's   :13


# X7WinsUp
# Min.   :0.0000
# 1st Qu.:0.0000
# Median :0.0000
# Mean   :0.4375
# 3rd Qu.:1.0000
# Max.   :1.0000
# NA's   :13


# Let us run a logistic regression to examine if the odds of winning
# seven or more games is dictated by the conference AFC or NFC
# Use the following code
ConferenceWinsModel <- glm(X7WinsUp ~ Conference,data=NFLafcnfc,family=binomial)


# Get the summary
summary(ConferenceWinsModel)
# This is the output
# Call:
# glm(formula = X7WinsUp ~ Conference, family = binomial, data = NFLafcnfc)
# Deviance Residuals:
#    Min     1Q Median     3Q    Max
# -1.073  -1.073  -1.073  1.286  1.286
# Coefficients:
#             Estimate Std. Error z value Pr(>|z|)
# (Intercept) -2.513e-01  5.039e-01  -0.499    0.618
```

```
# Conference   3.165e-16  7.127e-01   0.000    1.000
# AIC: 47.86
# Number of Fisher Scoring iterations: 3


# Let us run a linear regression model to examine PCT by conference
regression<-lm(NFLafcnfc$PCT~ NFLafcnfc$Conference)
summary(regression)
# Call:
# lm(formula = NFLafcnfc$PCT ~ NFLafcnfc$Conference)
# Residuals:
#      Min       1Q   Median       3Q      Max
# -0.27269 -0.13606 -0.05769  0.15631  0.48781
# Coefficients:
#                         Estimate Std. Error t value Pr(>|t|)
# (Intercept)              0.48669    0.05141   9.466 1.62e-10 ***
# NFLafcnfc$Conference 0.02550    0.07271   0.351    0.728
# ---
# Signif. codes:  0 *** 0.001 ** 0.01 * 0.05 . 0.1   1
# Residual standard error: 0.2057 on 30 degrees of freedom
# Multiple R-squared: 0.004083,  Adjusted R-squared: -0.02911
# F-statistic: 0.123 on 1 and 30 DF,  p-value: 0.7283
# There is no statistical significance by Conference on PCT
# This is good as it means that they are equally challenged


# To further verify we can run an ANOVA model to determine
# if there are any group differences on PCT by AFC or NFC conference
PCTbyConferenceANOVAmodel<-aov(NFLafcnfc$PCT~NFLafcnfc$Conference)
summary(PCTbyConferenceANOVAmodel)
#                      Df Sum Sq Mean Sq F value Pr(>F)
# NFLafcnfc$Conference  1 0.0052 0.00520   0.123  0.728
# Residuals            30 1.2688 0.04229
# The results confirm the previous findings.
```

6

Slam Dunk Analytics

"I've missed more than 9,000 shots in my career. I've lost almost 300 games. Twenty-six times I've been trusted to take the game winning shot and missed. I've failed over and over and over again in my life. And that is why I succeed."

—MICHAEL JORDAN

Basketball as we know it today was developed by James Naismith of Springfield, Massachusetts in 1891. According to reports, he was given fourteen days to come up with a game that could be played indoors as well as outdoors. Rumor has it he devised the original thirteen rules of the game within an hour.

Basketball was originally played using peach baskets. In 1906, the peach baskets were replaced by backboards with metal hoops. It is interesting to note that the original ball used to play the game was a soccer ball. It was not until a few decades later that the brown-orange ball was used.

As the game of basketball evolved, so did its fan base around the world. In 1932, eight countries came together to form the International Basketball Federation or FIBA (from the French Fédération Internationale de Basketball Amateur). Initially the organization was intended to oversee amateur players only. It held its first world championship for men's basketball in 1950 in Argentina.

Although basketball debuted at the 1904 Olympics, it was not officially included as an Olympic sport until the 1936 games held in Berlin. In 1989, FIBA began to include professional players in the league, making them eligible to play for the first time in the 1992 Olympic Games. During these games, the best and most recognized players from the NBA came together to form the "Dream Team."

The largest international basketball organizations include the NBA, Euroleague, and FIBA. Many all-star NBA basketball players have been imported from the Euroleague and FIBA. They include Manu Ginobili from Argentina, Jose Calderon from Spain, Yao Ming from China, Pau and Marc Gasol from Spain, Juan Carlos Navarro also from Spain, Dirk Nowitzki from Germany, and Tony Parker from France. All-time legends of the game include Larry Bird, Scottie Pippen, Charles Barkley, Magic Johnson, Larry Bird, Karl Malone, and John Stockton among others. Michael Jordan, who broke multiple records and won six championship rings over the course of his career, is considered to be the greatest basketball player of all time.

Since the original rules of basketball were established in 1892 by James Naismith, they have undergone several revisions and additions throughout the years. The official rules include not only the parameters of the game, but also regulations regarding equipment and apparel. The equipment required includes a backboard that is six feet wide and three-and-a-half feet high, and a rim that is located ten feet above the ground with a diameter of eighteen inches. The game is played on a court that is ninety-four feet long and fifty feet wide. The official ball in the NBA has a circumference of twenty-nine and one-half inches (74.93 cm) and a weight of twenty-two ounces (623.6 grams). Uniforms consist of long shorts and a jersey, typically with a number and the team name on both the front and back sides (though there are exceptions), along with a pair of high-top sneakers.

The objective of the game is to score more points than the opposing team. Points are earned by making shots into the opponent's basket or net. A shot that goes through the basket can be worth one, two, or three points, based upon where it is taken from and the situation. For instance, a shot that goes through the basket is worth one point when taken from the free throw as a result of a foul or penalty. Shots made throughout the game are worth two points from inside the three-point line and three points from outside the three-point line. Shots that go through the basket are called field goals.

An NBA basketball game lasts forty-eight minutes, consisting of four twelve-minute quarters, whereas an FIBA game consists of four ten-minute quarters. Both leagues allot a fifteen-minute half-time break between the second and the third quarters, at which time the teams switch sides on the court. If both teams are tied by the end of four quarters, a five minute overtime period is added. The clock is stopped when timeouts or fouls occur, so an NBA game ends up lasting much longer than forty-eight minutes, and an FIBA game longer than forty minutes.

The start of a basketball game is cued by the tip-off, with the ball being tossed up between two players, one from each team. In the second half of the game, the team that failed to win the tip-off is given first possession of the ball. As in football, the team with possession of the ball is called the offense and the other team the defense. But unlike football, there are only five players on each team, and they play both offense and defense. Basketball play is continuous, interrupted only by fouls, timeouts, and between-quarter breaks. See the basketball glossary (page 201) for definitions about the game.

If you choose to be a data scientist for basketball, you should learn about player positions and the physicality involved with each position. You should know the fundamentals of the game. A basketball team consists of five players, each with a designated role: point guard (PG), shooting guard (SG), center (C), power forward (PF), and small forward (SF). The top players in today's game include LeBron James (small forward), Kevin Durant (small forward), Steph Curry (point guard), Russell Westbrook (point guard), and James Harden (shooting guard), among others.

The point guard is responsible for leading, dribbling, and passing. Players in this position, although tall, are usually the shortest players on the team. The role of point guard requires the ability to call plays as well as to execute them. While on offense, the player in this position needs to be a good passer as well as quick on his feet. When on defense, his role is to prevent shots from being made and to steal the ball from the other team.

For the point guard, measures of speed and agility are fundamental. The three-cone agility drill, lane agility drill, or three-quarter sprint may be used to assess change of direction (COD) and speed. In addition, this position requires both aerobic and anaerobic power. Thus a player should be tested for cardiorespiratory fitness through either a laboratory assessment such as the VO_2 max or a field test such as the Cooper 1.5 mile run/walk submaximal test. Anaerobic power should be assessed using the Wingate cycle test, the maximal vertical reach, countermovement jump, static squat vertical jump, or maximal vertical jump. Psychological constructs that should be examined for this player position include team cohesion, confidence, decision-making ability, and leadership skills. Recommended psychological assessments include the GEQ, CSAI-2R, and the IAT.

The shooting guard is recognized as the best shooter on the team. His role requires attributes such as great eye-hand coordination, the ability (psychologically) to move on quickly from a missed shot, and outstanding shooting skills. He should be able to shoot from anywhere on the court and have good court sense to get open and make shots. When playing defense, the player in this position is responsible for guarding the other team's shooting guard, so he also needs the ability to anticipate the moves of other players and be quick enough to get to the ball before the opposing players take shots.

The measures integral to the shooting guard position include coordination, shooting skill, anaerobic power, speed, and agility. To better assess coordination and shooting skill, drills that simulate on-court dribbling and shooting are useful for predicting a shooting guard's game-time performance. The spot-up shooting and non-stationary shooting assessment are appropriate. Anaerobic power may be assessed through maximal vertical reach or other jump tests mentioned previously. Speed may be assessed by the shuttle run or the three-quarter sprint. To test agility, the lane agility drill is appropriate, along with the pro agility or three cone drill assessments. Primary psychological constructs that should be assessed include confidence, anxiety, and resilience. Recommended psychological measures include the SOQ, CSAI-2R, BDI, and the 16PF.

Small forwards are typically taller than guards, shorter than power forwards, and much shorter than centers. The small forward requires great athletic ability, if not the most among the five positions in basketball. The small forward must be strong and fast enough to get near the perimeter to take shots, drive the ball to the hoop, and get offensive rebounds.

Additionally, the small forward must be strong in defense and possess incredible balance, to prevent drives from the opposing team as well as obtain defensive rebounds. Finally, since the small forward position is multifaceted and requires great endurance, CRF should also be considered an influential factor.

Measures recommended for a small forward include assessments of upper body muscular strength, power, and endurance (see chapter 3). Small forwards should also be assessed for anaerobic power through the measurement of vertical jump height, maximal vertical reach, and agility through the measurement of the lane agility assessment. Psychological variables to be considered for this player position include competitiveness and aggressiveness, which can be assessed using the CAAS, the 16PF, and the TAT psychological assessments.

The power forward is usually very tall, only second in height to a center. As a consequence, they are known to rebound fairly well. Some power forwards are so versatile that they might be considered hybrid players. For instance, the term "stretch four" refers to a shooting power forward who conceptually stretches out the floor because of his shooting ability.

Measures recommended for power forwards include using the bench press for assessment of muscular strength, power, and endurance. Measures of anaerobic power such as the vertical jump height and maximal vertical reach are recommended. In addition, measures of agility such as the lane agility assessment, or three-cone agility assessment, should be incorporated to examine speed of change of direction for this player position.

Psychological variables to be considered for the power forward are anxiety and confidence. Psychological measures such as the CSAI-2R, SAS, and the SCAT are recommended for the assessment of confidence and anxiety.

Like other players, the center is expected to get open and make shots, but most of these shots will be close to the basket. The center is typically the tallest player on the team and consequently his role consists of obtaining rebounds. On defense, he is expected to block shots and rebound. The center's height is a big help in this regard.

For the center, measures of muscular strength, muscular power, anaerobic power, flexibility and reach are recommended. For muscular power, it is recommended to use a pneumatic machine for the bench press because of the explosive nature of this assessment (through the concentric portion of the bench press). Assessments of anaerobic power include the max vertical jump and the vertical leap. Measures of flexibility and reach such as the trunk rotation test and the sit and reach assessment are recommended. Psychological assessments recommended for the center include self-efficacy, 16PF, and SOQ.

Interestingly, the fascination with player profiles has even led the world of technology to incorporate sports performance parameters. It is interesting to see that video gamers have picked up on the concept of distinct characteristics across player positions. Height restrictions have been incorporated in the video game NBA 2K. Visual Concepts, the game developer, has gone as far as to implement style-of-play parameters in NBA 2K16:

- **Player Height**
  - Point Guard. 5'7"– 6'7"
  - Shooting Guard. 5'10" – 6'8"
  - Small Forward. 6'3" – 6'10"
  - Power Forward. 6'5" – 7'0"
  - Center. 6'8" – 7'3"
- **Style of Play**
  - Outside. Mid-range and three-point shooting
  - Inside. Hook, dunk, and fade away shots
  - Balanced. A combination of both inside and outside play

Although several major sports attempt to assess speed, agility, muscular strength, and reaction time, there is no consensus about how to measure these constructs across various sports. The NBA has developed a set of measures to assess player strengths and weaknesses using not only shooting percentage statistics, but also additional physical fitness, anthropometric, and shooting skill assessments. The NBA draft is somewhat similar to the NFL Combine, but still differs on several physical measures.

For agility, the NFL uses the three-cone agility drill and the 20-yard shuttle, whereas the NBA uses the lane agility drill. For muscular strength, the NFL uses bench press repetitions lifting 225 pounds, whereas the NBA uses the same assessment with a lower resistance load of 185 pounds. Speed is quantified differently between the two sports. Rather than recording the time required to complete the forty-yard dash as in the NFL Combine, the NBA measures speed with a three-quarter sprint.

The five basketball positions are sufficiently distinct to require individual attention. To identify players for each position and to compare players at a particular position, we need to utilize measures appropriate for that position. Measurement of physical and psychological constructs can better provide us with insights on what measures should be utilized or weighed more heavily by player position. Player profiles will allow for better prediction of basketball performance as well as talent identification for future recruits.

For further discussion of basketball analytics, refer to works by Berri (1999), Berri, Brook, and Fenn (2011), Shea and Baker (2013), and Shea (2014). Of special note is *Basketball on Paper* by Oliver (2004a), which reviews measures of basketball player performance on the court. There are a number of key measures to consider, as documented in table 6.1.

Exhibit 6.1 (page 110) shows an R program and listing for analyzing data from the NBA draft data. Figure 6.1 shows agility quantified using the lane agility drill by player position during the NBA draft. Figure 6.2 shows muscular strength and endurance quantified using the bench press test with a load of 185 pounds by player position during the NBA draft. Figure 6.3 shows anaerobic power quantified using the maximal vertical leap by player position during the NBA draft. Figure 6.4 shows anaerobic power quantified using the standing vertical leap by player position. Figure 6.5 shows anaerobic power quantified using the three quarter sprint by player position. And figure 6.6 shows anaerobic power, speed, and agility quantified using the shuttle run by player position.

Exhibit 6.2 (page 114) shows an additional R program and listing. This second program looks at NBA game time performance across player positions. Figure 6.7 shows steals by player position. Figure 6.8 shows defensive rebounds by player position. Figure 6.9 shows offensive rebounds by player position. Figure 6.10 shows assists by player position. Figure 6.11 shows shooting percentage by player position. And figure 6.12 shows player efficiency by player position.

Table 6.1. *Basketball Performance Measures*

Performance Measure	Abbreviation
3 point field goal percentage	3P%
3 point field goals attempted	3PA
3 point field goals made	3PM
Assists	AST
Assists per game	APG
Blocks	BLK
Defensive rebound rate	DRR
Defensive rebounds	DREB
Estimated wins added: Value added divided by 30, giving the estimated number of wins a player adds to a team's season total above what a replacement playe would produce.	EWA
Field goal percentage	FG%
Field goals attempted	FGA
Field goals made	FGM
Free throw made	FTM
Free throw percentage	FT%
Free throws attempted	FTA
Minutes	MIN
Offensive rebound rate	ORR
Offensive rebounds	OREB
Player efficiency rating is the overall rating of a player's per-minute statistical production. The league average is 15.00 every season.	PER
Plus/minus point differential	+/-
Points	PTS
Points per game	PPG
Rebound rate = (100 x (Rebounds x Team Minutes)) divided by [Player Minutes x (Team Rebounds + Opponent Rebounds)]	REBR
Rebounds	REB
Rebounds per game	RPG
Steals	STL
Steals per game	SPG
True shooting percentage = Total points / [(FGA + (0.44 x FTA)]	TS%
Turnovers	TOV
Usage rate = {[FGA + (FT Att. x 0.44) + (Ast x 0.33) + TO] x 40 x League Pace} divided by (Minutes x Team Pace)	USG
Value Added = ([Minutes * (PER - PRL)] / 67). PRL (Position Replacement Level) = 11.5 for power forwards, 11.0 for point guards, 10.6 for centers, 10.5 for shooting guards and small forwards	VA
Win or Lose	W/L

Figure 6.1. Lane Agility Drill by Player Position (NBA Draft Data)

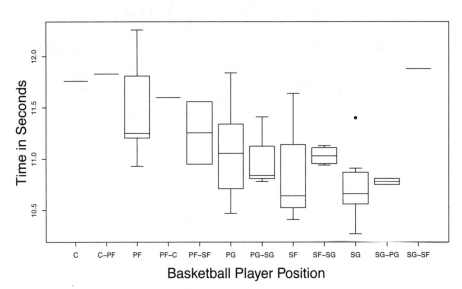

Figure 6.2. Bench Press by Player Position (NBA Draft Data)

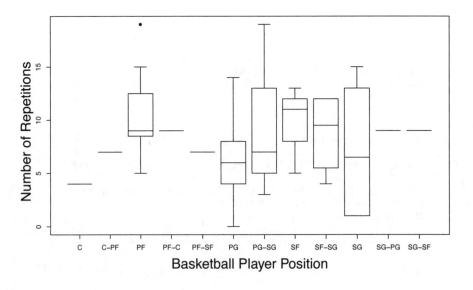

Figure 6.3. Max Vertical Leap by Player Position (NBA Draft Data)

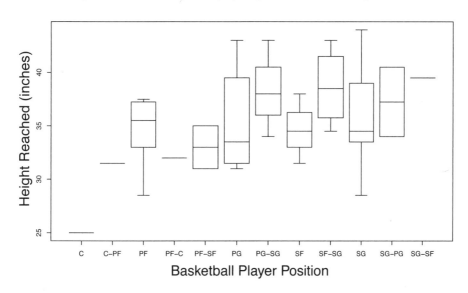

Figure 6.4. Standing Vertical Leap by Player Position (NBA Draft Data)

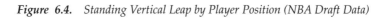
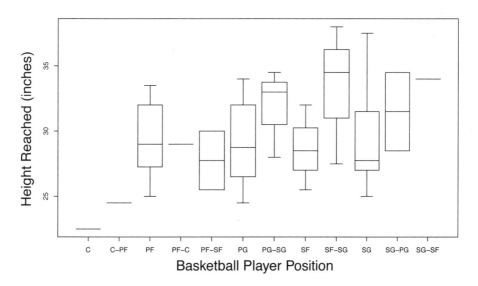

Figure 6.5. Three Quarter Sprint by Player Position (NBA Draft Data)

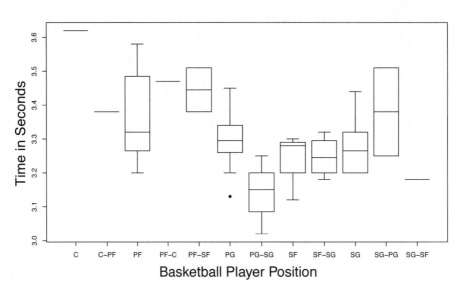

Figure 6.6. Shuttle Run by Player Position (NBA Draft Data)

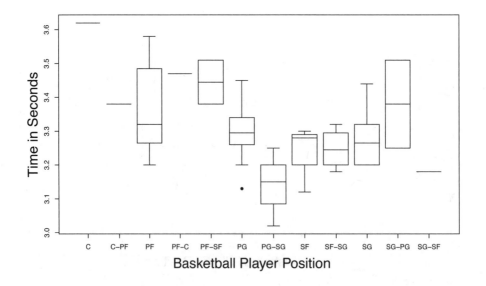

Figure 6.7. *Steals by Player Position (NBA)*

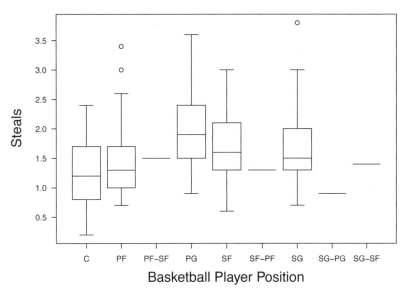

Figure 6.8. *Defensive Rebounds by Player Position (NBA)*

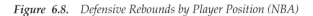
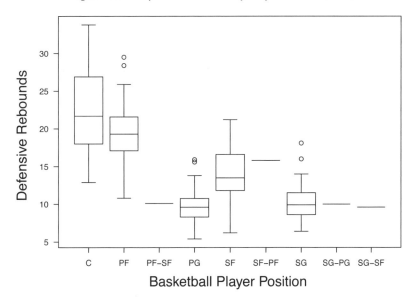

Figure 6.9. *Offensive Rebounds by Player Position (NBA)*

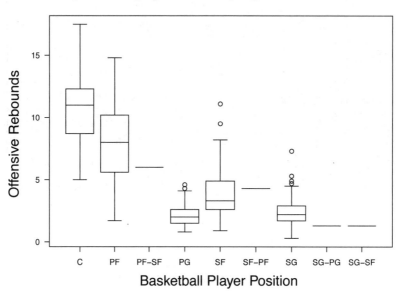

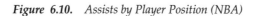

Figure 6.10. *Assists by Player Position (NBA)*

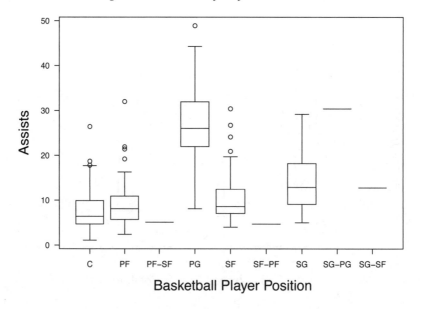

Figure 6.11. *Shooting Percentage by Player Position (NBA)*

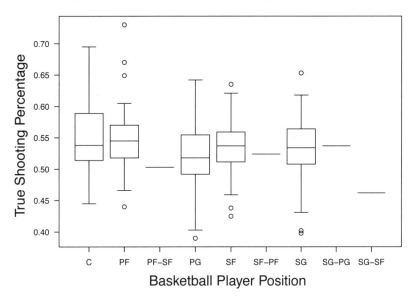

Figure 6.12. *Player Efficiency Rating by Player Position (NBA)*

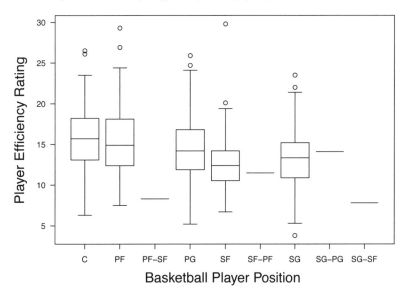

Exhibit 6.1. *Analyzing NBA Draft Data (R)*

```
# Analyzing NBA Draft Data (R)

#####################################
##   Slam Dunk Analytics R code   ##
#####################################

# Read in the file
Basketball<-read.csv(file.choose())
# Get a glimpse at what is in the dataset (use the function summary)
summary(Basketball)

# To get the names of the variables use the following function
names(Basketball)
# [1]  "Player"   "Position" "Age"      "Team"   "Games"  "Minutes"
# [7]  "PER"      "TS"       "ORB"      "DRB"    "TRB"    "AST"
# [13] "STL"      "BLK"      "TOV"      "USG"    "ORtg"   "DRtg"
# [19] "OWS"      "DWS"      "WS"


# Let us examine differences in number of assists by player position
# after controlling for age
# To do this we will use an ANCOVA model
ancovabyage<-aov(AST~Position + Age, data=Basketball)


# Then use summary to see the actual results of the model you ran
summary(ancovabyage)


# Example of the output obtained from running an ANCOVA
#             Df   Sum Sq Mean Sq F value           Pr(>F)
# Position     8   15884  1985.5  54.789 <0.0000000000000002 ***
# Age          1   157    157.1   4.336              0.0381 *
# Residuals  332   12031  36.2

# Signif. codes:  0 '***' 0.001 '**' 0.01 '*' 0.05 '.' 0.1 ' ' 1


# Let us run a multiple linear regression and compare our findings
lmbyage<-lm(AST~Position + Age, data=Basketball)
summary(lmbyage)

# Call:
# lm(formula = AST ~ Position + Age, data = Basketball)

# Residuals:
# Min      1Q  Median      3Q     Max
# -18.301  -3.912  -1.304   2.936  22.528
```

```
# Coefficients:
#                Estimate Std. Error t value          Pr(>|t|)
# (Intercept)      3.4080     2.2367   1.524          0.128539
# PositionPF       1.2393     1.0451   1.186          0.236522
# PositionPF-SF   -2.8003     6.0693  -0.461          0.644815
# PositionPG      19.1661     1.0814  17.724 < 0.0000000000000002 ***
# PositionSF       2.6826     1.0511   2.552          0.011155 *
# PositionSF-PF   -2.3684     6.0786  -0.390          0.697057
# PositionSG       6.6190     1.0544   6.277    0.00000000108 ***
# PositionSG-PG   22.4997     6.0693   3.707          0.000246 ***
# PositionSG-SF    3.7350     6.1002   0.612          0.540780
# Age              0.1664     0.0799   2.082          0.038076 *

# Signif. codes:  0 '***' 0.001 '**' 0.01 '*' 0.05 '.' 0.1 ' ' 1

# Residual standard error: 6.02 on 332 degrees of freedom
# Multiple R-squared:  0.5714,Adjusted R-squared:  0.5598
# F-statistic: 49.18 on 9 and 332 DF,  p-value: < 0.00000000000000022




# To check your reference code put the name of the dataset
# followed by a dollar sign followed by the name of the variable
# within the summary function


summary(Basketball$Position)
# C    PF PF-SF   PG   SF SF-PF   SG SG-PG SG-SF
# 61    73     1   63   71     1   70     1     1
# The reference group is C abbreviation for Center


# Run a model without player position
temp =  lm(AST~Age, data=Basketball)
# Check and see if there are significant differences between the model
# that includes the covariate age or not
# use the following code
anova(temp, lmbyage)


# The following output will be displayed

# Analysis of Variance Table
# Model 1: AST ~ Age
# Model 2: AST ~ Position + Age
# Res.Df   RSS Df Sum of Sq      F             Pr(>F)
# 1    340 28000
# 2    332 12031  8     15969 55.082 < 0.00000000000000022 ***

# Signif. codes:  0 '***' 0.001 '**' 0.01 '*' 0.05 '.' 0.1 ' ' 1
```

```
###################################################
##  NBA Draft Performance and Player Positions  ##
###################################################

nbadraft<-read.csv(file.choose())
summary(nbadraft)

# position        lane            shuttle   threequartersprint
# PF     :11   Min.    :10.27           : 3   Min.    :3.020
# PG     :10   1st Qu.:10.77   3.12   : 3   1st Qu.:3.220
# SG     :10   Median :11.11   3.15   : 3   Median :3.280
# SF-SG  : 4   Mean    :11.15   2.88   : 2   Mean    :3.308
# PG-SG  : 3   3rd Qu.:11.47   2.93   : 2   3rd Qu.:3.380
# SF     : 3   Max.    :12.26   3.05   : 2   Max.    :3.620
# (Other): 8   NA's    :1      (Other):34

# verticalleap   maxverticalleap     bench
# Min.    :22.50   Min.    :25.0   Min.    : 0.000
# 1st Qu.:26.50   1st Qu.:32.0   1st Qu.: 5.000
# Median :28.50   Median :34.5   Median : 8.000
# Mean    :29.58   Mean    :35.3   Mean    : 8.362
# 3rd Qu.:32.50   3rd Qu.:38.0   3rd Qu.:11.500
# Max.    :38.00   Max.    :44.0   Max.    :19.000
#                                 NA's    :2

# Make simple boxplots to get a picture of the different
# physical measures by basketball player position

attach(mtcars)

pdf('AgilitybyPlayerPosition.pdf',
    height = 7, width = 11)
plot(nbadraft$position, nbadraft$lane,
     main="Lane Agility by Player Position",
     xlab="Basketball Player Position", ylab="Time in Seconds", pch=16)
dev.off()

pdf('VerticalLeapAnaerobicPowerbyPlayerPosition.pdf',
    height = 7, width = 11)
plot(nbadraft$position, nbadraft$verticalleap,
     main="Standing Vertical Leap by Player Position",
     xlab="Basketball Player Position", ylab="Height Reached (inches)", pch=16)
dev.off()

pdf('MaxVerticalLeapAnaerobicPowerbyPlayerPosition.pdf',
    height = 7, width = 11)
plot(nbadraft$position, nbadraft$maxverticalleap,
     main="Max Vertical Leap by Player Position",
     xlab="Basketball Player Position", ylab="Height Reached (inches)", pch=16)
dev.off()
```

```
pdf('BenchPressMuscularEndurancebyPlayerPosition.pdf',
    height = 7, width = 11)
plot(nbadraft$position, nbadraft$bench,
    main="Bench Press by Player Position",
    xlab="Basketball Player Position", ylab="Number of Repetitions", pch=16)
dev.off()


pdf('ThreeQuarterSprintSpeedbyPlayerPosition.pdf',
    height = 7, width = 11)
plot(nbadraft$position, nbadraft$threequartersprint,
    main="Three Quarter Sprint by Player Position",
    xlab="Basketball Player Position", ylab="Time in Seconds", pch=16)
dev.off()


pdf('ShuttleSpeedAnaerobicPowerbyPlayerPosition.pdf',
    height = 7, width = 11)
plot(nbadraft$position, nbadraft$threequartersprint,
    main="Shuttle Run by Player Position",
    xlab="Basketball Player Position", ylab="Time in Seconds", pch=16)
dev.off()


# These are examples of various analyses of NBA draft data.
# As we can see from the box plots, there are substantial
# differences across positions on most physical performance
# tests. As with the NFL Combine data, there are also times
# when only one draft player at a particular position is tested.
# This explains the existence of horizontal lines in box plots.
# These are median lines with no surrounding boxes.
```

Exhibit 6.2. *Analyzing NBA Game Time Performance Data (R)*

```
# Analyzing NBA Game Time Performance Data (R)

############################################################
##   NBA Basketball Player Gametime Performance R code   ##
############################################################

Basketball <- read.csv("BasketballDatasetAnalysis.csv")

DRBmodel = aov(DRB ~ Position + Age , data = Basketball)
summary(DRBmodel)
# Results
#            Df Sum Sq Mean Sq F value Pr(>F)
# Position    8   8185  1023.2   83.59 <2e-16 ***
# Age         1      4     3.6    0.29   0.59
# Residuals 332   4064    12.2

# Signif. codes:  0 *** 0.001 ** 0.01 * 0.05 . 0.1   1

# Position is significant on DRB after we control for age
# Diagnosis of the ANCOVA model
# Check if the residuals follow normal distribution by ploting QQ plot
qqnorm(mod$residuals)
# approximately follows a straight line

# Run a model on offensive rebounds by NBA player position
ORBmodel = aov(ORB ~ Position, data = Basketball)
summary(ORBmodel)
#            Df Sum Sq Mean Sq F value Pr(>F)
# Position    8   3694   461.7   99.39 <2e-16 ***
# Residuals 333   1547     4.6

# Signif. codes:  0 *** 0.001 ** 0.01 * 0.05 . 0.1   1
# There are significant differences by NBA player position on offensive rebounds

ASTmodel = aov(AST ~ Position, data = Basketball)
summary(ASTmodel)
#            Df Sum Sq Mean Sq F value Pr(>F)
# Position    8  15884  1985.5   54.25 <2e-16 ***
# Residuals 333  12188    36.6

# Signif. codes:  0 *** 0.001 ** 0.01 * 0.05 . 0.1   1
# There are significant differences by NBA player position on number of assists

STLmodel = aov(STL ~ Position, data = Basketball)
summary(STLmodel)
# Df Sum Sq Mean Sq F value  Pr(>F)
# Position    8  22.11  2.7642   8.491 1.6e-10 ***
# Residuals 333 108.41  0.3255

# Signif. codes:  0 *** 0.001 ** 0.01 * 0.05 . 0.1   1
# There are significant differences by NBA player position on number of steals
```

```
PERmodel = aov(PER ~ Position, data = Basketball)
summary(PERmodel)
# Df Sum Sq Mean Sq F value   Pr(>F)
# Position     8    564   70.47   4.405 4.42e-05 ***
# Residuals  333   5327   16.00


# Signif. codes:  0 *** 0.001 ** 0.01 * 0.05 . 0.1   1
# There are significant differences by NBA player position on PER

Minutesmodel = lm(Minutes ~ Age, data = Basketball)
summary(Minutesmodel)
# Call:
# lm(formula = Minutes ~ Age, data = Basketball)


# Residuals:
# Min       1Q   Median      3Q      Max
# -1394.30  -642.19     8.06  587.91  1484.41


# Coefficients:
# Estimate Std. Error t value Pr(>|t|)
# (Intercept) 1501.885    257.669   5.829  1.3e-08 ***
# Age            5.428      9.631   0.564    0.573


# Signif. codes:  0 *** 0.001 ** 0.01 * 0.05 . 0.1   1


# Residual standard error: 731.7 on 340 degrees of freedom
# Multiple R-squared:  0.0009333,  Adjusted R-squared:  -0.002005
# F-statistic: 0.3176 on 1 and 340 DF,  p-value: 0.5734
# There are no significant differences by NBA player age on minutes played


TSmodel = aov(TS ~ Position, data = Basketball)
summary(TSmodel)
# Df Sum Sq  Mean Sq F value Pr(>F)
# Position     8 0.0460 0.005745   2.557 0.0102 *
# Residuals  333 0.7482 0.002247


# Signif. codes:  0 *** 0.001 ** 0.01 * 0.05 . 0.1   1
# There are significant differences by NBA player position on TS%


# Plots
# Defensive Rebounds by NBA Player Position
pdf("plot_nba_defensive_rebounds.pdf", width = 9, height = 7)
par(las = 1, cex = 1.1, mar = c(5, 4, 4, 2) + 0.1)
boxplot (DRB ~ Position, data = Basketball,
        xlab = "Basketball Player Position", ylab = "Defensive Rebounds")
dev.off()


# Assists by NBA Player Position
pdf("plot_nba_assists.pdf", width = 9, height = 7)
par(las = 1, cex = 1.1, mar = c(5, 4, 4, 2) + 0.1)
boxplot (AST ~ Position, data = Basketball,
        xlab = "Basketball Player Position", ylab = "Assists")
dev.off()
```

```
# Offensive Rebounds by NBA Player Position
pdf("plot_nba_offensive_rebounds.pdf", width = 9, height = 7)
par(las = 1, cex = 1.1, mar = c(5, 4, 4, 2) + 0.1)
boxplot (ORB ~ Position, data = Basketball,
        xlab = "Basketball Player Position", ylab = "Offensive Rebounds")
dev.off()

# Steals by NBA Player Position
pdf("plot_nba_steals.pdf", width = 9, height = 7)
par(las = 1, cex = 1.1, mar = c(5, 4, 4, 2) + 0.1)
boxplot (STL ~ Position, data = Basketball,
        xlab = "Basketball Player Position", ylab = "Steals")
dev.off()

# Player Efficiency Rating by NBA Player Position
pdf("plot_nba_player_efficiency.pdf", width = 9, height = 7)
par(las = 1, cex = 1.1, mar = c(5, 4, 4, 2) + 0.1)
boxplot (PER ~ Position, data = Basketball,
        xlab = "Basketball Player Position",
        ylab = "Player Efficiency Rating")
dev.off()

# True Shooting Percentage by NBA Player Position
pdf("plot_nba_shooting_percentage.pdf", width = 9, height = 7)
par(las = 1, cex = 1.1, mar = c(5, 4, 4, 2) + 0.1)
boxplot (TS ~ Position, data = Basketball,
        xlab = "Basketball Player Position",
        ylab = "True Shooting Percentage")
dev.off()

# Although some models may not yield statistical significance, the findings
# are still very relevant to player position. The findings demonstrate the
# importance of meaningful differences versus statistical significance.
```

7

Home Run Analytics

"During my eighteen years I came to bat almost 10,000 times. I struck out about 1,700 times and walked maybe 1,800 times. You figure a ballplayer will average about 500 at bats a season. That means I played seven years without ever hitting the ball."

—MICKEY MANTLE

America's favorite pastime, baseball, is said to have originated on American soil. For a while baseball historians argued that it originated from a game called *rounders* in England. Baseball may well be derived from English rounders, cricket, or other bat-and-ball games across the globe, but it was in America that baseball became the fascination of a country. It is Americans who love the words "take me out to the ball game."

In the 19th century, baseball became very popular. The Brotherhood of Professional Baseball was formed in 1885. Players demanded better salaries and formed a union, the Players Protective Association, to protect their rights. The American League was formed in 1901, giving way to better contracts and higher salaries for baseball players. A great deal of change took place domestically in the United States, as well as internationally during this time. Although the United States was established as a world power, there were ongoing labor market battles, increasing levels of poverty and immigration, and safety concerns related to the labor force.

Player frustration led to the creation of the Players' Fraternity, which was established in 1912. After failed attempts to negotiate better on- and off-the-field conditions, the first players' strike occurred that same year. Management became upset with players who participated in the strike and sought street players as substitutes. To make matters worse, World War I broke out on July 28, 1914. Although league owners lobbied to prevent their players from being drafted, the secretary of war mandated that Major League Baseball (MLB) players participate in the draft.

During this period of turmoil the Black Sox Scandal erupted, in which Black Sox team members accepted money to throw the 1919 World Series against the Cincinnati Reds. There were consequences, of course, and certain players were banned for life from playing Major League Baseball. As a result, new rules were introduced in 1920. The new rules significantly improved a batter's chance at making contact with the ball. This gave rise to the interesting statistic that, for nearly a decade from 1921–1930 batting less than .280 became nearly unheard of. Many credit this new rule for the unexpected increase in baseball's attendance and popularity, which in turn gave rise to economic prosperity.

This was a period in which many great players became known, including Babe Ruth, the "Great Bambino," for his massive accumulation of home runs. But this was also a time during which many great players went unnoticed because of their skin color. The need for representation of minorities in the league was apparent and, as a result, several smaller leagues emerged. The Negro National League was formed in 1920 by Rube Foster, and in 1923 the Eastern Colored League began and later morphed into the American Negro League in 1929.

The Great Depression brought famine not only to our country but also to the sport of baseball. By 1932, the United States was encumbered with unemployment and lack of job security. Baseball saw an immense drop in sport participation as well as the fan base attending games. Amidst this tumult, the President of the United States supported baseball. A fanatic of the game, Franklin D. Roosevelt is remembered for throwing more first pitches than any other president in our history.

Baseball's first All-Star Game was played at Comiskey Park in Chicago, Illinois in 1933, with the first night game played in 1935 at Crosley Field in

Cincinnati, Ohio. Another milestone was the unveiling of the Baseball Hall of Fame, which took place in 1939. The first players inducted to the Hall of Fame were Ty Cobb, Babe Ruth, Honus Wagner, Christy Mathewson, and Walter Johnson.

By this time World War II had begun. It is interesting to note that in parallel with the ongoing war, a battle was taking place in baseball between the US and Japan. The Japanese government began throwing slights aimed at American baseball and banning commonly used terms such as "safe," "out," and "strike." The Japanese government went as far as to denounce the game of baseball, and supposedly even put a curse on Babe Ruth.

Within the United States, chewing gum "shark" and Chicago Cubs owner Philip Wrigley focused on keeping the sport popular. His initiatives included the conversion of semi-pro female softball players to baseball players. Wrigley hosted tryouts in May 1932, and the following women's teams were formed: the Rockford Peaches, Racine Belles, Kenosha Comets, and the South Bend Blue Sox. Known for a pet peeve that women players should be feminine through and through, Wrigley went as far as to state, "No pants-wearing, tough-talking, female softballer will play on any of our four teams." The league was terminated in 1954.

Fast forward several years to 1971 and the Society for American Baseball Research was developed. This group focused on developing new and novel methods aimed at advancing the game of baseball. They took pride in research and the utilization of statistics. In 1980, Bill James coined the new term "Sabermetrics," referring to "the search for objective knowledge about baseball." Proponents of Sabermetrics sought to arrive at meaningful measures of player performance. They developed measures of hitting, fielding, and pitching performance and applied these measures to past and current professional players.

Some names you should be well acquainted with include the following legends of the game: Joe DiMaggio, Lou Gehrig, Babe Ruth, Willie Mays, Hank Aaron, Mickey Mantle, Randy Johnson, Roger Clemens, Pedro Martinez, Cal Ripken, and future hall of famer, Derek Jeter. An important name for data scientists to be familiar with is Henry Chadwick, baseball's first statistician, who was also inducted into the Baseball Hall of Fame.

The initial rules of baseball, known as "Knickerbocker Rules," were established in 1857, however they have evolved throughout the years. The game as we know it today is based on the majority of rules set by the year 1893. Modifications continued to occur even as recently as 2008.

The game of baseball is played by two opposing teams, consisting of nine players each. Unlike sports in which time is quantified in intervals of quarters, baseball utilizes the structure of innings. There are a total of nine innings that are terminated whenever a team gets three outs. Each team continues to send players to bat until three outs are accumulated. Outs are a result of being struck out while at bat, tagged out before touching base, or having the ball caught in the air. The team on offense scores by making runs. Runs occur when the batter makes a hit and runs through first, second, third, and home base. The pitcher throws the ball to the player at bat with the intention of striking him out (or sometimes making him walk). The fielding team, also known as the defense, is focused on causing the other team three outs as soon as possible, in order to complete the inning and switch roles to the offensive position. The term "fielder" is used to refer to either infielders or outfielders who are on defense. The infield consists of first, second, and third bases, the pitcher's mound, and home plate. Outfielders are further than infielders from home base in the left, center, and right fields. At the end of nine innings, the team with the higher score wins.

Balls and strikes are called by the umpire behind home plate. A batter gets three strikes before being called out on strikes. Foul balls count as strikes until the player has two strikes. Pitches outside the strike zone are called balls, and the batter is awarded first base if he receives four balls.

Equipment used in baseball consists of helmets, wooden baseball bats (at the professional level), gloves specifically tailored to player positions, and cleats. Catchers require additional specific equipment due to their at-risk positions, including a helmet with facemask, knee guards (because of the constant squat-like stance), mitt, and a chest protector. The ball is hard in texture. It consists of an outer layer of stitched cowhide, a middle layer made of a combination of wool, polyester, cotton yarn, and an inner layer with a round cork center. The official ball used in Major League Baseball weighs in the range of 141.75–148.83 grams, and typically has a circumference of 22.86–23.49 centimeters.

Although the outfield dimensions of baseball fields vary from one stadium to the next, the infield diamond is a standard ninety square feet. The pitching mound lies in the center of the diamond, eighteen feet in diameter and ten inches higher than home plate. The first, second, and third bases are fifteen square inches, compared to the home plate which is seventeen square inches. The distance between all bases is a standard ninety feet. Additional details about the game are reviewed in the baseball glossary (page 209), with official rules provided by Major League Baseball (2015).

Research on measures of professional baseball players has long focused on body composition and anthropometrics. Both are commonly examined in the field of sports performance, but findings reveal that these attributes may not be as important as physical or psychological constructs when seeking out clutch performers. Although the literature on physical measures relative to player position is scarce, there have been a few studies examining anthropometrics and body composition profiles for various player positions.

Carda et al. (1994) examined the physical characteristics for various player positions within college baseball to determine whether or not player position profiles exist. According to their findings, pitchers tended be taller and had less musculature than other positions. They found outfielders to have a more mesomorph-type body. Among infielders, differences within positions such as first, second, and third basemen were also apparent. They found that first basemen and shortstops tended to be taller than second basemen. Finally, this study found catchers weighed more than second basemen. Carvajal et al. (2009) provide additional discussion of body type and baseball prowess.

Many coaches utilize assessments of flexibility and speed to predict the performance of baseball players. Hoffman et al. (2009) found that performance measures, and not anthropometric assessments, account for twenty-five to thirty-one percent of the variance in baseball performance. Findings from this study revealed that, for professional baseball players, grip strength, anaerobic power, agility, and speed are better predictors of performance than body composition.

Another study focused on age as a covariate (Mangine et al. 2013). The study examined associations among anthropometric and performance measurements on fielding performance. It revealed that the maximal vertical jump and pro agility drill were better predictors of performance than body composition or anthropometrics.

Overall, professional baseball players have been found to possess the physical attributes of anaerobic power, speed, and agility. For instance, research has shown that grip strength is significantly greater for MLB players compared with rookies and semi-professional baseball players. MLB players also exhibit significantly higher anaerobic power, evident in their vertical jump peak power and vertical jump mean values. In addition, agility and speed, as quantified by the pro agility assessment and the 10-yard sprint, were also strong predictors of performance for professional baseball players compared to non-professional baseball players (Coleman and Lasky 1992; Carda and Looney 1994; Carvajal et al. 2009; Hoffman et al. 2009).

Understanding various player positions is essential for determining which measures are most suitable for predicting performance for a particular position. Let us take a look at the role of the pitcher. The pitcher must be able to throw the ball continuously. Thus, he must have great range of motion in his throwing arm, as well as muscular endurance, muscular power, and anaerobic power. Pitchers are also responsible for covering the area in the middle of the field near the pitcher's mound. With this in mind, it is imperative that assessments of flexibility (range of motion), upper body muscular endurance, muscular power, and anaerobic power be implemented. It is suggested that the throwing arm's external rotation and shoulder flexion be assessed using a goniometer. Pitchers should exhibit greater range of motion than the non-athletic population, which typically displays ninety degrees range of motion for external rotation. Professional baseball pitchers have been reported to have external rotation values ranging from 124 degrees to 148 degrees, and flexion of a minimum of 180 degrees, thus emphasizing the importance of upper body flexibility for this position. Although muscular endurance and power are usually assessed using the bench press, for overhead (throwing) athletes such as pitchers, the bench press may actually hinder performance as well as predispose them to injury.

There is scarce research on optimal measures of muscular endurance and muscular power for overhead athletes. Further research is needed to fill the gap in this area. Implementation of measures of muscular endurance and power, while performing isokinetic testing in a laboratory setting or using a shoulder press as a field measure, should be performed cautiously and under the supervision of a strength and conditioning coach. Moreover, assessments of internal and external rotation using manual muscle testing are strongly recommended. For anaerobic power, typical assessments may be utilized wherein the pitcher incorporates his core and entire body into the pitch in an explosive manner. Anaerobic power assessments mentioned in chapter 2 may be used, although assessments specific to the position of pitcher should be developed.

The position of a catcher requires squatting for prolonged periods of time. The catcher must be able to react quickly to stolen base attempts, throw the ball to infielders, and repeatedly use his legs in an explosive manner moving from a squat to a standing position. Additionally, he must be alert for any foul balls or pop-ups. Accordingly, measures appropriate for assessing catchers include assessment of lower body muscular strength, power, and endurance. Assessment of vision, coordination, and anaerobic power are also recommended.

The shortstop is responsible for covering balls between second and third bases. His role includes backing up the second baseman when a player from the opposing team tries to steal a base. It would be beneficial to assess anaerobic power and reaction time.

For the most part, the outfielder's responsibilities are to catch balls hit into the outfield, be able to throw the ball long distances, and prepare for the following play. Although each fielding position is different, many of the assessments covered in chapter 2 can be used to assess the fielder's overall muscular strength, power, and endurance, as well as anaerobic power. Measures for infielders should include assessments of reaction time and coordination in addition to the physical measures already mentioned. Finally, psychological measures such as the IAT or the Dot-Probe Task are ideal to assess reaction time. Also, confidence and anxiety should be assessed using the SOQ or CSAI-2R.

Improved accuracy in measurement, paired with analytics, can help us better predict performance of baseball players in different positions. Of all the sports listed in this book, baseball has a long-standing history of using analytics to assess and predict performance. Throughout the history of the sport, baseball researchers have provided insight into the game using statistics. Important contributors include Allan Roth, Ferdinand Cole, Henry Chadwick, Bill James, and others associated with the Society for American Baseball Research.

For further discussion of baseball analytics, refer to Costa, Huber, and Saccoman (2007, 2009) and Baumer and Zimbalist (2014). For extensive treatment of baseball analytics with R, see Marchi and Albert (2014). Miller (2016) reviews issues concerning various on-field performance measures. There are many measures to consider, as documented in table 7.1.

Exhibit 7.1 on page 128 shows a sample R program and output for analyzing baseball player performance measures. These are statistics examining differences in runs, hits, slugging, and home runs by player position. Figure 7.1 shows the number of hits by MLB player position. Figure 7.2 shows the number of RBIs by MLB player position. Figure 7.3 shows the number of runs by MLB player position. And figure 7.4 shows the number of home runs by MLB player position. It is evident that there are significant differences in performance across player positions.

Exhibit 7.2 on page 130 shows the R code and listing for analyzing Major League Baseball game time batting performance measures. It explores relationships among various measures of hitting prowess, including batting average, on-base percentage, runs batted in, and home runs.

Table 7.1. *Baseball Performance Measures*

Performance Measure	Abbreviation
Assists	A
At bats	AB
Base on balls (walks)	BB
Batting average (hits per at bat)	AVG or BA
Double plays	DP
Earned run average by a pitcher ((ER x 9)/IP)	ERA
Errors	E
Fly outs	AO
Number of games completed by starting pitcher	CG
Number of games finished as a relief pitcher	GF
Number of games played	G
Number of hits	H
Number of losses charged to a pitcher	L
Number of pitches	NP
Number of runs	R
Number of sacrifice bunts	SAC
Number of stolen bases	SB
Number of times a batter appeared at the plate	PA
Number of times a batter has been hit by a pitch	HBP
Number of times a batter was walked intentionally	IBB
Number of times caught stealing a base	CS
Number of times made it to first base on hit (singles)	1B
Number of times made it to 2nd base (doubles)	2B
Number of times made it to 3rd base (triples)	3B
Number of times made it to home plate (home runs)	HR
Number of wins credited to a pitcher	W
OBP + SLG	OPS
On base percentage (reach base per plate appearance)	OBP
Putouts	PO
Range factor	RF
Runs batted in	RBI
Strikeouts	SO
Slugging percentage (total bases divided by at bats)	SLG
Total number of bases	TB
Total number of batters faced as a pitcher	TBF
Total number of innings pitched	IP
Total number of innings played by an infielder	INN
Total number of triples, doubles, and home runs	XBH

Figure 7.1. *Hits by Player Position (MLB)*

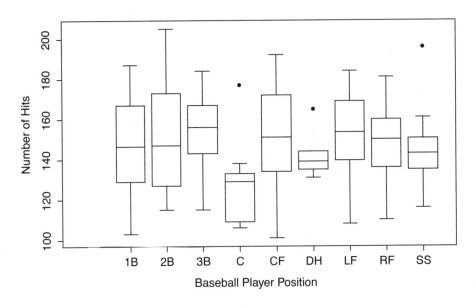

Figure 7.2. *RBIs by Player Position (MLB)*

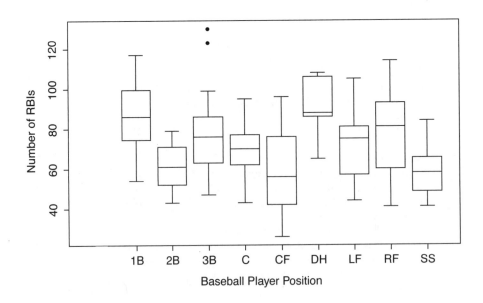

Figure 7.3. *Runs by Player Position (MLB)*

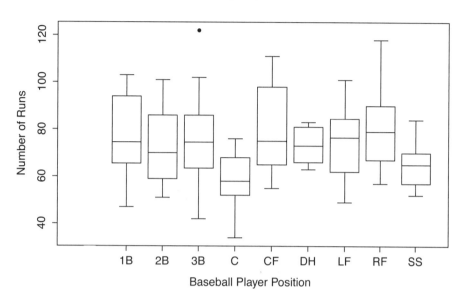

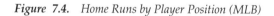

Figure 7.4. *Home Runs by Player Position (MLB)*

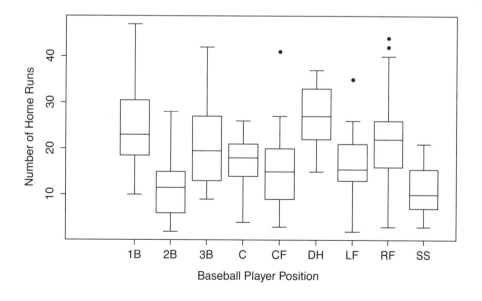

Exhibit 7.1. *Analyzing MLB Player Performance (R)*

```
# Analyzing Baseball Player Performance (R)

####################################
##   Home Run Analytics R code  ##
####################################

# Reading in the data
MLBdata<-read.csv(file.choose())

# Get the summary of descriptives
summary(MLBdata)
# The output is shown here for demonstration purposes

# RK               Team          Pos           G
# Min.   :  1.00         : 83          :83   Min.   :116.0
# 1st Qu.: 36.25   CHC   :  7    RF     :21   1st Qu.:140.2
# Median : 71.50   KC    :  7    1B     :20   Median :150.5
# Mean   : 71.48   TOR   :  7    3B     :20   Mean   :147.3
# 3rd Qu.:106.75   NYY   :  6    SS     :19   3rd Qu.:155.8
# Max.   :142.00   OAK   :  6    2B     :18   Max.   :162.0
# NA's   : 83      (Other):109  (Other):44   NA's   : 83


# AB               R               H               X2B
# Min.   :429.0    Min.   : 34.00  Min.   :101.0   Min.   :14.00
# 1st Qu.:505.0    1st Qu.: 63.00  1st Qu.:133.0   1st Qu.:24.00
# Median :549.0    Median : 73.00  Median :146.5   Median :29.00
# Mean   :544.6    Mean   : 74.13  Mean   :148.5   Mean   :29.06
# 3rd Qu.:586.0    3rd Qu.: 85.00  3rd Qu.:164.8   3rd Qu.:33.75
# Max.   :638.0    Max.   :122.00  Max.   :205.0   Max.   :45.00
# NA's   : 83      NA's   : 83     NA's   : 83     NA's   : 83


# X3B              HR              RBI             BB
# Min.   : 0.00    Min.   : 2.00   Min.   : 26.00  Min.   : 13.00
# 1st Qu.: 1.00    1st Qu.:11.00   1st Qu.: 56.00  1st Qu.: 32.25
# Median : 2.50    Median :17.00   Median : 70.50  Median : 45.00
# Mean   : 3.12    Mean   :18.39   Mean   : 71.28  Mean   : 49.27
# 3rd Qu.: 5.00    3rd Qu.:23.00   3rd Qu.: 84.00  3rd Qu.: 58.00
# Max.   :12.00    Max.   :47.00   Max.   :130.00  Max.   :143.00
# NA's   : 83      NA's   : 83     NA's   : 83     NA's   : 83


# SO               SB              CS              AVG_
# Min.   : 38.00   Min.   : 0.000  Min.   : 0.000  Min.   :0.2100
# 1st Qu.: 85.25   1st Qu.: 2.000  1st Qu.: 1.000  1st Qu.:0.2560
# Median :106.50   Median : 6.500  Median : 3.000  Median :0.2705
# Mean   :109.34   Mean   : 9.859  Mean   : 3.711  Mean   :0.2719
# 3rd Qu.:134.50   3rd Qu.:15.750  3rd Qu.: 5.750  3rd Qu.:0.2900
# Max.   :208.00   Max.   :58.000  Max.   :20.000  Max.   :0.3380
# NA's   : 83      NA's   : 83     NA's   : 83     NA's   : 83
```

```
# OBP              SLG              OPS
# Min.   :0.2580   Min.   :0.3200   Min.   :0.5870
# 1st Qu.:0.3093   1st Qu.:0.3925   1st Qu.:0.7115
# Median :0.3340   Median :0.4350   Median :0.7635
# Mean   :0.3350   Mean   :0.4378   Mean   :0.7728
# 3rd Qu.:0.3590   3rd Qu.:0.4733   3rd Qu.:0.8217
# Max.   :0.4600   Max.   :0.6490   Max.   :1.1090
# NA's   :83       NA's   :83       NA's   :83



# Make simple plots to get a picture of your data
attach(mtcars)
plot(MLBdata$Pos, MLBdata$R, main="Runs by Baseball Player Position",
     xlab="Baseball Player Position", ylab="Number of Runs", pch=16)

plot(MLBdata$Pos, MLBdata$H, main="Hits by Baseball Player Position",
     xlab="Baseball Player Position", ylab="Number of Hits", pch=16)

plot(MLBdata$Pos, MLBdata$HR, main="Home Runs by Baseball Player Position",
     xlab="Baseball Player Position", ylab="Number of Home Runs", pch=16)

plot(MLBdata$Pos, MLBdata$RBI, main="RBI by Baseball Player Position",
     xlab="Baseball Player Position", ylab="Number of RBIs", pch=16)

plot(MLBdata$Pos, MLBdata$SO, main="Strikeouts by Baseball Player Position",
     xlab="Baseball Player Position", ylab="Number of Strikeouts", pch=16)

# There are evident differences in performance outcomes by player position.
```

Exhibit 7.2. *Analyzing MLB Game Time Batting Performance (R)*

```
# MLB Batting Performance by Player Position (R)

###############################################################################
##   MLB Player Game Time  Performance Correlation and Regression R code ##
###############################################################################

# Let us examine some gametime performance variables with Rank
# Run a correlation using the code below
# Examine the relationship between Rank and Hits
cor.test(Baseball$RK, Baseball$H)
# The results of running a correlation yield the following output
# Pearson's product-moment correlation
# data:  Baseball$RK and Baseball$H
# t = -14.3143, df = 140, p-value < 2.2e-16
# alternative hypothesis: true correlation is not equal to 0
# 95 percent confidence interval:
# -0.8301014 -0.6941799
# sample estimates:
# cor
# -0.7707694


# Now let us take a look at a scatterplot
plot(Baseball$RK, Baseball$H,
main="Correlation MLB Rank with Hits",
        xlab = "MLB Rank", ylab = "Hits")

# Since there was a strong correlation let us run a regression model
# To determine how much variance in Rank is accounted for by hits.
# Use the following code
RankbyHitslinearmodel<-lm(Baseball$RK~Baseball$H)
summary(RankbyHitslinearmodel)

# Call:
# lm(formula = Baseball$RK ~ Baseball$H)
# Residuals:
#    Min      1Q  Median      3Q     Max
# -75.388 -16.708   2.953  20.246  57.880
# Coefficients:
#             Estimate Std. Error t value Pr(>|t|)
# (Intercept) 282.67155   14.91804   18.95   <2e-16 ***
# Baseball$H   -1.42265    0.09939  -14.31   <2e-16 ***
# ---
# Signif. codes:  0 *** 0.001 ** 0.01 * 0.05 . 0.1   1
# Residual standard error: 26.3 on 140 degrees of freedom
# Multiple R-squared:  0.5941,  Adjusted R-squared:  0.5912
# F-statistic: 204.9 on 1 and 140 DF,  p-value: < 2.2e-16
# The linear regression model revealed that there is a
# statistically significant variance accounted for by number of hits.
# This can be interpreted as 59% of the variance in Rank is accounted for
# by number of hits.
```

```
# Let us examine the association between Rank and Home Runs.
cor.test(Baseball$RK, Baseball$HR)
# Pearson's product-moment correlation
# data:  Baseball$RK and Baseball$HR
# t = 0.0882, df = 140, p-value = 0.9299
# alternative hypothesis: true correlation is not equal to 0
# 95 percent confidence interval:
# -0.1574690  0.1719677
# sample estimates:
# cor
# 0.007451552


# Let us get a better picture by plotting the data
plot(Baseball$RK, Baseball$HR,
main="Correlation MLB Rank with Home Runs",
         xlab = "MLB Rank", ylab = "Home Runs")

# Let us run a regression model
RankbyHomeRunslinearmodel<-lm(Baseball$RK~Baseball$HR)
summary(RankbyHomeRunslinearmodel)
# Call:
# lm(formula = Baseball$RK ~ Baseball$HR)

# Residuals:
#     Min      1Q  Median      3Q     Max
# -70.467 -35.513  -0.053  35.172  70.296
# Coefficients:
#             Estimate Std. Error t value Pr(>|t|)
# (Intercept) 70.93497    7.07458  10.027   <2e-16 ***
# Baseball$HR  0.02958    0.33549   0.088     0.93
# ---
# Signif. codes:  0 *** 0.001 ** 0.01 * 0.05 . 0.1   1
# Residual standard error: 41.27 on 140 degrees of freedom
# Multiple R-squared: 5.553e-05,  Adjusted R-squared:  -0.007087
# F-statistic: 0.007774 on 1 and 140 DF,  p-value: 0.9299
# The linear regression model was not statistically significant


# Now let us examine the relationship between Rank and RBIs.
cor.test(Baseball$RK, Baseball$RBI)
# Pearson's product-moment correlation
# data:  Baseball$RK and Baseball$RBI
# t = -2.2021, df = 140, p-value = 0.0293
# alternative hypothesis: true correlation is not equal to 0
# 95 percent confidence interval:
# -0.33752164 -0.01880671
# sample estimates:
# cor
# -0.1829672


# Let us examine the plot
plot(Baseball$RK, Baseball$RBI,
     main="Correlation MLB Rank with RBIs",
     xlab = "MLB Rank", ylab = "RBIs")
```

```
# Run a regression model on Rank by RBIs
RankbyRBIslinearmodel<-lm(Baseball$RK~Baseball$RBI)
summary(RankbyRBIslinearmodel)

# Call:
# lm(formula = Baseball$RK ~ Baseball$RBI)
# Residuals:
#     Min      1Q  Median      3Q     Max
# -78.949 -29.746   0.103  34.583  73.409
# Coefficients:
#              Estimate Std. Error t value Pr(>|t|)
# (Intercept)  98.1805    12.5947   7.795 1.32e-12 ***
# Baseball$RBI -0.3746     0.1701  -2.202   0.0293 *
# ---
# Signif. codes:  0 *** 0.001 ** 0.01 * 0.05 . 0.1   1
# Residual standard error: 40.58 on 140 degrees of freedom
# Multiple R-squared: 0.03348,  Adjusted R-squared: 0.02657
# F-statistic: 4.849 on 1 and 140 DF,  p-value: 0.0293
# The linear regression model revealed that there is a
# statistically significant variance accounted for by RBIs.
# This can be interpreted as 3% of the variance in Rank is
# accounted for by RBI.


# Let us Examine the association between Rank and OBP
cor.test(Baseball$RK, Baseball$OBP)
# Pearson's product-moment correlation
# data:  Baseball$RK and Baseball$OBP
# t = -11.5397, df = 140, p-value < 2.2e-16
# alternative hypothesis: true correlation is not equal to 0
# 95 percent confidence interval:
# -0.7739211 -0.6028090
# sample estimates:
# cor
# -0.6982052


# Now let us make a plot
plot(Baseball$RK, Baseball$OBP,
    main="Correlation MLB Rank with OBP",
    xlab = "MLB Rank", ylab = "OBP")

# Run a linear regression model on Rank by OBP
RankbyOBPlinearmodel<-lm(Baseball$RK~Baseball$OBP)
summary(RankbyOBPlinearmodel)
# Call:
# lm(formula = Baseball$RK ~ Baseball$OBP)
# Residuals:
#     Min      1Q  Median      3Q     Max
# -53.012 -21.558  -2.978  18.228  79.611
# Coefficients:
#              Estimate Std. Error t value Pr(>|t|)
# (Intercept)    346.94      24.00   14.46   <2e-16 ***
# Baseball$OBP  -822.27      71.26  -11.54   <2e-16 ***
```

```
# ---
# Signif. codes:  0 *** 0.001 ** 0.01 * 0.05 . 0.1   1
# Residual standard error: 29.55 on 140 degrees of freedom
# Multiple R-squared:  0.4875,  Adjusted R-squared:  0.4838
# F-statistic: 133.2 on 1 and 140 DF,  p-value: < 2.2e-16
# The linear regression model revealed that there is a
# statistically significant variance accounted for by OBP on Rank.
# This can be interpreted as 49% of the variance in Rank is
# accounted for by OBP.


# Examine the relationship between Rank and AVG.
cor.test(Baseball$RK, Baseball$AVG_)
# Pearson's product-moment correlation
# data:  Baseball$RK and Baseball$AVG_
# t = -61.8568, df = 140, p-value < 2.2e-16
# alternative hypothesis: true correlation is not equal to 0
# 95 percent confidence interval:
# -0.9871974 -0.9752558
# sample estimates:
# cor
# -0.9821926
# This is a very strong correlation


# Plot the data
plot(Baseball$RK, Baseball$AVG_,
     main="Correlation MLB Rank with AVG",
     xlab = "MLB Rank", ylab = "AVG")
# This plot is almost perfect

# Run a regression model on Rank by AVG.
RankbyAVGlinearmodel<-lm(Baseball$RK~Baseball$AVG_)
summary(RankbyAVGlinearmodel)
# Call:
# lm(formula = Baseball$RK ~ Baseball$AVG_)
# Residuals:
#    Min      1Q  Median      3Q     Max
# -27.773  -5.945  -1.770   5.792  34.342
# Coefficients:
#                 Estimate Std. Error t value Pr(>|t|)
# (Intercept)      503.008      7.007   71.79   <2e-16 ***
# Baseball$AVG_  -1586.834     25.653  -61.86   <2e-16 ***
# ---
# Signif. codes:  0 *** 0.001 ** 0.01 * 0.05 . 0.1   1
# Residual standard error: 7.754 on 140 degrees of freedom
# Multiple R-squared:  0.9647,  Adjusted R-squared:  0.9645
# F-statistic:  3826 on 1 and 140 DF,  p-value: < 2.2e-16
# As evident from the plot AVG is a great predictor of Rank.
# The linear regression model revealed that there is a
# statistically significant variance accounted for by AVG on Rank.
# This can be interpreted as 96% of the variance in Rank
# is accounted for by AVG.
```

```
# Run a correlation on Rank and OPS.
cor.test(Baseball$RK, Baseball$OPS)
# Pearson's product-moment correlation
# data:  Baseball$RK and Baseball$OPS
# t = -8.1836, df = 140, p-value = 1.521e-13
# alternative hypothesis: true correlation is not equal to 0
# 95 percent confidence interval:
# -0.6707184 -0.4458943
# sample estimates:
# cor
# -0.5688397


# Plot Rank by OPS
plot(Baseball$RK, Baseball$OPS,
     main="Correlation MLB Rank with OPS",
     xlab = "MLB Rank", ylab = "OPS")

# Run a regression model on Rank by OPS
# RankbyOPSlinearmodel<-lm(Baseball$RK~Baseball$OPS)
# summary(RankbyOPSlinearmodel)
# Call:
# lm(formula = Baseball$RK ~ Baseball$OPS)
# Residuals:
#     Min     1Q Median     3Q     Max
# -71.644 -24.634  -1.681 23.856  80.445
# Coefficients:
#               Estimate Std. Error t value Pr(>|t|)
# (Intercept)     274.99      25.03  10.986  < 2e-16 ***
# Baseball$OPS   -263.35      32.18  -8.184 1.52e-13 ***
# ---
# Signif. codes:  0 *** 0.001 ** 0.01 * 0.05 . 0.1   1
# Residual standard error: 33.94 on 140 degrees of freedom
# Multiple R-squared:  0.3236,  Adjusted R-squared:  0.3187
# F-statistic: 66.97 on 1 and 140 DF,  p-value: 1.521e-13
# The linear regression model revealed that there is a
# statistically significant variance accounted for by OPS on Rank.
# This can be interpreted as 32% of the variance in Rank
# is accounted for by OPS.

# Examine Rank and SLG.
cor.test(Baseball$RK, Baseball$SLG)
# Pearson's product-moment correlation
# data:  Baseball$RK and Baseball$SLG
# t = -5.4978, df = 140, p-value = 1.768e-07
# alternative hypothesis: true correlation is not equal to 0
# 95 percent confidence interval:
# -0.5480639 -0.2757957
# sample estimates:
# cor
# -0.4213792
```

```
# Make a plot
plot(Baseball$RK, Baseball$SLG,
     main="Correlation MLB Rank with SLG",
     xlab = "MLB Rank", ylab = "SLG")

# Conduct a linear regression on Rank by SLG
RankbySLGlinearmodel<-lm(Baseball$RK~Baseball$SLG)
summary(RankbySLGlinearmodel)
# Call:
# lm(formula = Baseball$RK ~ Baseball$SLG)
# Residuals:
#     Min      1Q  Median      3Q     Max
# -74.999 -26.424  -1.709  28.642  70.927
# Coefficients:
#              Estimate Std. Error t value Pr(>|t|)
# (Intercept)    193.63      22.44   8.629 1.22e-14 ***
# Baseball$SLG  -279.03      50.75  -5.498 1.77e-07 ***
# ---
# Signif. codes:  0 *** 0.001 ** 0.01 * 0.05 . 0.1   1
# Residual standard error: 37.43 on 140 degrees of freedom
# Multiple R-squared: 0.1776,  Adjusted R-squared: 0.1717
# F-statistic: 30.23 on 1 and 140 DF,  p-value: 1.768e-07
# The linear regression model revealed that there is a
# statistically significant variance accounted for by SLG on Rank.
# This can be interpreted as 18% of the variance in Rank
# is accounted for by SLG.


# Let us run a multiple linear regression using
# all the predictor variables we examined using the following code
mlr<-lm(Baseball$RK ~ Baseball$H + Baseball$HR + Baseball$RBI +
         Baseball$OBP + Baseball$AVG_ + Baseball$OPS + Baseball$SLG)
# Get the summary
summary(mlr)
# Call:
# lm(formula = Baseball$RK ~ Baseball$H + Baseball$HR + Baseball$RBI +
#          Baseball$OBP + Baseball$AVG_ + Baseball$OPS + Baseball$SLG)
# Residuals:
#    Min      1Q  Median      3Q     Max
# -29.502  -5.891  -1.577   5.220  33.215
# Coefficients:
#               Estimate Std. Error t value Pr(>|t|)
# (Intercept)   5.028e+02  7.684e+00  65.431   <2e-16 ***
# Baseball$H   -1.302e-02  6.162e-02  -0.211    0.833
# Baseball$HR   6.847e-02  2.887e-01   0.237    0.813
# Baseball$RBI -5.205e-02  6.660e-02  -0.782    0.436
# Baseball$OBP  1.160e+03  1.366e+03   0.849    0.397
# Baseball$AVG_ -1.580e+03  9.130e+01 -17.304   <2e-16 ***
# Baseball$OPS -1.151e+03  1.363e+03  -0.844    0.400
# Baseball$SLG  1.150e+03  1.359e+03   0.846    0.399
```

```
# ---
# Signif. codes:  0 *** 0.001 ** 0.01 * 0.05 . 0.1   1
# Residual standard error: 7.871 on 134 degrees of freedom
# Multiple R-squared:  0.9652,  Adjusted R-squared:  0.9634
# F-statistic: 530.8 on 7 and 134 DF,  p-value: < 2.2e-16
# The results of this multiple linear regression show that
# AVG is still the most important variable for predicting Rank
# after controlling for the other performance variables.


# The results of all these analyses reveal that it is important
# to understand not only the variables given but the sport and
# how the combination of several performance variables can modify your model.
```

8

Golden Goal Analytics

"It took me seventeen years and 114 days to become an overnight success."

—Lionel Messi

The sport we call soccer is recognized around the world as "Futbol." Although there are many different versions of the early beginnings of soccer, written text has been found referring to a similar game in China more than three thousand years ago. The game went by the name of "Tsu Chu" and involved kicking a leather ball into an empty hole. Other soccer historians note that, while this game was being played in the Eastern hemisphere, Native American tribes in the Western hemisphere were playing a kicking game called "pasuckuakohowog," which translates to "they gather to play ball with the foot." Researchers have also found traces of the game in Japan, Egypt, and Greece prior to its becoming popular in Europe and the Americas. In fact, kicking games may have been used to prepare warriors for battle.

Around 600-1600 AD versions of a kicking game were recorded in the Americas. Mesoamerican civilizations formed teams and set up baskets around a designated area with the objective of kicking a rubber ball into them. Ultimately, modern soccer originated in England, although among royalty it was frowned upon as a sport. English royalty were even known to imprison players of the game because of the ruckus it caused and its violent nature, which eventually led to its banning.

In spite of these events, rules for play were codified at the University of Cambridge in 1848 and were known as the Cambridge Rules. The sport grew and began to be played in schools and universities all over the country. Official soccer rules, known as the *Laws of the Game*, were drawn up by Cobb Morley, now recognized as the "father of soccer." These rules were eventually accepted by the Football Association in 1863 and have withstood the test of time. The first governing body of soccer was the Football Association, as the game was originally called association football. With time, the long name was shortened to "soccer."

The first official Football Association Cup was played in 1872. Leagues began to emerge in the late 1800s and early 1900s. The governing body of association football in Europe was the Union of European Football Association (UEFA) which was initiated in 1971. A few decades later the popularity of soccer spread to the United States and, in 1996, the organization of Major League Soccer (MLS) was developed.

In addition to league playoffs, countries participate in an international playoff every four years, the World Cup of the Fédération Internationale de Football Association (FIFA), the most watched sporting event worldwide. Common names of soccer legends to be well acquainted with include the likes of Pele, Diego Maradona, Ronaldo, Ronaldinho, David Beckham, Zinedine Zidane, Luis Enrique, Roberto Carlos, and future legends of the game, Lionel Messi and Cristiano Ronaldo.

The sport of soccer is played with eleven players on each team. It is a game in which hands are not allowed to touch the ball, with the exception of the goalie. The objective is to score as many goals as possible against the opposing team, and have the higher score by the end of the game. There is a ninety-minute clock, split in two halves, with halftime in the middle. After a fifteen-minute halftime, teams switch sides. The common goal is to score as many goals as possible and prevent the other team from scoring.

A team is considered to have scored a goal when the soccer ball crosses the goal line. In soccer, there is a sudden-death overtime that involves additional time for each team to score a goal. The winning goal in overtime is called the "golden goal." If neither team has scored in the two additional fifteen-minute overtime periods, penalty kicks take place to decide the game. Penalty shots also occur when a player commits a foul within the area of his own penalty box. Consequences of foul play include receiving a yellow or red card. A yellow card from the referee represents a warning. Two yellow cards are the equivalent of a red penalty card. A red card is given to a player when he has done something significantly wrong. The player is then required to leave the field immediately, and is suspended for the following game.

Equipment utilized in modern day soccer includes a pressurized spherical soccer ball, the inner layer of which is a latex bladder, and the outer layer stitched along the edges. The soccer ball's official dimensions are twenty-two centimeters in diameter and between sixty-eight to seventy centimeters in circumference.

A FIFA-approved soccer ball is the highest quality ball, as grueling tests of water absorption, air retention, air flight, and shape retention have been performed to make sure it is match-ready. The ball weighs between 410 and 450 grams.

Dimensions of the official soccer field are typically 115 yards in length, by 74 yards in width. The field consists of several landmarks including the goal line, halfway line, center circle, center spot, penalty box (eighteen-yard box), penalty spot, penalty arc, goal box (six-yard box), corner arc, and the technical area. Finally, soccer uniforms are fairly simple and consist of a jersey with the name and number of the player on the back, shorts, shin guards, and soccer-specific cleats. The goalie requires additional padding and gloves with which to catch the ball.

Although soccer technically consists of eleven positions, there are four distinct categories in which they can be placed. The first category is the goalie, second are the defenders (full backs), third includes midfielders (half-backs), and the fourth category is that of forwards (strikers).

The eleven positions can be shifted a bit, meaning that based on the formation, there may be more or fewer defenders, midfielders, or forwards on the field. There are two very popular formations common in today's game. There is the 4-4-2 formation, which consists of four defenders, four midfielders, two forwards, and the goalie. Then there is a 4-3-3 formation that has four positions as defenders, three as midfielders, three forwards, and of course the goalie.

The number of fullbacks, midfielders, and forwards may deviate based on the strategy of play, according to whether the coach wants to incorporate a more offensive or defensive style of play. It is important to understand formations, as most often they are indicators of a team's style of play, whether offensive, balanced, or defensive. A team that has an offensive style of play is always trying to find a way to score and is on the attack. Typical formations of teams that play using a more offensive style include the 4-4-2, 4-3-3, 4-2-4, 3-4-3, and 3-5-2. On the other hand, a team whose goalie may not be strong or a team facing an opposing team whose offense is extremely strong may be better off using a defensive style of play. As a result, the team may implement a 4-5-1, 5-3-2 or the versatile 4-4-2 formation. See the soccer glossary (page 227) for additional information about the game.

Literature on physical and psychological measures for professional soccer players reveals very interesting findings. Rampinini et al. (2007) examined whether a repeated-sprint ability (RSA) protocol, which consisted of maximal sprints lasting from one to seven seconds with interspersed short recovery period. They found RSA to be a more accurate assessment of anaerobic power than a single sprint assessment of match performance for soccer players. The assessment was quantified by a video-computerized match analysis image recognition system called ProZone. The RSA measure was found to be a more precise measure of match performance due to its ability to simulate real-time soccer matches. Another study examining anthropometrics and age characteristics of professional soccer players found no significant differences in match performance by age. The Rampinini et al. (2007) study suggests that today's goalies, central defenders, and center forwards are older and taller than players in those positions forty years ago. Additionally, this study found that midfielders and wing players displayed lower BMI and reciprocal ponderal index (a measure of leanness) compared with players in positions centrally located on the soccer field.

In 2010, a protocol simulating soccer games was developed and termed the ball-sport endurance and sprint test, nicknamed the BEAST90 protocol by Williams et al. (2010). This assessment measures movement patterns and physical demands replicating those that occur in a real-life soccer match. Amateur soccer players were tested to assess the validity and reliability of this protocol. Validity and reliability were established by comparing the values obtained from two separate assessments (with a gap of seven days in between) of fifteen amateur soccer players on distance, movement, peak heart rate, and oxygen uptake. The values in the two trials were comparable and did not significantly differ, confirming the reliability and validity of the BEAST90 protocol. This protocol is recommended for assessment of cardiorespiratory endurance and anaerobic power typically evidenced in a ninety-minute soccer match.

The literature is scarce pertaining to psychological assessments for soccer. Filaire et al. (2001) examined seventeen male professional soccer players' mood states. The findings revealed that professional soccer players who played well displayed the positive attributes of the iceberg profile and performed optimally during their soccer matches. Additionally, they found a significant decrease in vigor, paired with increased levels of tension and depression in professional soccer players who performed poorly.

Some scientists have found that exhibiting a negative attitude and an absence of strong psychological skills is associated with a predisposition to injury, as well as delayed injury recovery in athletes (Woods et al. 2003). It is important to know that soccer players have a tendency, because of the nature of sport, to suffer disproportionately from pulled muscles in the thigh area (twenty-three percent more), knee injuries (seventeen percent more), and ankle injuries (also seventeen percent more) compared to athletes in other sports.

Another study examined the relationship between lower body muscles and anaerobic power in soccer players (Robineau et al. 2012). Researchers specifically assessed the quadriceps and hamstring muscle groups as they relate to sprint speed, squat jump, and countermovement jump height reach. They found that over the length of a soccer match, squat jump height and sprint speed were significantly reduced, while no changes were found in countermovement jump. This implies that the squat jump may be a more relevant measure of anaerobic power for soccer.

Chamari et al. (2008) examined lower body explosiveness utilized the squat jump and countermovement jump with a modification that included five consecutive strides prior to, and post, the actual jump. They called the five consecutive strides jump test the "5JT" and implemented it with fifteen elite soccer players. They found that the 5JT had a significant positive correlation with both the standard squat jump measure and countermovement jump.

Chamari et al. (2008) suggested that the 5JT could also be used as an assessment of anaerobic power. Additionally, these researchers noted that distance covered during a soccer game significantly differed between player positions, with midfielders and forwards covering approximately twelve kilometers compared to defenders who typically cover about ten kilometers. Although research on performance measures of soccer players is more abundant than for other sports, there is still a long way to go.

Speed, agility, and anaerobic power are typically assessed for all soccer positions. The UEFA training ground and FIFA websites are great resources often utilized in the MLS soccer combine, as well as by other teams seeking to measure and assess soccer performance. But it must be recognized that measures and assessments should be designed for specific player positions. Taking a closer look at the role of each position, information can be extracted and utilized to develop more relevant and predictive assessments of soccer performance.

The position of defender typically requires greater anaerobic power capacity rather than aerobic capacity. Defenders also tend to be lower in technical skill, but have greater tackling ability in comparison to midfielders and strikers. As mentioned previously, players in center positions, particularly center defenders, are taller than right and left defenders. Athletes playing the sweeper position are usually smaller and quicker. Anaerobic power, agility, and lower body muscular strength should be assessed for defenders, utilizing the assessments designated in chapter 2. Additionally, the psychological makeup of a defender has been recognized to include high levels of motivation, persistence, and resiliency. Relevant psychological assessments include SMS-6, MMPI, and the 16PF.

A midfielder, regardless of whether designated to play in a more offensive or defensive style, should possess extremely high cardiorespiratory endurance and anaerobic power. A midfielder may have some advantage if he is tall, such as in winning headers. Conversely, a short midfielder may be quicker and more agile in eluding defenders. The midfielder position also requires the ability to see the game, spot teammates, make accurate passes, and set up plays. Of all soccer positions, midfielders are considered to control the pace of the game. They must be versatile enough to transition from defense to offense, pass the ball to the striker, and take the shot themselves. Assessments of cardiorespiratory endurance, as well as anaerobic power are strongly recommended. Additionally, the BEAST90 protocol is recommended for assessment and training, as it encompasses both aerobic and anaerobic capacity characteristics. Lower body muscular endurance and power assessments are also recommended for players in this position. The midfielder position requires that the athlete have high levels of vigor, the ability to think under pressure, create plays, as well as possess quick reflexes and decision-making ability. Thus, it is recommended that midfielders be assessed on the iceberg profile, the CSAI-2R, the Wonderlic, and the IAT to assess confidence and anxiety levels, cognitive ability, and reaction time reflexes.

Forwards get much of the credit for making goals. There are tall forwards and short forwards. The position of a forward requires quick decision making skills and the ability to score goals. Thus, forwards should have high levels of anaerobic power, extremely high shooting accuracy, great vision, anticipatory skills, and killer instincts. They must have the ability to handle pressure and be able to finish the play by scoring the goal. Measures of anaerobic power such as jump tests, RSA, and agility are strongly recommended for this position.

As for assessing the skill and technique needed for the scoring ability that is crucial to the position of a striker, incorporating a game-like simulation similar to that used by the NBA (for spot-up shooting and shooting off the dribble) should be implemented. For instance, for a forward it might be useful to incorporate drills and assessments that include dribbling and passing defenders, shooting from each side of the field, and scoring. Drills such as these will help to better assess skills and predict future in-game performance for the forward position. Also assessments of vision and reaction time using the IAT are recommended.

The SOQ and the TSCI are great assessments of confidence that are known to be reflective of handling high-pressured situations. The MMPI, TAT, and 16PF may be used to assess player personality, but there is yet to be a diagnostic that quantifies the "killer instinct."

A goalie requires great anticipatory skill, eye-hand coordination, flexibility, and anaerobic power. Recommended associations include the IAT, back scratch test, trunk rotation test, and the static squat jump. Additionally, a goalie should possess certain psychological traits specific to this position. The goalkeeper's position is very solitary. Thus, the player should display some degree of independence which may be assessed using the 16PF or the MMPI.

At the end of the soccer match, goalies have been said to feel one of two ways: like a winner, or like a failure. Goalies must have extreme concentration, thus an ability to get into the zone and remain in a state of flow should be assessed using either the Flow Questionnaire or the Flow State Scale. Finally, when it comes to being scored on, the goalie should have what is called a "short-term memory," so as not to affect future performance.

Combining the assessment of physical and psychological constructs with analytics, a new and better way of strategizing and predicting performance in soccer can be developed. Until recently, soccer analytics have been silent or dormant. A book about soccer, *The Numbers Game* (Anderson and Sally 2013), reveals that soccer analysts have been examining events when players have possession of the ball. Shockingly, 99 percent of the time players do not have the ball, and 98.5 percent of the time they run without it. The typical soccer player has possession of the ball for an average of 53.4 seconds throughout the entire course of a soccer match (Anderson and Sally 2013).

Sports analytics revolution has been at the forefront of sports science and technology, utilized by players, coaches, and team management to optimize performance and, consequently, the chances of winning. To illustrate this point, Peter Vermes, head coach of MLS team Sporting Kansas City is known to utilize sports data science to optimize performance and prevent injury in his players. He was quoted saying, "You're looking at what type of training sessions, or even exercises, that you may do with the players that are either extremely useful for your model of play, or actually detrimental.... No matter how you play, if you understand the science of it, you can train your team in the model of your play" (Schaerlaeckens 2015).

For additional information about the physiology of soccer, see Bangsbo (1993) and Stølen et al. (2005). Taskin (2008) reviews physical assessments relevant to the sport. And Bangsbo and Peitersen (2000) and Anderson and Sally (2013) discuss soccer analytics and strategy.

Table 8.1 (page 146) shows UEFA Champions League tournament phase leading scorers. Table 8.2 (page 147) shows UEFA Champions League tournament phase leaders in assists. And table 8.3 (page 148) shows key performance measures in soccer and their abbreviations.

Exhibit 8.1 (page 151) shows an R program and listing for analyzing performance of the UEFA Champions League leaders in assists and goals scored. Figure 8.1 (page 149) is a boxplot that displays the number of assists by player position (UEFA). And figure 8.2 (page 149) is a boxplot that displays the number of goals scored by player position (UEFA).

Continuing with the exploration of these data, exhibit 8.2 (page 154) shows an R program and listing for additional analyses of performance of the UEFA Champions League leading soccer players. Figure 8.3 (page 150) is a boxplot detailing passes attempted by player position (UEFA). And figure 8.4 (page 150) is a boxplot detailing passes completed by player position (UEFA).

Table 8.1. UEFA Champions League Tournament Phase Leading Scorers

Player	Team	Position	Total Points	Playing Time (minutes)
Neymar	Barcelona	3	10	1026
Cristiano Ronaldo	Real Madrid	3	10	1065
Lionel Messi	Barcelona	3	10	1147
Luiz Adriano	Shakhtar Donetsk	3	9	628
Jackson Martínez	Porto	3	7	629
Thomas Müller	Bayern	2	7	777
Luis Suárez	Barcelona	3	7	827
Carlos Tévez	Juventus	3	7	1156
Sergio Agüero	Man. City	3	6	550
Karim Benzema	Real Madrid	3	6	664
Edinson Cavani	Paris	3	6	920
Robert Lewandowski	Bayern	3	6	932
Klaas-Jan Huntelaar	Schalke	3	5	663
Yacine Brahimi	Porto	2	5	682
Álvaro Morata	Juventus	3	5	744
Mario Mandžukić	Atlético	3	5	832
Ciro Immobile	Dortmund	3	4	404
Nani	Sporting CP	2	4	449
Mario Götze	Bayern	2	4	747
Adrián Ramos	Dortmund	3	3	98
Lukas Podolski	Arsenal	4	3	127
Vincent Aboubakar	Porto	3	3	271
Marco Reus	Dortmund	4	3	341
Franck Ribéry	Bayern	2	3	387
Aaron Ramsey	Arsenal	2	3	404
Seydou Doumbia	CSKA Moskva	3	3	405
Gervinho	AS Roma	3	3	434
Ricardo Quaresma	Porto	2	3	469
Danny Welbeck	Arsenal	3	3	500
Lasse Schöne	Ajax	3	3	501

Note: Position numbers from the traditional 4-4-2 formation are as follows:
2 = right fullback, 3, 5, and 6 = left fullback, 4 = defensive midfielder, 7 = right midfielder,
8 = central/attacking midfielder, 9 = striker, 10 = second/support striker, 11 = left midfielder.

Source. http://www.uefa.com/uefachampionsleague/season=2015/statistics/round=2000548/players/type=topscorers/index.html.

Table 8.2. UEFA Champions League Tournament Phase Leaders in Assists

Player	Team	Position	Total Assists	Playing Time (minutes)
Lionel Messi	Barcelona	3	6	1147
Andrés Iniesta	Barcelona	2	5	786
Bastian Schweinsteiger	Bayern	2	4	456
Cesc Fàbregas	Chelsea	2	4	696
Koke	Atlético	2	4	833
Dani Alves	Barcelona	1	4	961
Cristiano Ronaldo	Real Madrid	3	4	1065
Pajtim Kasami	Olympiacos	3	3	391
Łukasz Piszczek	Dortmund	1	3	392
Pedro Rodríguez	Barcelona	4	3	397
Eden Hazard	Chelsea	4	3	654
Fabian Frei	Basel	3	3	670
Yacine Brahimi	Porto	4	3	682
Karim Bellarabi	Leverkusen	2	3	712
Thomas Müller	Bayern	3	3	777
Hector Herrera	Porto	2	3	789
Gregory van der Wiel	Paris	2	3	812
Luis Suárez	Barcelona	3	3	827
Paul Pogba	Juventus	2	3	833
Juanfran	Atlético	2	3	930
Robert Lewandowski	Bayern	3	3	932
Toni Kroos	Real Madrid	3	3	968
Jérôme Boateng	Bayern	1	3	990
Carlos Tévez	Juventus	3	3	1156
Rafinha	Barcelona	2	2	114
Bernard	Shakhtar Donetsk	4	2	158
Ricardo Kishna	Ajax	3	2	241
Juan Manuel Iturbe	Roma	3	2	244
Arkadiusz Milik	Ajax	3	2	256
Jefferson	Sporting CP	1	2	270

Note: Position numbers from the traditional 4-4-2 formation are as follows:
2 = right fullback, 3, 5, and 6 = left fullback, 4 = defensive midfielder, 7 = right midfielder, 8 = central/attacking midfielder, 9 = striker, 10 = second/support striker, 11 = left midfielder.

Source. http://www.uefa.com/uefachampionsleague/season=2015/statistics/round=2000548/players/type=assists/index.html.

Table 8.3. *Soccer Performance Measures*

Performance Measure	Abbreviation
Assists	A
Average goals expected per shot	ExpG
Completed percentage	CMP%
Corner kicks	CK
Forward completed percentage	Forward Comp %
Forward pass percentage	Forward Pass %
Fouls committed	FC
Fouls suffered	FS
Game winning goals	GWG
Games played	GP
Games started	GS
Goal percentage	GP%
Goals	G
Goals above average	GAA
Goals against	GA
Goals for	GF
Minutes	Min
Offsides	OFF
Passes attempted	PA
Passes completed	PC
Penalty kick attempts	PKA
Penalty kick goals	PKG
Penalty kick saves	PKS
Saves	SV
Shots	SHT
Shots on goal	SOG
Shutouts	SO

Figure 8.1. *Number of Assists by Player Position (UEFA)*

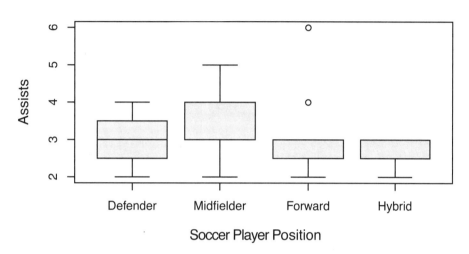

Figure 8.2. *Number of Goals Scored by Player (UEFA)*

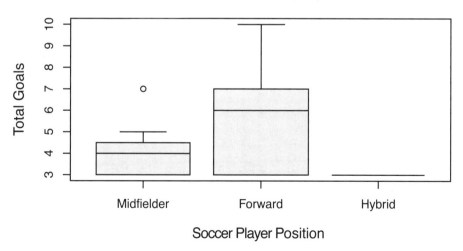

Figure 8.3. Number of Passes Attempted by Player Position (UEFA)

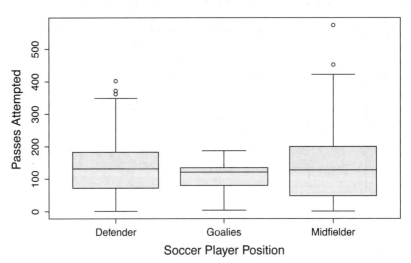

Figure 8.4. Number of Passes Completed by Player Position (UEFA)

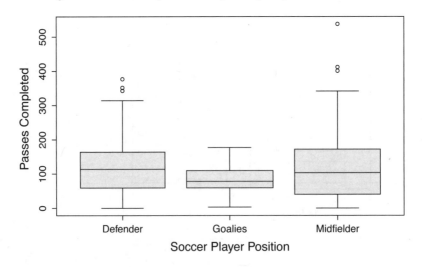

Exhibit 8.1. *Analyzing UEFA Assists and Goals Scored (R)*

```
# Analyzing UEFA  Assists and Goals Scored (R)


####################################
## Golden Goal Analytics R code   ##
####################################
# Reading in the data
setwd('/Users/Desktop/PerformanceMeasurementAnalytics/soccer')
SoccerAssists <- read.csv('goalassist.csv')
SoccerGoalsScored <- read.csv('goalscored.csv')

# Checking the structure of the data
str(SoccerAssists)
str(SoccerGoalsScored)

# Changing the positions variable to character
SoccerAssists$Position <- as.character(SoccerAssists$Position)
SoccerGoalsScored$Position <- as.character(SoccerGoalsScored$Position)

# Testing for a relationship between Time and Assists,
# since there is no relationship using this dataset,
# we can now ignore it in the regression model
AssistsTimeModel1 <- lm(Time ~ Position, data = SoccerAssists)

# Check summary for significance
summary(AssistsTimeModel1)

#####################################################
##    UEFA Champions League Leaders in Assists    ##
#####################################################

# Assists by position - simple linear regression model
AssistsbyPositionLinearModel2 <- lm(Assists ~ Position, data = SoccerAssists)

# Check summary for significance
summary(AssistsbyPositionLinearModel2)

# Assists by position -  ANOVA
AssistsbyPositionANOVAModel3 <- aov(Assists ~ Position, data = SoccerAssists)

# Check summary for significance
summary(AssistsbyPositionANOVAModel3)

# Robust alternative - Kruskal Wallis use if data is not normally distributed
kruskal.test(Assists ~ factor(Position), data = SoccerAssists)

# Count data -> use a Poisson regression. Uses a log link to model data.
AssistsbyPositionsPoissonModel4 <- glm(Assists ~ Position,
                                    data = SoccerAssists, family = poisson)

# Check summary for significance
summary(AssistsbyPositionsPoissonModel4)
```

```
# Examining the boxplot below we see that
# there seem to be differences by player position.
# However they are not statistically significant.
# The boxplot does show a trend of
# greater number of assists by the midfielder position.

# Figure
# Creates a space to save the figure
pdf('SoccerAssists.pdf', height = 4, width = 4 * (1 + sqrt(5)) / 2)
# Which variables to use
with(SoccerAssists, boxplot(Assists ~ Position,
                    # Changes x and y labels
                    xlab = 'Soccer Player Position', ylab = 'Assists',
                    # Names under the boxplots
                    names = c('Defender', 'Midfielder', 'Forward', 'Hybrid'),
                    # Color - see color chart
                    col = 'gray92',
                    # Main title
                    main = 'Number of Assists by Player Position (UEFA)',
                    # Size of x and y labels
                    cex.lab = 1.2))
# Closes the figure space
dev.off()

############################################################
##    UEFA Champions League Leaders in Goals Scored    ##
############################################################

# Total by position - regression linear model (same as ANOVA)
SoccerGoalsScoredLinearModel1 <- lm(Total ~ Position, data = SoccerGoalsScored)
SoccerGoalsScoredANOVAModel2 <- aov(Total ~ Position, data = SoccerGoalsScored)

# Robust alternative - Kruskal Wallis since data is not normally distributed
kruskal.test(Total ~ factor(Position), data = SoccerGoalsScored)

# Count data -> use a Poisson regression. Uses a log link to model data.
SoccerGoalsScoredPoissonModel3 <- glm(Total ~ Position,
                            data = SoccerGoalsScored, family = poisson)

# Examining the boxplot below we see
# that there seem to be differences by player position.
# However they are not statistically significant.
# The boxplot does show a trend of greater number
# of goals scored by the forward position.
# The lack of statistical significance could be due to the small sample size.
# These data are based on only the world leading scorers
# At that level midfielders also have a high scoring record.

# Figure
# Creates a space to save the figure
pdf('SoccerGoalsScored.pdf', height = 4, width = 4 * (1 + sqrt(5)) / 2)
# Which variables to use
```

```
with(SoccerGoalsScored, boxplot(Total ~ Position,
                       # Changes x and y labels
                       xlab = 'Soccer Player Position', ylab = 'Total Goals',
                       # Names under the boxplots
                       names = c('Midfielder', 'Forward', 'Hybrid'),
                       # Color - see color chart
                       col = 'gray92',
                       # Main title
                       main = 'Number of Goals Scored by Player (UEFA)',
                       # Size of x and y labels
                       cex.lab = 1.2))
# Closes the figure space
dev.off()


################################################################
##  UEFA Champions League Performance by Player Position   ##
################################################################

# Reading in the data
setwd('/Users/Desktop/PerformanceMeasurementAnalytics/soccer')
UEFAdefenders <- read.csv('UEFAdefense.csv')
UEFAgoalies <- read.csv('UEFAgoalies.csv')
UEFAmidfielders <- read.csv('UEFAmidfielder.csv')

# Combine the rows for the three files read in and named the new file uefa
uefa <- rbind(UEFAdefenders, UEFAgoalies, UEFAmidfielders)
uefa$Position <- c(rep('Defender', nrow(UEFAdefenders)),
                   rep('Goalie', nrow(UEFAgoalies)),
                   rep('Midfielder', nrow(UEFAmidfielders)))

# Get rid of rows with NA (missing values) across
uefa <- uefa[!is.na(uefa$PA), ]

# This presents a summary of your data.
summary(uefa)
```

Exhibit 8.2.   Analyzing UEFA Passes Attempted and Completed (R)

```
# Analyzing UEFA Passes Attempted and Completed (R)

####################################
## Golden Goal Analytics R code    ##
####################################
# Reading in the data
setwd('/Users/Desktop/PerformanceMeasurementAnalytics/soccer')
SoccerAssists <- read.csv('goalassist.csv')
SoccerGoalsScored <- read.csv('goalscored.csv')

# Checking the structure of the data
str(SoccerAssists)
str(SoccerGoalsScored)

# Changing the positions variable to character
SoccerAssists$Position <- as.character(SoccerAssists$Position)
SoccerGoalsScored$Position <- as.character(SoccerGoalsScored$Position)

# Reading in the data
setwd('/Users/Desktop/PerformanceMeasurementAnalytics/soccer')
UEFAdefenders <- read.csv('UEFAdefense.csv')
UEFAgoalies <- read.csv('UEFAgoalies.csv')
UEFAmidfielders <- read.csv('UEFAmidfielder.csv')

# Combine the rows for the three files read in and named the new file uefa
uefa <- rbind(UEFAdefenders, UEFAgoalies, UEFAmidfielders)
uefa$Position <- c(rep('Defender', nrow(UEFAdefenders)),
                   rep('Goalie', nrow(UEFAgoalies)),
                   rep('Midfielder', nrow(UEFAmidfielders)))

# Get rid of rows with NA (missing values) across
uefa <- uefa[!is.na(uefa$PA), ]

# Presents a summary of your data
summary(uefa)

#######################################################################
##  UEFA Champions League Passes Attempted by Player Position    ##
#######################################################################

# Use a linear model to regress player position on pass attempts
PassAttemptsbyPositionLinearModel1 <- lm(PA ~ Position, data = uefa)

# If you do not want to include outliers then
# check the Median using tapply function because the
# mean will be skewed by outliers
tapply(uefa$PA, uefa$Position, median)
tapply(uefa$PA, uefa$Position, mean)

# Kruskal Wallis Test (a non-parametric equivalent of anova)
kruskal.test(PA ~ factor(Position), data = uefa)
```

```
# The following output is displayed
# Kruskal-Wallis rank sum test
# data:  PA by factor(Position)
# Kruskal-Wallis chi-squared = 2.7198, df = 2, p-value = 0.2567
# There was no significant difference by player position on
# passes attempted with the sample from this dataset.
# Examining the boxplot below we can tell that certain positions
# do attempt to pass more although the results
# were not statistically significant.

# Figure
# Creates a space to save the figure
pdf('UEFAPA.pdf', height = 4, width = 4 * (1 + sqrt(5)) / 2)
# Which variables to use
with(uefa, boxplot(PA ~ Position,
                    # Changes x and y labels
                    xlab = 'Position', ylab = 'Soccer Player Position',
                    # Color - see color chart
                    col = 'gray92',
                    # Main title
                    main = 'Number of Passes Attempted by Player Position (UEFA)',
                    # Size of x and y labels
                    cex.lab = 1.2))
# Closes the figure space
dev.off()


######################################################################
##   UEFA Champions League Passes Completed by Player Position   ##
######################################################################

# Use a linear model to regress player position on pass attempts
PassesCompletedbyPositionLinearModel1 <- lm(PC ~ Position, data = uefa)

# Get rid of rows with NA (missing values) across
uefa <- uefa[!is.na(uefa$PC), ]

# Use a linear model to regress player position on passes completed
PassAttemptsbyPositionLinearModel1 <- lm(PC ~ Position, data = uefa)

# If you do not want to include outliers then check the Median
# using tapply function because the mean will be skewed by outliers.
tapply(uefa$PC, uefa$Position, median)
tapply(uefa$PC, uefa$Position, mean)

# Kruskal Test
kruskal.test(PC ~ factor(Position), data = uefa)

# The following output is displayed
# Kruskal-Wallis rank sum test
# data:  PC by factor(Position)
# Kruskal-Wallis chi-squared = 6.5932, df = 2, p-value = 0.03701
```

```
# There is a significant difference by player position
# on passes completed p=0.03

# Figure
# Creates a space to save the figure
pdf('UEFApassescompleted.pdf',
    height = 4, width = 4 * (1 + sqrt(5)) / 2)
# Which variables to use
with(uefa, boxplot(PC ~ Position,
                   # Changes x and y labels
                   xlab = 'Soccer Player Position',
                   # Color - see color chart
                   col = 'gray92',
                   # Main title
                   main = 'Number of Passes Completed by Player Position (UEFA)',
                   # Size of x and y labels
                   cex.lab = 1.2))
# Closes the figure space
dev.off()
```

9

Game, Set, Match Analytics

"You've got to take the initiative and play your game. In a decisive set, confidence is the difference."

—Chris Evert

All over the world, tennis is known as the sport of kings. Originally played in France, it is documented as having begun early in the thirteenth century in French monasteries as *jeu de paume*, game of the palm. Many believe that the name tennis derived from *tenez*, the old French word for play. As kings from various countries became involved in the sport, it gained a reputation for being an elite game which only royalty could play. The word *real*, meaning "royal," was integrated into the name of the sport which came to be known as *real tennis* in England.

Tennis is documented as evolving from a game played with the palm of the hand, to wearing a webbed glove, to being played with a paddle. Finally, in the 1500s, the paddle developed into a wooden racquet strung with sheep's gut. The game also moved from indoors to outdoors. The tennis ball was originally composed of an inner cork core surrounded by sand, and an outer layer of sheepskin. It was not until the middle of the nineteenth century that a rubber-type ball was developed and endorsed by players of real tennis.

The evolution of the game was led by Major Walter Clopton Wingfield. Known for having experimented with different sizes of courts and nets, he later came up with a court-type game called *Sphairistike*. Eventually he came to be recognized as the inventor of lawn tennis, which quickly gained in popularity. The first men's world championship was played at Wimbledon in Great Britain in 1877, with the first women's championship taking place seven years later in 1884.

The US Open, French Open, and Australian Open were established after Wimbledon. A Grand Slam occurs when these four championships are won within a calendar year, a feat that very few players have achieved. Among those few who have won the Grand Slam include Don Budge, Maureen Connolly, Rod Laver, Margaret Court, and Steffi Graf. Then there is the non-calendar year Grand Slam that consists of winning four consecutive major titles that are not within a calendar year. Winners of the non-calendar year Grand Slam include the likes of Martina Navratilova and Serena Williams. Then there is the Golden Slam, which only one person has ever accomplished—Steffi Graf who won all four slams and the Olympic gold medal in one calendar year. Slightly less prestigious is the Career Golden Slam, which occurs when a player wins all four slams throughout their careers along with winning a gold medal. Players who have accomplished this feat include Andre Agassi, Serena Williams, and Rafael Nadal, among others. Finally, there is the Super Slam, which consists of winning all four slams, the Olympic gold medal, and a final event at the end of the year. No player has yet achieved a Super Slam in one calendar year. However, Steffi Graf did achieve all the criteria for a Super Slam, but not in the same calendar year, thus achieving a non-calendar year Super Slam. Finally, there is the Career Super Slam, meaning having met all the criteria required to win the Super Slam but over a longer period of time.

Few changes to the game have occurred since the original rules were established in 1875 by the governing authority, Marylebone Cricket Club. At the time, the court dimensions were designated as thirty feet in width by seventy-eight feet in length, whereas current day dimensions are twenty-seven feet by seventy-eight feet. In 1884 the net height was established as three feet six inches. The official yellow balls were introduced in 1970, and were restricted to weigh between two ounces and two and 1/16th ounces.

Surprisingly, it was not until 1976 that rules were set for the size and dimensions of tennis racquets. At first, only wooden racquets were allowed. In 1996, regulations were put in place for the racquet length, width, and frame, not to exceed twenty-nine inches in length, and no more than twelve and a half inches in width. Although the Association for Tennis Professionals (ATP) and the Women's Tennis Association (WTA) have their own rulebooks. The overarching governing body of tennis is the International Tennis Federation, which maintains the official Rules of Tennis.

The game is played by having individual athletes at opposite sides of the net of the tennis court, rallying back and forth. The objective of the game is to return the ball back once more than the opponent. The match begins with one player serving the ball into the court. An ace is a serve that lands within the service box area but the receiver fails to touch. It is a fundamental rule of the game that the ball bounces no more than one time before it is hit. The goal is to win enough points by either hitting the last ball in or having the opponent hit the ball out. Overall, winning a match is a consequence of winning a large number of points at the right time.

You may have heard tennis players use the word "love" in lieu of zero. According to literary scholars, this custom is rumored to have developed from the phrase "not for love nor money." Scorekeeping in a game of tennis follows the pattern of a clock as the game was originally based on time. Later, during competitions, forty-five was shortened to forty, resulting in the scoring we have today of 0, 15, 30, 40, and game. Players must win a minimum of four points in order to win a game. If both players have three points each, a score of 40 to 40 (also referred to as deuce), two additional points are needed to gain the advantage and win the game. Typically, the first player to win six games wins the set. A player must win two out of three sets to win the match. Exceptions do exist. For instance, during grand slam tournaments in men's professional tennis, players are required to win three out of five sets to win a match. See the tennis glossary (page 241) for additional definitions of tennis terms.

Tennis is a well-rounded, complete sport as tennis players must possess high levels of anaerobic and aerobic capacity. A tennis player needs to be able to sprint to the ball, as well as endure the perils of a three- or five-set match.

Agility is key, and a player must be able to change direction quickly. Rallying from the baseline relies heavily on lateral movement. Muscular strength, power, and endurance are also needed for the repeated explosive movements required in a tennis match.

The sport of tennis is also considered to weigh heavily on the *mental* game. Psychological skills and decision-making abilities are required to become a world class tennis player. These individuals are able to make decisions quickly based on court sense. In addition, balance and coordination are required for the complex skills and technique that must be developed for the serve, forehand, and backhand.

There are a variety of playing styles: serve and volleyers, counterpunchers, aggressive baseliners, and all-court players. Although all styles of play require a minimum of the aforementioned attributes, each has its own specific formula for success, with emphasis on different physical and psychological attributes. This implies that measures should be incorporated correspondingly, based on the style of game.

The serve and volleyer relies heavily on the strength, spin, speed, and location of his or her serve, as well as the volley technique and touch at the net. These players have great forward running speed, as their style requires them to sprint from the baseline to the net. It is documented that this style of play requires more overall muscular power and endurance. And although balance is an often overlooked component, research by the International Tennis Federation has found that as many as eighty percent of errors are due to a lack of balance. This is particularly important when bending down to hit a low volley, as it is essential for executing volleys with precision. The player's ability to balance over the body's center of mass is crucial when making contact with the ball. Physical measures recommended for this style of play include assessment of upper body muscular strength, power, and endurance, as the shoulders are depended heavily upon for power and speed in the serve.

Players require the transfer of muscular leg power into the service motion, first step explosiveness in their trajectory toward the net, and lower body muscular endurance to repeatedly get down for low volleys (lunge style). Accordingly, measures of lower body muscular strength, power, and endurance should also be assessed.

The serve and volleyer style of play requires the player to be mentally strong. Persistence is key, because the players have to perform the same pattern over and over again, even if the ball passes them repeatedly. Measures of resilience have yet to be validated, however the BDI can be used as a diagnostic of how depressed a tennis player can become after continuously being passed when attempting to serve and volley. Additional psychological assessments recommended include the SOQ or the CSAI-2R to examine confidence and anxiety, and the IAT for evaluation of reaction time. Successful serve and volleyers include former players Pete Sampras, Goran Ivanisevic, Patrick Rafter, Boris Becker, Martina Navratilova, and Jana Novotná.

Counterpunchers rely on their footspeed, placing a lot of wear and tear on their bodies. They run and return balls, and win by outlasting their opponent during rallies. They are frugal with unnecessary errors and are frustratingly consistent. They have a reputation of not giving away any free points. Among the most relevant physical factors in their performance is their anaerobic and aerobic capacity. Counterpunchers are more resistant to fatigue than other players.

Preferred assessments of anaerobic capacity for counterpunchers are respiratory rate and lactate threshold tests. In addition to having a high lactate threshold capacity, these athletes must also possess great cardiorespiratory endurance. Counterpunchers should be assessed using the VO_2 max test to verify that they are ready to endure matches lasting three to five sets. Additionally, anaerobic power should be assessed with either the Wingate test or the 40-yard dash.

Another factor that should be assessed for counterpunchers is agility, using the pro agility drill, because this style of play consists of constantly running from side to side on the baseline. Muscular endurance and power are also important, as many of the movements require constant repetitive motions and explosiveness. Of the three muscular components (strength, power, and endurance), muscular endurance takes precedence for this playing style, with muscular power second, followed by muscular strength. Lastly, but not least, balance in these players should be good enough in order to return hard shots.

Recommended psychological assessments include the CSAI-2R, MMPI, and 16PF. Counterpunchers are known to be grinders. Typical counterpunchers include former players Michael Chang and Aranxta Sanchez Vicario, and current player Rafael Nadal.

The aggressive baseliner is the most commonly seen style of play in today's game. These tennis players enjoy the comfort of the baseline but don't wait for the opponent to make the mistake; they are strategically trying to put the opponent in a bad position, so that they can strike and go in for the kill. They are known to dominate and control the rally. Aggressive baseliners entertain long rallies but can also come to the net and put away the shot. They return shots in an aggressive manner, sometimes taking the ball on the rise and giving their opponents less time to recover.

Aggressive baseliners rely more on anaerobic power than cardiorespiratory endurance. Thus, greater emphasis should be placed on values obtained from anaerobic power and speed assessments such as the short shuttle and 40-yard dash. Out of the three muscular components, muscular power takes precedence for this playing style; muscular endurance is second, followed by muscular strength. Psychological measures that should be utilized include the CAAS (aggression) and the CSAI-2R. Examples of aggressive baseliners include former players Andre Agassi and Monica Seles, and current players Novak Djokovic, Serena Williams, Venus Williams, Andy Murray, and David Ferrer.

Finally, the fourth type of playing style is that of the all-court player. These players are typically well rounded with no real penetrable weakness to be found in their style of play. They can play from baseline, as well as from the net. They also possess excellent footwork and like to mix up their game with a variety of shots. They possess more cardiorespiratory endurance than the serve and volleyer, but less than an aggressive baseliner or counterpuncher. Additionally, they possess moderate to high levels of anaerobic power and should be assessed using measures mentioned throughout this chapter, such as the 20-yard shuttle and 40-yard dash.

Psychological measures to be assessed for the all-court player are decision-making skills, confidence level, and anxiety. Assessments such as the Wonderlic, IAT, and CSAI-2R should be utilized for this type of tennis player.

The strokes of these players are solid, all around. The all-court player can adapt his or her game based on whether he or she is winning or losing. If an all-court player is losing from the baseline, he or she will not be afraid to come to the net more often. Examples of all-court players include two former World No.1s, Roger Federer and Martina Hingis (both Swiss). It might be worthwhile to see if country of origin, as a variable, affects a player's style of game.

For additional reading about tennis physiology, see Smekal et al. (2001). And for information about tennis analytics, refer to Klaassen and Magnus (1998, 2003, 2014) and O'Donoghue (2001). Regarding tennis player performance on the court, there are a number of key measures to consider, as documented in table 9.1.

A taboo topic, not often discussed, is the investment required to become a professional tennis player. This is a major contributing factor to a tennis player's success. There are some who ignore the financial data and argue that tennis is open to everybody. They maintain that everybody has an equal opportunity to play, when in fact this is hardly the case for the underprivileged and minority populations. Tables 9.2 and 9.3 show annual costs to attempt to become a professional tennis player.

Regardless of which estimate you believe, you need over a hundred and forty thousand dollars ($140,000) to attempt to compete at the professional level in tennis. To put things in perspective, note the annual incomes of minorities within the United States, as shown in table 9.4. None of the three minority annual household incomes is sufficient to cover the expenses of one year's worth of training and tournaments required to make it to the professional level. As a matter of fact, it would take more than the annual incomes of two Asian households or the annual incomes of three Black or Hispanic households.

Yet many still wonder why the U.S. has a drought of rising tennis stars, and why the best athletes are not choosing the sport of tennis. Hopefully, these facts will enlighten us and open our eyes to what is really going on in the tennis world. For additional details, see the article *Is Socioeconomic Status a Contributing Factor to Tennis Players' Success?* (Martin 2015).

Table 9.1. *Tennis Performance Measures*

Performance Measure	Abbreviation
Aces	A
Backhand unforced errors	BUE
Backhand winners	BW
Break points	BP
Break points converted	BPC
Double faults	DF
First serve percentage	FS%
Forced errors	FE
Forehand unforced errors	FUE
Forehand winners	FW
Number of times approached the net	NAN
Points won approaching the net	PWAN
Points won on first serve	PWFS
Points won on second serve	PWSS
Return of serve percentage	RS%
Second serve percentage	SS%
Serve percentage	S%
Speed of serve	SoS
Unforced errors	UE
Winners	Wn

Table 9.2. *Annual Cost for Playing Professional Tennis*

Item	Cost
Coaching (travel)	$70,000
Physical Training	$12,000
Mental Training	$1,000
Travel	$60,000
Total	$143,000

Additional Variables	Cost
Travel	
Number of tournaments per year	20
Cost per tournament	$3,000
Coaching	
Salary	$50,000
Travel ($1,000 per tournament)	$20,000
Physical Training:	
Top level training (at least $1,000 per month)	$12,000

Source. Martin (2015).

Table 9.3. *Annual Expenses for the 100th-Ranked Tennis Player*

Item	Cost
Coach (annual salary $60k + $30k travel expenses)	$90,000
Meals	$6,000
Racquet Expenses	$5,000
Miscellaneous	$3,000
Taxes	$54,000
Travel for Player	$25,000
Total	**$183,000**

Source. Martin (2015).

Table 9.4. *U.S. Minority Group Income and Education*

Race or Ethnic Group	Median Annual Household Income (dollars)	Percentage Living in Poverty	Percentage with at Least Some College
Hispanics	39,005	25.6	2.0
Blacks	32,229	27.6	3.5
Asians	70,644	13.0	21.0

Source. U.S. Census Bureau 2012.

Player earnings are an important topic for discussion. The data show that the top fifty to one hundred players can make a living from their earnings. Lower ranked players, who would otherwise be earning enough to make a living in any of the other four sports discussed in this book, do not make enough in tennis to cover their costs of play.

Exhibit 9.1 on page 169 shows the R program and listing used to analyze player earnings. Figure 9.1 shows ATP and WTA earnings by player nationality. And exhibit 9.2 on page 172 shows the R program for producing figure 9.2 comparing earnings of the top professional tennis players in the world—ATP rankings for men and WTA rankings for women. Chapter 10 provides additional discussion about earnings of professional athletes across various sports.

Figure 9.1. *Professional Tennis Player Earnings by Nationality (ATP, WTA)*

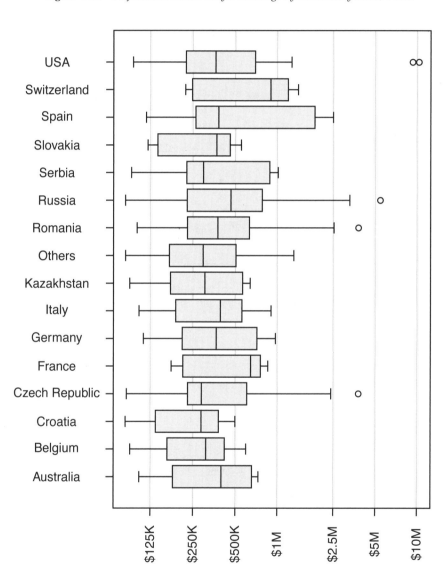

Figure 9.2. *Professional Tennis Player Earnings by Rank and Sex (Top 100 ATP, WTA)*

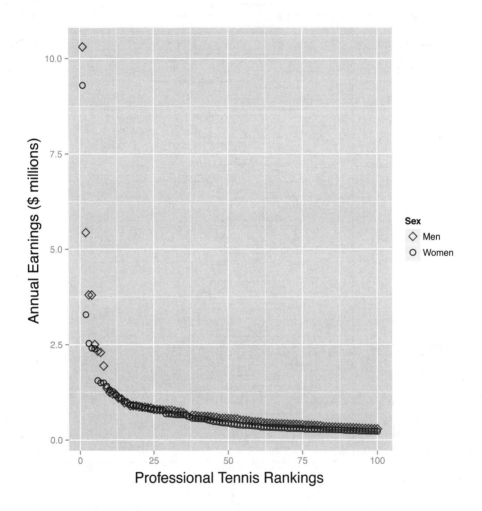

Exhibit 9.1. *Analyzing ATP and WTA Player Earnings by Country (R)*

```
# Analyzing Tennis Player Earnings (R)

##########################################
## Game, Set, Match Analytics R code ##
##########################################

library(MASS)
library(scales)

# Read in the data
setwd()
ATP <- read.csv('ATPearnings.csv')
WTA <- read.csv('WTAearnings.csv')

# Get descriptives
summary(ATP)
summary(WTA)

##########################
## Earnings by Country ##
##########################

# Merge the rows from the ATP and WTA
MergedATPWTA <- rbind(ATP, WTA)

# The variable country within the Mergedfile, make it a character
MergedATPWTA$Country = as.character(WTA$Country)
group = NULL
for(i in 1:nrow(MergedATPWTA)){
  if (MergedATPWTA$Country[i] %in%
        names(table(MergedATPWTA$Country))
      [table(MergedATPWTA$Country) >= 9]){
    group[i] = MergedATPWTA$Country[i]
  } else{
    group[i] = "Others"
  }
}
MergedATPWTA$group = as.character(group)

EarningsbyCountryLinearModel1 <- lm(Earnings ~ group, data = MergedATPWTA)

# Diagnostics for this model are poor
# outliers having an effect on the fit
summary(EarningsbyCountryLinearModel1)

# Call:
# lm(formula = Earnings ~ group, data = MergedATPWTA)

# Residuals:
# Min      1Q   Median    3Q      Max
# -883123 -339451 -141100  130104 9326844
```

```
# Coefficients:
#               Estimate Std. Error t value Pr(>|t|)
# (Intercept)     435176     319946   1.360    0.175
# Belgium        -131998     452473  -0.292    0.771
# Croatia        -158764     452473  -0.351    0.726
# Czech Republic  199282     364795   0.546    0.585
# France          109632     452473   0.242    0.809
# Germany           9787     375170   0.026    0.979
# Italy           -10583     391853  -0.027    0.978
# Kazakhstan      -64606     452473  -0.143    0.887
# Others          -59105     341064  -0.173    0.863
# Romania         302848     404704   0.748    0.455
# Russia          473017     382409   1.237    0.217
# Serbia           30346     423249   0.072    0.943
# Slovakia       -104775     423249  -0.248    0.805
# Spain           482146     423249   1.139    0.256
# Switzerland     413441     452473   0.914    0.362
# USA             542344     357711   1.516    0.131

# Residual standard error: 959800 on 284 degrees of freedom
# Multiple R-squared:  0.06122,   Adjusted R-squared:  0.01163
# F-statistic: 1.235 on 15 and 284 DF,  p-value: 0.2448

# Taking a look at the summary statistics we can see that
# The countries leading in earnings are USA, Spain, Russia, and Switzerland
# Three ways to deal with it:

# Perform a log transformation
EarningsbyCountryLinearModel1log <- lm(log(Earnings) ~ group,
                         data = MergedATPWTA)

# Use a non-parametric test
kruskal.test(Earnings ~ factor(group), data = MergedATPWTA)

# Utilize a Negative Binomial model
EarningsbyCountryLinearModel1nb <- glm.nb(Earnings ~ group,
                         data = MergedATPWTA)
# uses a log link. Use exp() to get covariates back on the original scale

# To extrapolate and interpret findings use the following code
# For example, USA vs. Switzerland
exp(coef(EarningsbyCountryLinearModel1nb)[16] -
    coef(EarningsbyCountryLinearModel1nb)[15])
# Means that USA makes about 15% more than Switzerland

# Figure
# Creates a space to save the figure
pdf('EarningsbyCountry.pdf', height = 8, width = 6)
par(mar = c(5.1, 6.8, 4.1, 2.1))
# Which variables to use
```

```
with(MergedATPWTA, boxplot(log(Earnings) ~ group,
                   # Changes x and y labels
                   xlab = '', ylab = '',
                   # Color - see color chart
                   col = 'gray92',
                   # Main title
                   main = 'Earnings by Country',
                   # Size of x and y labels
                   cex.lab = 1.2,
                   # Makes the plot horizontal
                   horizontal = T,
                   # Removes axis labels / tick marks
                   yaxt = 'n', xaxt = 'n'))

# adds in vertical lines
abline(v = log(c(125000, 250000, 500000, 1000000, 2500000,
                 5000000, 10000000)),
       col = 'lightgray', lty = 'dotted')
# Which variables to use
with(MergedATPWTA, boxplot(log(Earnings) ~ group,
                   # Changes x and y labels
                   xlab = '', ylab = '',
                   # Color - see color chart
                   col = 'gray92',
                   # Main title
                   main = 'Earnings by Country',
                   # Size of x and y labels
                   cex.lab = 1.2,
                   # Makes the plot horizontal
                   horizontal = T,
                   # Removes axis labels / tick marks
                   yaxt = 'n', xaxt = 'n',
                   # Re-draws the boxplots over the lines
                   add = T))

# Adds tick marks
axis(side = 1, at = log(c(125000, 250000, 500000, 1000000, 2500000,
                          5000000, 10000000)),
     lab = FALSE)
text(x = log(c(125000, 250000, 500000, 1000000, 2500000,
               5000000, 10000000)),
     labels = paste('$', c("125K", "250K", "500K", "1M",
                           "2.5M", "5M", "10M"), sep = ''),
     srt = 90, y = par("usr")[3] - 1.3, xpd = TRUE)
axis(side = 2, at = 1:16, label = rep('', 16))
text(y = 1:16, x = 10.2,
     labels = sort(unique(group)),
     xpd = TRUE)
# All of this is to make those plots
# Closes the figure space
dev.off()
```

Exhibit 9.2. *Analyzing ATP and WTA Player Earnings by Rank and Sex (R)*

```
# Professional Tennis Player Earnings by Rank and Sex (R)

#########################################
## Game, Set, Match Analytics R code ##
#########################################

library(ggplot2)

# Reading in the data
setwd()
ATP <- read.csv('ATPtop100earnings.csv')
WTA <- read.csv('WTAtop100earnings.csv')

# Add Sex to data frames
ATP$Sex <- rep("Men", length = nrow(ATP))
WTA$Sex <- rep("Women", length = nrow(WTA))

players <- rbind(ATP, WTA)
players$Sex <- factor(players$Sex)
players$EarningsMM <- players$Earnings/1000000

# Examine the structure of the combined data frame
print(str(players))

pdf("fig_ysports_08_earnings_by_sex.pdf", width = 7, height = 7)
# Scatter plot of Earnings against Rank by Sex
ggplot_object <- ggplot(data = players,
    aes(x = Rank, y = EarningsMM, shape = Sex,
        colour = Sex)) +
    geom_point(size = 3) +
    scale_shape_manual(values = c(5, 1)) +
    scale_colour_manual(values = c("darkred", "darkblue")) +
    labs(x = "Professional Tennis Rankings",
         y = "Annual Earnings ($ millions)")
print(ggplot_object)
dev.off()

# This graph shows shows that men and women are similar in
# annual earnings overall. In comparison to other sports, however,
# there is greater inequality between the top ten ranked
# players and lower ranked players.
```

10

Performance and Market Value

"Being number two sucks."

—ANDRE AGASSI

In sports there can only be one victor. Athletes play to win, to be victorious, and ultimately to be the last man or woman standing. The winner of a competition is not always the best or highest ranked player. Sometimes athletes of lower caliber surprise us. This is part of the excitement and beauty of sport. Why is this? Because in sports there is always a degree of unpredictability.

As data scientists, our goal is to determine the ingredients for the recipe of success in sports. Why? Because we want both to improve and predict performance. This chapter is full of answers and many more questions about the future of sports analytics. We will cover the rating and ranking methods used today, from simple description to how they determine market value and relate to sport performance.

Although the terms rating and ranking are often used interchangeably, they are distinct terms. A score assigned to a specified item refers to its *rating*. For instance, a hotel may receive three stars out of a five-star star rating. The term *ranking* refers to the order (rank) by which items or lists of objects are organized. A list of the top ten five-star hotels is an example of a ranking.

Tennis players such as Pete Sampras and Roger Federer were always seeking to break the record for length of time ranked world No. 1. In tennis, it is well known that there is a big difference between ratings and rankings (Rankin and Grube 1980). The United States Tennis Association (USTA) even has a designated web page to educate tennis players on the difference between ratings and rankings. The USTA defines ratings as the level of play that is self-identified by an athlete (National Tennis Rating Program includes a scale with eight levels, beginner to advanced), whereas rankings reflect the level of play of an athlete in comparison to his or her competition. When players see their names on a list, they are seeing a ranking, not a rating. More specifically, a ranking is a hierarchy established through earned results of performance. For instance, the men's professional tennis organization, ATP, uses a formula that includes only the points earned from twelve obligatory tournaments and six tournaments of the player's choice within fifty-two weeks. This is specifically for higher ranked male professional tennis players. Lower ranked male tennis players choose which eighteen tournaments to include, since they cannot get into the higher-level tournaments.

It is important to be aware that greater numbers of points are earned from more prestigious tournaments. For instance, a player who gets to the quarterfinals of the French Open still earns more points than the player who actually wins an ATP Tour 250 Series tournament, such as the IF Stockholm Open in Sweden. This method of determining rank differs slightly from the women's professional tennis tour, WTA, in which rankings are based on cumulative results of the sixteen best tournaments played over a rolling fifty-two week period. Evidently there are issues with the ranking system currently in place, which became obvious to many when Caroline Wozniaki held the ranking of World No. 1 for over a year without having won a grand slam (Miladinovic 2008; Klaassen and Magnus 2014; Blackburn 2013). Mathematicians and other academicians have raised concerns about the predictive ability of current ranking methods in place (McHale and Morton 2011; Clarke and Dyte 2000; Crespo, Reid, Miley, and Atienza 2003).

There is controversy over ratings and rankings and whether they are valid reflections of performance as well as team strength. Rating teams in team sports is similar to rating individuals in individual sports, with the exception that rating the specific positions within a team requires an additional level of complexity because of team cohesion variables (Hughes, Shank, et al. 2005; Stefani and Pollard 2007). An example of a complex rating system is the EA Sports Player Performance Index. This index rates all soccer players based on team wins. Of course this causes a bias in that players who are on winning teams lead in this type of rating system (Stefani and Pollard 2007). A ranking system popular among athletes, coaches, analysts and sports fans is the Fédération Internationale de Football Association (FIFA) world rankings. FIFA has even developed a great online resource, displaying the most up-to-date rankings lists and soccer-specific ratings on their website, `http://www.fifa.com/worldfootball/ranking/index.html`. Finally, the most well known example of sports ratings within the United States is in the sport of baseball. The Oakland A's instituted Sabermetrics and utilized their very own novel methodology to obtain undervalued players and build an efficient team with limited resources (Lewis 2003; McHale and Davies 2007; McHale, Scarf, and Folker 2012).

Many stakeholders in the sports industry use rating and ranking systems because they are perceived as a tool to judge the quality of a player, assign market value, and predict performance. The term "rating" is used when a value has been designated or assigned to the variable of interest, whether that be a restaurant, a hotel, an athlete, or a team. Typically, sports rankings are determined by wins versus losses.

How should we interpret rankings? How do we know what they are meant to represent? Are we sure that rankings reflect those who are the best in every sport? It is seldom that we speculate how ratings and rankings are developed. Here are some methods that can be applied when developing ratings and rankings. The Massey rating method is named after Kenneth Massey, who developed a model for rating teams and is currently used in the Bowl Championship Series (BCS) for college football. Massey uses rank to predict point scores, which results in a final score used to rate teams. The Colley rating method utilizes winning percentage (number of wins per number of games played by a team) to rate teams. Since this method is based only on the win/loss record and not point score data, many professional leagues currently use it. There is a caveat: This method does not factor in the strength of the opposition.

A more commonly used method of rating is called the Markov model, which has recently been used to rate both basketball and football teams. The Markov method is based on "votes." What exactly does this mean? Well, there are many things that can count as a vote for the winning team: the number of wins, the margin of victory when matched against a higher-ranked opponent, the number of points scored, and so forth. Simpler rating methods include the Matrix and the Redmond methods. They have been shown to be effective when all teams in the league play the same number of games.

Methods that utilize a network approach include the Park-Newman method and the Hochbaum method. The Park-Newman method was named after its developers, Park and Newman, who devised a unique model used in football which takes into consideration both direct and indirect wins. Hochbaum developed a method for network optimization based on linear algebraic expressions. Hochbaum (2015) was quoted as saying, "I like to take two approaches to finding the 'best method' for solving a problem. One tries to devise an efficient algorithm for the problem, and the other tries to establish limits on the efficiency of the algorithm."

Several other popular methods include the Elo Ratings, the logistic regression/Markov chain method, and Monte Carlo simulation. The Elo Ratings system is a fairly simple method in which player performance is quantified by the ability to win against the competition (Langville and Meyer 2012; Miller 2016). Logistic regression/Markov chain method is unique in that it utilizes logistic regression along with the properties of the Markov model of transient states. It has been used successfully in basketball to predict the outcomes during March Madness, as well as to rank college teams. Finally, history holds that the Monte Carlo simulation method originates from the games of chance played in the casinos of Monaco. It is commonly used to examine variables that change from state to state. Repeated random sampling is used to approximate the mean value of the variable of interest.

Overall, linear regression is a popular method that is used for ratings. Assuming that there is linearity within the data, least squares reveal the smallest variance within each sample. Least squares ratings are among the most commonly used analytic models in sports. There are a variety of methods, including Keener's method for ratings, the analytic hierarchy process (AHP), and those based on offensive-defensive ratings and point spreads.

Ratings and rankings have been discussed by numerous sport researchers. Langville and Meyer (2012) provide a detailed review of the available methods in *Who's #1? The Science of Rating and Ranking*. For additional discussion, see Stefani (1987, 1997), Thompson (1975), Groeneveld (1990), Appleton (1995), Carlin (1996), West (2006), Ovadia (2004), Stefani and Pollard (2007), and Paruolo, Saisana, and Saltelli (2013).

Athletes, coaches, spectators, analysts, and sports managers alike have a vested interest in rankings. Why is this? Rankings are an indicator of performance and therefore the market value of the athlete. Let us take a look at the market values of athletes from different sports. The market value of athletes within the United States is as follows, in order from the highest paid to the least: MLB, NBA, NFL, ATP, WTA, and MLS. Interestingly, international soccer players such as Cristiano Ronaldo and Lionel Messi are among the highest paid athletes in the world, with annual salaries higher than many MLB, NBA, and NFL players (Einolf 2004; Scully 2004; Simmons 2007; Fry, Galanos, and Posso 2014). Tables 10.1 through 10.7 at the end of this chapter show annual salaries of the top athletes in the world in various professional leagues.

Although incomes vary from sport to sport, there is much greater disparity among athletes due to gender and socioeconomic status. Coming from a physiological perspective, and not condoning such disparities, I understand the physiological differences and capacity of female and male athletes. I find it fascinating to see how far males can push the boundaries in sport. In general, men have greater upper body strength. Their power and endurance is due to anatomical differences in the upper body, as well as to physiological differences that include much higher levels of testosterone. This is not to say that watching women compete is not exciting. In fact, it is more intriguing to see that the physiology of women has exceeded the beliefs and limitations superimposed by gender and stereotyped roles. Examples of this include Dara Torres winning an Olympic silver medal at the age of forty-one, and Dyana Nyad, who at the age of sixty-four swam from Cuba to Florida without the aid of a shark cage. Nyad swam one hundred and eleven miles in fifty-three hours, from Havana to Key West, and was recognized as the world's greatest long distance swimmer. We also now have Ronda Rousey excelling in the Ultimate Fighting Championship (UFC), traditionally a male-dominated sport (Komi and Bosco 1978; Mayhew and Salm 1990; Mayhew et al. 2001).

Although great strides have been made toward gender equality in tennis, much remains to be done regarding socioeconomic status (SES). A major problem faces the sport of tennis in the form of SES inequality. Although many may argue that there are great opportunities today for anyone in the sport of tennis, it is a very different story when we consider opportunities to compete at the professional level. Chances are significantly skewed in favor of those of higher SES. Player investments and SES disparity in the sport of tennis are discussed in the article *Is Socioeconomic Status a Contributing Factor to Tennis Players' Success?* by Martin (2015). Additionally, there is an earnings disparity between higher and lower ranked professional tennis players. There is a significant decrease in professional tennis players' earnings when ranked below the top 50, unlike other sports covered in this book. For additional information about tennis player salaries, please refer to tables 10.4 and 10.5.

When sports commentators and fans use the term "sports analytics," they are usually thinking of statistics that describe player and team performance in games. After reading this book, you now know that sports analytics is much more than statistics computed from box scores or play-by-play logs. Performance on the field depends on training and conditioning—preparing the body and the mind for peak performance. And the first step toward understanding what contributes to peak performance is to do a good job of measurement, followed by choosing the correct statistical model and understanding what findings are relevant to each sport.

Table 10.1.   *Salaries of Top MLB Players*

Rank	Player	Annual Earnings (millions of dollars)
1	Clayton Kershaw	30.0
2	Jon Lester	30.0
3	Justin Verlander	28.0
4	Ryan Howard	25.0
5	Cliff Lee	25.0
6	Albert Pujols	24.1
7	Felix Hernandez	24.1
8	Prince Fielder	24.1
9	Robinson Cano	24.0
10	Zack Greinke	23.0
11	Joe Mauer	23.0
12	C.C. Sabathia	23.0
13	Mark Teixeira	22.5
14	Masahiro Tanaka	22.0
15	Hanley Ramirez	22.0
16	Miguel Cabrera	22.0
17	Jacoby Ellsbury	21.1
18	Alex Rodriguez	21.0
19	Matt Kemp	21.0
20	Jayson Werth	21.0
21	Adrian Gonzalez	21.0
22	Carl Crawford	20.5
23	Matt Cain	20.0
24	Pablo Sandoval	20.0
25	David Wright	20.0
26	Adam Wainwright	19.5
27	Mark Buehrle	19.0
28	Hunter Pence	18.5
29	Andre Ethier	18.0
30	Jered Weaver	18.0
31	C.J. Wilson	18.0
32	Tim Lincecum	18.0
33	Matt Holliday	17.0
34	Brian McCann	17.0
35	Brandon McCarthy	17.0
36	Elvis Andrus	17.0
37	Buster Posey	16.6
38	Jordan Zimmermann	16.5
39	Carlos Gonzalez	16.1
40	Adrian Beltre	16.0
41	Ian Kinsler	16.0
42	Anibal Sanchez	16.0
43	David Ortiz	16.0
44	Curtis Granderson	16.0
45	Yasmany Tomas	15.9
46	Max Scherzer	15.2
47	Nelson Cruz	15.1
48	Yadier Molina	15.1
49	Jhonny Peralta	15.0
50	Carlos Beltran	15.0

Source. http://www.spotrac.com/rankings/mlb/

Table 10.2. *Salaries of Top NBA Players*

Rank	Name	Team	Annual Earnings (dollars)
1	Kobe Bryant, SG	Los Angeles Lakers	25,000,000
2	Joe Johnson, SF	Brooklyn Nets	24,894,863
3	LeBron James, SF	Cleveland Cavaliers	22,970,500
4	Carmelo Anthony, SF	New York Knicks	22,875,000
5	Dwight Howard, C	Houston Rockets	22,359,364
6	Chris Bosh, PF	Miami Heat	22,192,730
7	Chris Paul, PG	Los Angeles Clippers	21,468,695
8	Kevin Durant, SF	Oklahoma City Thunder	20,158,622
9	Derrick Rose, PG	Chicago Bulls	20,093,064
10	Dwyane Wade, SG	Miami Heat	20,000,000
11	LaMarcus Aldridge, PF	San Antonio Spurs	19,689,000
12	Kevin Love, PF	Cleveland Cavaliers	19,689,000
13	Marc Gasol, C	Memphis Grizzlies	19,688,000
14	Blake Griffin, PF	Los Angeles Clippers	18,907,726
15	Paul Millsap, PF	Atlanta Hawks	18,671,659
16	Paul George, SF	Indiana Pacers	17,120,106
17	Russell Westbrook, PG	Oklahoma City Thunder	16,744,218
18	Kawhi Leonard, SF	San Antonio Spurs	16,407,500
19	Enes Kanter, C	Oklahoma City Thunder	16,407,500
20	Jimmy Butler, SG	Chicago Bulls	16,407,500
21	Tobias Harris, SF	Orlando Magic	16,000,000
22	John Wall, PG	Washington Wizards	15,851,950
23	DeMarcus Cousins, C	Sacramento Kings	15,851,950
24	James Harden, SG	Houston Rockets	15,756,438
25	Roy Hibbert, C	Los Angeles Lakers	15,592,217
26	Eric Gordon, SG	New Orleans Pelicans	15,514,031
27	Klay Thompson, SG	Golden State Warriors	15,501,000
28	David Lee, PF	Boston Celtics	15,493,680
29	Gordon Hayward, SG	Utah Jazz	15,409,570
30	Chandler Parsons, SF	Dallas Mavericks	15,361,500
31	Goran Dragic, SG	Miami Heat	14,783,000
32	Khris Middleton, SF	Milwaukee Bucks	14,700,000
33	Draymond Green, SF	Golden State Warriors	14,260,870
34	Danilo Gallinari, SF	Denver Nuggets	14,000,000
35	Reggie Jackson, PG	Detroit Pistons	13,913,044
36	Andrew Bogut, C	Golden State Warriors	13,800,000
37	DeMarre Carroll, SF	Toronto Raptors	13,600,000
38	Al Jefferson, C	Charlotte Hornets	13,500,000
39	Eric Bledsoe, PG	Phoenix Suns	13,500,000
40	Tony Parker, PG	San Antonio Spurs	13,437,500
41	Joakim Noah, C	Chicago Bulls	13,400,000
42	Nicolas Batum, SF	Charlotte Hornets	13,125,306
43	Nene Hilario, PF	Washington Wizards	13,000,000
44	Tyson Chandler, C	Phoenix Suns	13,000,000
45	Ricky Rubio, PG	Minnesota Timberwolves	12,700,000
46	Robin Lopez, C	New York Knicks	12,650,000
47	Ty Lawson, PG	Houston Rockets	12,404,495
48	Rudy Gay, SF	Sacramento Kings	12,403,101
49	Serge Ibaka, PF	Oklahoma City Thunder	12,250,000
50	Nikola Pekovic, C	Minnesota Timberwolves	12,100,000

Source. http://espn.go.com/nba/salaries

Table 10.3. Salaries of Top NFL Players

Rank	Name	Position	Annual Earnings (dollars)
1	Drew Brees	Quarterback	23,800,000
2	Philip Rivers	Quarterback	21,166,668
3	Calvin Johnson	Wide Receiver	20,558,000
4	Charles Johnson	Defensive End	20,020,000
5	Matt Ryan	Quarterback	19,500,000
6	Mario Williams	Defensive End	19,400,000
7	Aaron Rodgers	Quarterback	18,250,000
8	Matthew Stafford	Quarterback	17,721,250
9	Peyton Manning	Quarterback	17,500,000
10	Ben Roethlisberger	Quarterback	17,245,000
11	Robert Quinn	Defensive End	16,744,111
12	Jay Cutler	Quarterback	16,500,000
13	Darrelle Revis	Cornerback	16,000,000
14	Alex Smith	Quarterback	15,600,000
15	Adrian Peterson	Running Back	15,400,000
16	Colin Kaepernick	Quarterback	15,265,753
17	Tony Romo	Quarterback	14,973,000
18	Jason Pierre-Paul	Defensive End	14,813,000
19	Patrick Peterson	Cornerback	14,791,491
20	A.J. Green	Wide Receiver	14,750,000
21	Calais Campbell	Defensive End	14,750,000
22	Gerald McCoy	Defensive Tackle	14,595,000
23	Joe Flacco	Quarterback	14,550,000
24	Eli Manning	Quarterback	14,450,000
25	Tom Brady	Quarterback	14,000,000
26	J.J. Watt	Defensive End	13,969,000
27	Demaryius Thomas	Wide Receiver	13,200,000
28	Rodney Hudson	Center	13,000,000
29	Cam Newton	Quarterback	13,000,000
30	Sam Bradford	Quarterback	12,985,000
31	Brandon Carr	Cornerback	12,717,000
32	Clay Matthews	Inside Linebacker	12,700,000
33	Chris Long	Defensive End	12,500,000
34	Julio Jones	Wide Receiver	12,400,000
35	Vincent Jackson	Wide Receiver	12,209,777
36	Richard Sherman	Cornerback	12,200,000
37	Julius Peppers	Outside Linebacker	12,000,000
38	Ryan Kalil	Center	11,795,000
39	Johnathan Joseph	Cornerback	11,750,000
40	Joe Haden	Cornerback	11,700,000
41	D'Brickashaw Ferguson	Left Tackle	11,698,666
42	Vontae Davis	Cornerback	11,250,000
43	Larry Fitzgerald	Wide Receiver	10,850,000
44	Branden Albert	Left Tackle	10,725,000
45	Trent Williams	Left Tackle	10,680,388
46	Ryan Clady	Left Tackle	10,600,000
47	Cameron Wake	Defensive End	10,450,000
48	Nick Mangold	Center	10,407,100
49	Julius Thomas	Tight End	10,300,000
50	Joe Thomas	Left Tackle	10,200,000

Source. http://www.spotrac.com/nfl/rankings/

Table 10.4. *Salaries of Top ATP Players*

Rank	Player	Country	Points	Annual Earnings (dollars)
1	Novak Djokovic	Serbia	15,785	15,127,409
2	Andy Murray	Scotland	8,640	5,904,508
3	Roger Federer	Switzerland	8,420	6,135,034
4	Stan Wawrinka	Switzerland	6,495	5,032,607
5	Tomas Berdych	Czech Republic	4,910	2,786,099
6	Kei Nishikori	Japan	4,710	2,605,656
7	Rafael Nadal	Spain	4,060	2,760,423
8	David Ferrer	Spain	3,945	2,373,345
9	Milos Raonic	Canada	2,770	1,433,968
10	Kevin Anderson	South Africa	2,475	1,631,769
11	Richard Gasquet	France	2,400	1,875,600
12	Marin Cilic	Croatia	2,350	1,808,974
13	John Isner	United States	2,280	1,563,410
14	Gilles Simon	France	2,020	1,344,476
15	Jo-Wilfried Tsonga	France	1,990	1,443,611
16	David Goffin	Belgium	1,970	1,022,878
17	Feliciano Lopez	Spain	1,725	1,418,098
18	Dominic Thiem	Austria	1,600	1,018,677
19	Gael Monfils	France	1,590	953,884
20	Bernard Tomic	Australia	1,585	1,017,140
21	Ivo Karlovic	Croatia	1,575	987,747
22	Grigor Dimitrov	Bulgaria	1,555	914,699
23	Roberto Bautista Agut	Spain	1,510	1,090,898
24	Viktor Troicki	Serbia	1,499	1,064,725
25	Benoit Paire	France	1,471	843,261
26	Fabio Fognini	Italy	1,470	1,590,573
27	Andreas Seppi	Italy	1,440	1,019,721
28	Guillermo Garcia-Lopez	Spain	1,420	964,401
29	Jeremy Chardy	France	1,400	1,066,199
30	Tommy Robredo	Spain	1,290	724,507
31	Philipp Kohlschreiber	Germany	1,230	717,011
32	Nick Kyrgios	Australia	1,215	976,239
33	Jack Sock	United States	1,210	1,143,262
34	Thomaz Bellucci	Brazil	1,205	712,568
35	Pablo Cuevas	Uruguay	1,180	949,961
36	Gilles Muller	Luxembourg	1,140	767,121
37	Alexandr Dolgopolov	Ukraine	1,135	682,065
38	Leonardo Mayer	Argentina	1,090	725,957
39	Jiri Vesely	Czech Republic	1,067	703,904
40	Borna Coric	Croatia	1,051	595,531
41	Adrian Mannarino	France	1,050	758,519
42	Fernando Verdasco	Spain	1,040	772,604
43	Vasek Pospisil	Canada	995	1,218,245
44	Martin Klizan	Slovakia	990	775,495
45	Joao Sousa	Portugal	986	788,147
46	Marcos Baghdatis	Cyprus	943	573,734
47	Steve Johnson	United States	915	780,275
48	Donald Young	United States	871	664,357
49	Pablo Andujar	Spain	870	773,363
50	Mikhail Kukushkin	Kazakhstan	867	487,344

Source. http://www.tennis.com/earnings/ATP/

Table 10.5. Salaries of Top WTA Players

Rank	Player	Country	Points	Annual Earnings (dollars)
1	Serena Williams	United States	11285	10,582,642
2	Simona Halep	Romania	6580	3,615,642
3	Maria Sharapova	Russia	4691	3,299,284
4	Garbine Muguruza	Spain	4690	3,827,303
5	Petra Kvitova	Czech Republic	3860	2,146,237
6	Agnieszka Radwanska	Poland	3515	1,920,465
7	Lucie Safarova	Czech Republic	3405	2,579,546
8	Flavia Pennetta	Italy	3372	4,085,343
9	Angelique Kerber	Germany	3330	1,358,965
10	Timea Bacsinszky	Switzerland	3157	2,010,009
11	Caroline Wozniacki	Denmark	3151	1,106,475
12	Ana Ivanovic	Serbia	3145	1,418,973
13	Carla Suarez Navarro	Spain	3075	1,689,032
14	Venus Williams	United States	2982	1,692,556
15	Karolina Pliskova	Czech Republic	2950	1,286,293
16	Belinda Bencic	Switzerland	2900	1,483,574
17	Roberta Vinci	Italy	2655	2,185,843
18	Sara Errani	Italy	2525	1,263,820
19	Madison Keys	United States	2495	1,585,633
20	Andrea Petkovic	Germany	2445	1,046,532
21	Elina Svitolina	Ukraine	2410	1,116,439
22	Victoria Azarenka	Belarus	2276	1,369,657
23	Ekaterina Makarova	Russia	2250	1,705,438
24	Jelena Jankovic	Serbia	2125	1,154,864
25	Irina-Camelia Begu	Romania	1880	936,841
26	Anna Karolina Schmiedlova	Slovakia	1791	615,421
27	Kristina Mladenovic	France	1760	1,360,498
28	Samantha Stosur	Australia	1755	935,918
29	Anastasia Pavlyuchenkova	Russia	1755	754,972
30	Sloane Stephens	United States	1715	768,435
31	Sabine Lisicki	Germany	1597	1,005,884
32	Svetlana Kuznetsova	Russia	1477	898,885
33	Camila Giorgi	Italy	1395	578,956
34	Dominika Cibulkova	Slovakia	1336	663,358
35	Caroline Garcia	France	1315	849,955
36	Daria Gavrilova	Russia	1295	574,810
37	Lesia Tsurenko	Ukraine	1294	527,514
38	Barbora Strycova	Czech Republic	1290	777,690
39	Eugenie Bouchard	Canada	1273	784,628
40	Coco Vandeweghe	United States	1247	901,187
41	Annika Beck	Germany	1243	403,609
42	Madison Brengle	United States	1233	602,562
43	Alize Cornet	France	1205	663,375
44	Varvara Lepchenko	United States	1184	663,065
45	Monica Niculescu	Romania	1135	633,262
46	Teliana Pereira	Brazil	1107	317,279
47	Johanna Konta	England	1086	430,559
48	Tsvetana Pironkova	Bulgaria	1080	463,776
49	Mona Barthel	Germany	1065	522,332
50	Alison Van Uytvanck	Belgium	1062	588,717

Source. http://www.tennis.com/earnings/WTA/

Table 10.6. *Salaries of Top MLS Players*

Rank	Player	Position	Annual Earnings (dollars)
1	Ricardo Kaká	Midfielder	7,167,500
2	Sebastian Giovinco	Midfielder	7,115,556
3	Michael Bradley	Midfielder	6,500,000
4	Steven Gerrard	Midfielder	6,332,504
5	Frank Lampard	Midfielder	6,000,000
6	David Villa	Forward	5,610,000
7	Jozy Altidore	Forward	4,750,000
8	Clint Dempsey	Forward	4,605,942
9	Robbie Keane	Forward	4,500,000
10	Giovani Dos Santos	Midfielder	4,100,008
11	Jermaine Jones	Midfielder	3,052,500
12	Obafemi Martins	Forward	3,000,000
13	Andrea Pirlo	Midfielder	2,315,694
14	Shaun Maloney	Midfielder	1,586,000
15	Omar Gonzalez	Defender	1,450,000
16	Pedro Morales	Midfielder	1,410,900
17	Federico Higuain	Forward	1,175,000
18	Innocent Emeghara	Forward	1,040,000
19	Liam Ridgewell	Defender	1,000,000
20	Kennedy Igboananike	Forward	901,667
21	Octavio Rivero	Forward	890,850
22	Tesho Akindele	Midfielder	875,000
23	DaMarcus Beasley	Defender	813,333
24	Osvaldo Alonso	Midfielder	789,667
25	Maurice Edu	Midfielder	768,750
26	Mix Diskerud	Midfielder	750,000
27	Roger Espinoza	Midfielder	750,000
28	David Accam	Forward	720,938
29	Kyle Beckerman	Midfielder	700,000
30	Matt Besler	Defender	683,250
31	Graham Zusi	Midfielder	682,102
32	Chris Wondolowski	Forward	675,000
33	Fanendo Adi	Forward	664,000
34	Bradley Wright-Phillips	Forward	660,000
35	Diego Valeri	Midfielder	550,000
36	Sacha Kljestan	Midfielder	537,500
37	Kei Kamara	Forward	536,666
38	Aurélien Collin	Defender	525,000
39	Brek Shea	Midfielder	520,000
40	Dom Dwyer	Forward	518,750
41	Álvaro Saborío	Forward	493,333
42	Jose Goncalves	Defender	479,375
43	Mike Magee	Midfielder	467,500
44	Brad Davis	Midfielder	445,500
45	Mauro Díaz	Midfielder	442,400
46	Juan Agudelo	Forward	427,500
47	Marcelo Sarvas	Midfielder	425,000
48	Erick Torres	Forward	425,000
49	Bill Hamid	Goalkeeper	405,500
50	Laurent Ciman	Defender	401,667

Source. http://www.spotrac.com/mls/rankings/

Table 10.7. Salaries of Top FIFA Players

Rank	Player	Position	Annual Earnings (millions of dollars)
1	Lionel Messi	Forward	21.7
2	Cristiano Ronaldo	Forward	19.6
3	Zlatan Ibrahimovic	Forward	15.9
4	Radamel Falcao	Forward	15.4
5	Thiago Silva	Defender	13.2
6	Gareth Bale	Midfielder	10.3
7	Xavi Hernandez	Midfielder	8.8
8	Andres Iniesta	Midfielder	8.8
9	Wayne Rooney	Forward	8.4
10	Didier Drogba	Forward	8.1

Source. http://www.20minutos.es/graficos/los-10-jugadores-de-futbol-mejor-pagados-del-mundo-67/0/

Statistics Glossary

analysis of covariance (ANCOVA) A general linear model which blends ANOVA and regression, where the regression is used to control for a confounding variable. Also see *F-test*.

analysis of variance (ANOVA) A statistical method used to test differences between two or more means on a continuous dependent variable. Also see *F-test*.

Bayesian statistics Inferential statistics built on probability theory, in particular, Bayes Theorem, which provides a means by which probabilities may be updated based on additional information.

binary variable A variable that takes only two values, often coded as 0 and 1.

bootstrap sampling Resampling technique that involves repeated sampling with replacement from a sample. This provides a way to test hypotheses and construct confidence intervals when a theoretical sampling distribution is not available.

chi-square distribution Asymmetric continuous probability distribution used in chi-square tests.

chi-square test A variety of statistical tests rely on the chi-square statistic and distribution. One such test is the goodness-of-fit test that can be used with categorical variables.

classical statistics Alternative to Bayesian statistics. Most commonly associated with hypothesis testing in which a null (no-relationship or no-differences) hypothesis is set up to be tested relative to an alternative hypothesis. When we reject the null hypothesis, we say we have a statistically significant result. When no statistically significant result is observed, we say the null hypothesis was not rejected. We never accept the null hypothesis.

comma-delimited text (csv) File format and extension commonly used as input to spreadsheet programs and systems for statistical analysis.

cross-sectional data In statistics and econometrics, a type of data collected by observing many subjects (such as individuals, firms, countries, or regions) at the same point of time or without regard to differences in time. Units of study are organized in ways that assume independence from one unit to the next. Data items are not adjacent in time or geography, so they are not dependent or related to one another.

cross-validation   Resampling technique designed to test predictive models. A sample is split repeatedly into training and test subsamples. Each predictive model is fit to the training subsample and evaluated on the test subsample. Multi-fold cross validation splits the sample into K subsamples, and on each iteration, one of the K subsamples is used for testing and the other subsamples are used for fitting the model. Results for the K subsamples are averaged to provide an estimate of out-of-sample predictive accuracy. Leave-one-out cross-validation sets K equal to the size of the sample, so that only one sample observation is used as the test subsample on each iteration. Cross-validation is sometimes referred to as *internal cross-validation* because it is internal to the sample.

data visualization   General term for statistical graphics and information design graphics. Used for discovery (exploratory data analysis), diagnostics (model development and checking), and display (presentation, visual communication).

descriptive statistics   Traditional statistical methods that are intended to describe or characterize data and are not intended for drawing inferences. Statistical summaries of sample data that are neither explanatory nor predictive. Distinct from methods described as *inferential statistics*. Also called *descriptives*.

explanatory model   A model relating one or more explanatory variables to one or more response variables. An explanatory model is a useful description and explanation of why and how a thing works or an explanation of why a phenomenon is the way it is. This contrasts with a predictive model, which is used to forecast, estimate or predict a future outcome.

explanatory variable   Variable used to explain another variable (the response variable).

experimental research   The environment or aspects of the environment can be manipulated by the researcher. Distinct versions of the environment represent experimental treatments. There is randomization through random assignment of subjects to treatments. As much as possible, there is control of factors that can affect subject response.

F **distribution**   An asymmetric continuous probability distribution commonly used in F-tests and the ANOVA model.

F-**test**   Compares whether two variances are equal under a null hypothesis of equality.

generalized linear model   Class of predictive models (supervised learning models) from traditional statistics. These include linear regression, logistic regression, and Poisson regression, among other methods. The right-hand side of the prediction formula is a linear combination of explanatory variables that are connected to the dependent variable through a "link function." The model is linear in its parameters.

homogeneity of slopes   Assumption that the slopes run parallel to each other and that there is no interaction between the covariate and the independent variable.

homogeneity of variances   Assumption that variances are equal among groups. See Levene's test.

inferential statistics   Traditional statistical methods that draw inferences from samples to populations. The fitted models may be explanatory or predictive. Distinct from methods described as descriptive statistics.

levels of measurement   Distinctions across nominal (categorical), ordinal (ranks), interval, and ratio measures.

Levene's test   Statistical test for equality of variances.

linear mixed effects model   Used to model fixed and random effects linearly.

linear regression   Also called ordinary least-squares regression or just regression. A form of generalized linear model using a linear combination of explanatory variables to predict a continuous response variable or variable having meaningful magnitude. The model is linear in its parameters.

longitudinal data   Multiple observations for person or units of study across time periods, but also organized by cross-sections. Methods of analysis are called multiple time series, panel, or longitudinal data analysis. Adjacent units in time can be expected to be more highly related to one another than units more distant in time.

logistic regression   A generalized linear model using a linear combination of explanatory variables to predict a discrete binary response variable.

Markov model   Used when modeling a system with a random variable where there are a number of states in the model, probabilities for each state, and transition states. Model with the Markov property—the conditional probability of future states depends only on the present state.

model   Representation of the world in a quantified way that can be expressed by computer code. Examples are stochastic (probability) and statistical models, mathematical programming, and simulation models.

Monte Carlo simulation   A problem solving technique used to approximate the probability of certain outcomes by running multiple trial runs, called simulations, using random variables.

multi-level categorical variable   Categorical variable that takes more than two values, as opposed to a binary variable. Also called a multinomial variable.

multiple imputation   The preferred method of handling missing data is multiple imputation. That is, we create a number of alternative data sets using existing data to predict what the missing data values may be, and then we analyze each of the resulting data sets.

multivariate analysis of covariance (MANCOVA)   Group of statistical tests for equality of means on more than one dependent variable, controlling for differences across other variables.

multivariate analysis of variance (MANOVA)   Group of statistical tests for equality of means on more than one dependent variable.

nonlinear mixed model   Model used to model fixed and random effects nonlinearly. This type of model does not have all the parameters entering in a linear fashion.

normality of distribution   An assumption we check prior to using statistical analyses to determine whether the data are normally distributed.

observational research   Distinct from experimental research. The researcher is unable to control the environment or manipulate environmental conditions. Rather, the researcher observes events as they occur in the environment, making measures as things happen. Most business research is observational research.

outlier   Observed value of a variable that is outside the range of most other observed values. Outliers may be legitimate data, or they may be due to errors or unanticipated factors.

parameter   Quantitative characteristic of a population distribution, such as the population mean or variance.

Pearson product-moment correlation   Index of direction and strength of linear relationship that varies between -1 and +1. Also see *Spearman rank-order correlation.*

Poisson distribution   Probability distribution for a discrete variable taking non-negative integer values. Useful in modeling counts, including runs scored and points scored in sports. Gets its name from the French mathematician Siméon Denis Poisson.

Poisson regression   A form of generalized linear model using a linear combination of explanatory variables to predict a discrete response taking non-negative integer values (counts). Like the Poisson distribution, it gets its name from the French mathematician Siméon Denis Poisson.

population   A theoretical construct describing the domain or group of interest to the researcher. The complete set of observations of interest to the researcher. In actual research settings, a sampling frame is identified—this is a partial enumeration or list representing the population. Then samples are selected from the sampling frame, usually at random. Regardless, models of statistical inference make the assumption of *random sampling from the population.*

population distribution   The distribution of interest to the researcher. Characterized by population parameters.

posterior distribution   Probability distribution of a parameter. In Bayesian statistics, the posterior distribution is obtained by using Bayes theorem along with a prior distribution and the likelihood function for the sample data. It is "posterior" in the sense that it is the end product of a Bayesian data analysis, whereas the prior distribution begins the process. The Bayesian statistician uses Bayes theorem to revise his beliefs about population parameters, beginning with a prior distribution and ending with a posterior distribution.

prior distribution   Probability distribution of a parameter at the beginning of a Bayesian data analysis. The prior distribution (also referred to as the "prior") is in place before any data are collected or analyzed. It represents the researcher's prior belief about the population parameter.

predictive model   A model designed to predict as-yet unobserved values of a response variable using observed values of explanatory variables. The objective is for the model to predict the response accurately, whether or not the underlying mechanism relating explanatory and response variables is understood.

probability   Can be frequency-based, model-based, or subjective-based. A number between zero and one corresponding to the likelihood that an event will occur.

proportion   A relative frequency or ratio of counts. Like a probability, it is a number between zero and one.

psychographics   Demographics relating to psychological factors.

R   Open-source, object-oriented language for programming with data. Widely used for traditional statistics, machine learning, and data visualization. R programs do not require a compile cycle, so they are more quickly developed than programs in C/C++/C or Java.

regression   Group of supervised learning methods designed to predict the value of a variable with meaningful magnitude. Distinct from *classification*. In statistical modeling, regression analysis is a statistical process for estimating relationships among variables. It includes many techniques for modeling and analyzing several variables, when the focus is on the relationship between a dependent variable and one or more independent variables or predictors.

resampling   Statistical procedure that involves repeated sampling from a sample with replacement. See *bootstrap sampling* and *cross-validation*.

sampling   Process by which a subset of the population (rather than the entire population) is selected for analysis and modeling.

sampling distribution   Statistical term for the distribution of a sample statistic across all possible repeated samples from the population. Foundation for drawing inferences about the population using statistics from the sample.

scatter plot   Statistical graphic for displaying the values of two continuous variables. Useful for examining relationships between variables.

simulation   Capturing the essence of things in a computer program, so the computer program mimics or simulates behavior. Variations include discrete event simulation, process simulation, and agent-based modeling. Also see *Monte Carlo simulation*.

spatial data   Observations have geocodes or location data affixed. Common geocodes are longitude and latitude. Methods of analysis are called spatial data analysis. Adjacent units in space are expected to be more highly related to one another than units more distant in space.

Spearman rank-order correlation   Index of direction and strength of monotonic relationship between two ordinal variables that varies between -1 and +1. Also see *Pearson correlation*.

t **distribution**   Symmetric continuous probability distribution used in *t*-tests. Also called *Student's t distribution*.

*t***-test**   Classical hypothesis test used for testing hypotheses about one or two means when the population variance is unknown. Most relevant for normally distributed random variables and small sample sizes.

time series   Multiple observations for a person or unit of study across time periods. Methods of analysis are called time series analysis. Adjacent units in time can be expected to be more highly related to one another than units more distant in time.

traditional statistics   General term for both classical and Bayesian methods, as opposed to machine learning methods. With traditional statistics, we specify the model in advance of analysis and make assumptions about underlying population distributions prior to fitting the model to sample data.

Football Glossary

AstroTurf Artificial playing surface, named after the Astrodome in Houston, Texas.

audible Verbal commands shouted by the quarterback to his teammates at the line of scrimmage to change a play on short notice.

backfield Area behind the line of scrimmage.

back (running back) Halfback or fullback.

ball carrier Player who has possession of the ball.

beat Occurs when a player gets past an opponent trying to block or tackle him.

blackout Occurs when a regional network TV affiliate is forbidden from showing a local game because it is not sold out.

blitz Occurs when the defensive team sends players rushing toward the line of scrimmage as soon as the ball is snapped to try to sack the quarterback.

blocking Act of preventing a defensive player from getting to the ball carrier.

call a play To instruct players to execute a pre-planned play.

clipping An illegal block that is a personal foul, punishable by a fifteen-yard penalty.

complete pass Pass that is caught in the air by a teammate.

conference In the NFL, National Conference or American Conference.

controlling the game clock Tactics used by an offensive team to either save or use up time on the game clock.

This glossary follows the rules of NFL professional football in the United States (National Football League 2015). High school and college football rules differ from NFL rules.

coverage   Occurs when a defender prevents a receiver from catching a pass or when defensive team members prevent a long kick return.

cut back   Sudden change in direction taken in an effort to make it more difficult for defenders to follow and tackle a player.

defense (defensive team)   Team that does not have the ball. The job of the defense is to stop the offense. The eleven men on the defensive team work together to keep the offense from advancing toward the defense's end zone.

defensive players   Members of the defense. Defensive linemen battle directly against offensive linemen. Linebackers defend against a pass and push forward to stop a run or to tackle the quarterback. Cornerbacks and safeties defend against a pass from the quarterback to wide receivers and help to stop the run. There are eleven defensive players, with numbers of linemen, linebackers, and backs varying from one play to another.

division   In the NFL, divisions are sub-groups within conferences, such as the Eastern, Northern, Southern and Western Divisions.

double coverage   Occurs when two defensive players cover one receiver.

down   One of four chances a team on offense has to gain ten yards.

down the field   Direction of the opponent's goal line.

draft choice   Player that is picked by a professional sports team from a pool of candidates (usually college players) during the annual draft.

drive   Series of plays a team puts together in an attempt to score.

drop back   Occurs when a quarterback, after taking the snap, takes a few steps backward into an area called the pocket to get ready to pass the ball.

drop kick   Free kick in which a player drops the ball and kicks it right after it hits the ground.

eligible receiver   Offensive player, such as wide receiver and end, allowed to catch a forward pass. Linemen and the quarterback must notify the referee if they wish to become an eligible receiver, and they must stand at least one yard behind the line of scrimmage before the snap.

encroachment   Occurs when a player is in the neutral zone and contact occurs prior to the snap of the ball. Encroachment results in a foul punishable by a five-yard penalty.

end line   Boundary line that runs the width of the field along each end.

end zone   Area ten yards deep and fifty-three and one-third yards wide. This is the area between the end line and goal line bounded by the sidelines. It is the area in which the offense tries to score a touchdown and the area in which the defense can score by a touchback.

extra point   Additional point scored by a team after it has scored a touchdown, either by a point-after-touchdown (one point) or a two-point conversion (two points).

fair catch   Occurs when a kick returner decides only to catch a punt or kickoff and not advance it, protecting himself from being hit by an opponent; he signals for a fair catch by raising one hand in the air and waving it.

fair catch free kick   Rare event in football played by NFL rules. After a fair catch, the receiving team has the option of immediately executing a free kick (rather than starting its next play from the line of scrimmage. If a fair catch free kick goes through the opponent's goal post, the kicking team is awarded three points.

field   The field of play in the NFL measures one hundred yards long and fifty-three and one-third yards wide. Short white markings on the field called yard markers help the players, officials, and the fans keep track of the ball. Probably the most important part of the field is the end zone. It is an additional ten yards on each end of the field. When a team advances the ball into the opponent's end zone, six points are awarded to the team advancing the ball.

field goal   Place kick that passes above the crossbar and between the uprights of the goalpost, worth three points.

field position   Location of a team on the field relative to the two goal lines. It is considered good field position for an offensive team to be close to the defensive team's goal line, and conversely bad field position to be close to its own goal line.

first down   The first chance out of four that the offense has to advance the ball ten yards.

forward pass   Pass thrown by the offense that moves the offensive team closer to the opponent's goal line. An offense is allowed to throw only one forward pass per play, and it must be thrown from behind the offensive team's line of scrimmage.

forward progress   Location to which a ball carrier has advanced the ball, even if he was pushed backwards after getting there.

foul   Violation of NFL official rules by a team or player, punishable with a penalty.

franchise   Legal arrangement that establishes ownership of an NFL team.

free agent   Player whose contract with his most recent team has expired, allowing him to sign a new contract with any team that makes him an offer.

free kick   Kick from the ground or drop kick, rather than from a tee. Not a punt.

fumble   Occurs when a ball carrier loses possession by dropping the ball or having it knocked away before a play ends; the first player to regain possession of the loose ball is said to make the recovery, and his team becomes the offense.

goal line   Line drawn across the width of the field, ten yards inside each end line, which a team must cross with the ball to score a touchdown.

goal post Metallic structure that stands at the back of each end zone. Consists of a crossbar and two uprights that extend upward from it, supported directly above the end line by a base. Teams try to kick the ball above the crossbar and between the uprights to score a field goal or an extra point.

going for it Slang term for when a team facing a fourth down decides to try for a new first down instead of punting.

hand-off Running play in which the quarterback hands the ball to a back.

hang time Length of time a punt is in the air.

holding Foul in which a player impedes the movement of an opponent by grasping or hooking any part of the opponent's body or uniform; punishable by a penalty. In the NFL, holding by a member of the defense results in a five-yard penalty, with the offensive team being awarded a first down. Holding by a member of the offensive team results in a ten-yard penalty.

huddle Offensive team gathering prior to the snap of the ball. The quarterback is typically the leader, calling plays in the huddle.

in bounds Region of the field inside the sidelines and end lines.

incomplete pass Forward pass that touches the ground before being caught.

intentional grounding Foul called against a quarterback who purposely throws an incomplete forward pass solely to avoid a sack. Cannot be called if the pass lands at or beyond the line of scrimmage.

interception Pass caught in the air (picked off) by a defender whose team immediately gains possession of the ball and becomes the offensive team.

kickoff Occurs when a player on the kicking team kicks a ball to the receiving team using a tee (small stand that holds the ball). The tee is placed at the kicking team's thirty yard line. Often a player on the receiving team attempts to catch the ball and advance it the other direction. Used at the beginning of the game, the second half, and overtime, as well as to restart play after each score.

lateral Pass thrown to a teammate backwards from the team's line of scrimmage or parallel to it. Players may attempt a forward pass only once per play, but players may lateral the ball an unlimited number of times.

line of scrimmage Imaginary line which no player may cross before the snap. Each team has its own line of scrimmage, separated by the neutral zone.

live ball A ball becomes live as soon as it is free kicked.

loose ball A ball that is not in the possession of either team, such as after a fumble or kickoff. It may be recovered by either team.

loss of possession on downs   Occurs when the offensive team fails to reach the necessary line on a fourth down play, where the necessary line represents ten yards from the original line of scrimmage on first down.

midfield   Another word for the fifty yard line, which divides the length of the field in half. Also used to the positions nearby the fifty yard line.

moving the ball   Two ways to advance the ball—running and passing.

necessary line   Imaginary line the offense must cross to achieve a new first down.

neutral zone   Zone that contains the ball as it sits on the ground before each play. Area between the two lines of scrimmage.

NFL (National Football League)   The major professional football league in the U.S., comprised of thirty-two teams.

NFL Championship   Game held from 1933 through 1965 to decide the champion of professional football in the U.S. Renamed the Super Bowl in 1966.

offending team   The team that committed a foul.

offense (offensive team)   The team that has possession of the ball.

offensive players   Members of the offense. The usual composition of the offense includes players in the following roles: a quarterback responsible for passing the ball; a center responsible for snapping the ball to the quarterback and blocking the defense; two guards and two tackles responsible for blocking the defense; tight ends responsible for blocking the defense as well as catching a ball thrown by the quarterback; running backs responsible for taking the ball (handoff from the quarterback), running with it, and sometimes catching a ball thrown by the quarterback; and wide receivers responsible for catching a ball thrown by the quarterback. There are eleven offensive players with numbers of tight ends, running backs, and wide receivers varying from one formation to another.

offside   Occurs when any part of a player's body is beyond his line of scrimmage when the ball is snapped; a foul punishable by a five-yard penalty.

open receiver   Player who has no defender closely covering him.

out of bounds   Region of the field touching or outside the sidelines and end lines. When a ball carrier or the ball itself touches out of bounds, the play is over.

pass   Throwing the ball, usually done by the quarterback, although there are times when another player may pass the ball to confuse the defense. Actually, anyone on the offensive team is allowed to pass the ball as long as the pass is thrown from behind the line of scrimmage. A pass is complete if the ball is caught by another offensive player, usually a wide receiver or tight end, sometimes a running back. If the ball hits the ground before someone catches it, it is called an incomplete pass.

pass defender   Defensive player who covers an opposing receiver.

pass protection   Blocking by offensive players to keep defenders away from the quarterback on passing plays.

pass route   Predetermined path a receiver follows to help the passer quickly locate them, so the passer can more easily get the ball in the receiver's hands.

pass rush   Surge by defenders to get past blockers and sack the quarterback.

personal foul   Foul that could cause injury, punishable by a fifteen-yard penalty.

picked off   Another word for "intercepted," as in "intercepted pass."

pitch-out   Lateral toss from a quarterback to a running back. Not a forward pass.

place kick   Kick toward the goalpost for a field goal or extra point; held between the ground and another player's finger.

play   Action that begins with a snap.

players   Defensive team and offensive team participants, eleven from each team.

play clock   Clock displayed above each end zone that limits the time teams may take between plays to forty seconds; the ball must be snapped before the clock runs down to zero.

play-action pass   Passing play after the quarterback has faked a hand-off.

playoffs   Post-season tournament that determines the NFL champion.

pocket   Area behind the offensive line where the quarterback is protected by his blockers.

point-after-touchdown (PAT)   Place kick taken from the opponent's two yard line that is awarded to a team that has scored a touchdown. It is worth one point if it goes through the goalpost.

possession   Holding or controlling the football.

previous spot   Place where the ball was snapped to begin the play immediately prior to the current play.

punt   Occurs when a player ten yards behind the center catches a snap, drops it and kicks it before it hits the ground; an opponent tries to catch and advance it the other way. Not a free kick.

quarterback   Leader of a team's offense. Takes the snap from the center and either hands the ball to a running back to run with, passes it to a receiver, or runs with it.

reading the defense   Recognition by the quarterback of the defensive formation; he may then call an audible to adjust the offense.

receiver   Offensive player who catches or attempts to catch a forward pass.

recovery   To gain or regain possession of a fumble.

red zone   Imaginary area between the defense's twenty yard line and its goal line. Area from which the offense is most likely to score points.

return   Attempt by a player who has just caught an interception, punt, or kickoff to advance the ball in the other direction.

roll out   Occurs when a quarterback runs parallel up the line, looking for a receiver.

rookie   In the NFL or other league, a first-year player.

run   Occurs when the quarterback hands the ball off to a running back, who then tries to gain as many yards as possible by eluding defensive players. The quarterback is also allowed to run with the ball.

rush   For the offensive team, a running play. For the defensive team, a pass rush. See *pass rush*.

sack   Tackle of the quarterback behind the line of scrimmage.

safety   Occurs when a ball carrier is tackled in his own end zone after bringing the ball there under his own power; the defense earns two points and receives a free kick from the offense's own twenty yard line.

scoring   The object of the game is to score the most points. There are four ways to score points in football.

scrambling   Acts of the quarterback, attempting to avoid being tackled behind the line of scrimmage by the defense.

series   Group of four downs a team has to advance ten yards.

sideline   Boundary line that runs the length of the field along each side. A ball carrier or ball that touches or crosses the sideline is out of bounds.

single-elimination   Tournament in which a team is eliminated after one loss. The NFL playoffs are single-elimination tournaments.

snap   Occurs when the center while facing forward quickly hands the ball between his legs to a player standing behind him (usually the quarterback) to start each play.

special teams   Group of players who participate in kicking plays.

spike   Occurs when a player throws the ball at the ground to celebrate a touchdown.

spiral   Ball passed or kicked with a spin which propels it further with more accuracy; the ball points in the same direction throughout its flight.

spot   Location on the field marking the offensive team's forward progress or place of a foul.

stiff arm (straight arm)   A push by a ball carrier to ward off a tackler.

Super Bowl   The championship game of the NFL, played between the champions of the AFC and NFC at a neutral site each January. Last game of the NFL playoffs.

tackle   A player position on both the offensive and defensive lines. There is usually a left and right offensive tackle, and a left and right defensive tackle.

tackling   Contacting a ball carrier to cause him to touch the ground with any part of his body except his hands, thereby ending the play.

territory   The half of the field a team protects against its opponents.

third-and-long   Occurs when the offense faces a third down and is more than a short running play away from a first down. That is, third down and five or more yards from a first town.

tied game   Game that ends with two teams having the same score. Possible in regular season NFL games, which have only one fifteen minute overtime period.

touchback   Occurs when a player who gains possession of a ball in his own end zone kneels to the ground and automatically starts the next play at his own twenty yard line; also awarded if his opponent kicks the ball across the end line.

touchdown (TD)   The biggest single score in a football game. It is worth six points, and it allows the scoring team an opportunity to attempt to get an extra point. To score a touchdown, the ball must be carried across the goal line into the end zone, caught in the end zone, or a fumble recovered in the end zone, or an untouched kickoff recovered in the end zone by the kicking team.

turnover   Involuntary loss of possession of the ball during a play, either by a fumble or by throwing an interception.

two-point conversion   Occurs when a team that just scored a touchdown starts a play at the opponent's two yard line in the NFL and crosses the goal line to earn two points. When successful, it looks just like a touchdown. Introduced to the NFL in 1994.

Wild Card   NFL team that makes the playoffs by having one of the two best records among non-division winners in its conference.

winning percentage   The word "percentage" is used for what is actually a proportion. A common statistic across team sports. The proportion of games a team has won during a period of time. This formula accommodates ties, which are possible in NFL football regular season games:

$$\text{winning percentage} = \frac{\text{number of wins} + (\text{number of ties}/2)}{\text{number of games played}}$$

Basketball Glossary

air ball   A very poor shot, one that does not hit the rim or come close to the rim.

alley-oop pass   A pass thrown to another offensive player who is running toward the basket. That player leaps and catches the pass in midair, and then attempts to score a field goal on a layup or slam dunk.

assist   A pass that leads directly to a field goal by another player. Along with scoring, assists are an important aspect of a player's offensive performance. The count of assists in a game is often represented by the symbol *AST*.

assist percentage   Proportion of teammate field goals on which a player has assisted. Represented as *AST%*.

backcourt   Players, such as guards, who go back or remain back on defense (on the team's defensive half of the court) while other players play offense.

backdoor play   Occurs when one player passes to a teammate standing around the free throw line (high post). Then as defenders move toward the ball, another player cuts to the basket from the opposite side of the court to take a pass for an open shot.

bank shot   A shot aimed at a spot on the backboard, so that it bounces off the backboard and into the basket.

baseline (endline)   A line at each end of the court, under each basket.

basket   Physical structure through which field goals are made. Composed of a rim and a net affixed to the bottom center of the backboard.

bench   Players on reserve, not currently among the five players on the court.

This glossary defines terms as they apply to the National Basketball Association (2015a, 2015b), although most apply to high school and college play as well. See Oliver (2004a) for additional information about basketball statistics. And see McGuire (1958, 1960) and Gandolfi (2009) for a coaching perspective.

---

block   Preventing a shot from going in the basket. The count of the number of blocked shots in a game is often represented by the symbol *BLK*.

block percentage   Proportion of opponent field goal attempts blocked by a player.

bonus   A team being "in the bonus" means that the opposing team has exceeded its personal foul limit.

bounce pass   A pass from one player to another player on the same team that first bounces on the floor.

box out   Occurs when a player places his body between an opponent and the basket to be in a good position to make a rebound.

brick   A very poor shot, but distinct from an air ball. This shot hits the basket or backboard but does not go in.

charging   A rule violation that occurs when an offensive player initiates strong contact with a stationary opponent. This is a player control foul associated with a player on offense against a player on defense. After being called the team on offense loses control of the ball, but no free throws are awarded to the team on defense.

coast-to-coast   Going from one end of the court to the other with the ball.

collective bargaining agreement   An agreement negotiated between employers and employees, of which the agreement between the National Basketball Association (NBA) and the National Basketball Players Association (NBPA) is an example. This agreement governs terms and conditions of employment.

cut   Occurs when a player makes a quick move toward the basket to get in position for a shot.

dead-ball foul   Rule violation that occurs while the clock is stopped and the ball is not in play.

deny the ball   Preventing an opponent from getting the ball by guarding a player closely.

double dribble   A rule violation that occurs when a player dribbles the ball, stops, and then dribbles the ball again.

double foul   A rule violation in which players on opposing teams commit personal fouls at about the same time.

double-team   Occurs when two defensive players guard one offensive player.

downtown   Basketball slang for shooting from a distance, such as from behind the three-point line.

DPOY   Abbreviation for the NBA's Defensive Player of the Year.

draft Annual selection process by which NBA teams select players from colleges and other teams.

dribble Act of bouncing the ball. A player must dribble while moving with the ball. A player must start his dribble before his second step.

dunk (slam dunk) An aggressive shot thrown downward through the basket.

fast break Occurs when a team gains possession of the ball and moves the ball quickly from the defensive side of the court to the offensive side of the court. A fast break provides a strategic advantage for the team with the ball because the opposing team does not have time to set up its defense.

field goal A shot from the floor that goes through the basket, scoring two or three points. The count of the number of the number of two-point field goals is represented by the symbol $2P$. The count of the number of the number of three-point field goals is represented by the symbol $3P$. The total number of field goals is represented by the symbol FG. There are corresponding symbols for field goal attempts ($2PA$, $3PA$, and FG) and for the percentage of successful field goal attempts or shots made ($2PA\%$, $3PA\%$, and $FG\%$). While called percentages, these are actually computed as proportions.

flagrant foul A foul accompanied by excessive contact against an opponent.

foul A rule violation. A personal foul is the most common type of foul. It involves illegal physical contact with an opponent after the ball has become live and before the end of a period. It is an offensive personal foul if committed by the offensive team and a defensive personal foul if committed by the defensive team, or a loose ball foul if neither team has control of the ball. Personal fouls are called against an individual player and count against that player's personal foul limit. Technical fouls are distinct from personal fouls—officials call technical fouls for unsportsmanlike conduct.

foul out Each player has a personal foul limit. When he exceeds his personal foul limit, he is disqualified from participation in the remainder of the game.

foul trouble Occurs when a player is nearing the limit for personal fouls before he is ejected from the game, or a team is nearing the limit in each period after which all fouls become shooting fouls.

free agent A player's whose contract has been expired or was terminated by his team in accordance with NBA waiver procedures, or because he was eligible for an NBA Draft and was never signed to an NBA contract.

free throw A shot from fifteen feet, worth one point. A player gets two free throws if fouled during the act of shooting, one free throw otherwise. The count of free throw attempts is symbolized as FTA, and the count of free throws made by FT. The corresponding free throw percentage (FT%) is the proportion of free throws made of free throw attempts.

frontcourt Players not part of the backcourt. Another term for a team's center and forwards.

give-and-go   Occurs when a player passes to a second player and heads toward the basket, expecting a return pass. After receiving the return pass the first player may be better positioned to make a layup or dunk.

goaltending   A rule violation that occurs when a player interferes with a shot while the ball is on its downward trajectory toward the basket. The ball must have the possibility of going into the basket and it must be above the rim.

gunner   A player who shoots frequently.

hang time   The length of time a player is in the air (hangs) while attempting to make a shot.

high post   Area around the free throw circle.

hook shot   A shot taken with a sweeping, hook-like motion. Rather than facing the basket directly or head-on, the player taking the shot stands perpendicular to the basket.

hoop   The basket or place where points are scored.

jump ball   Occurs when players from opposing teams gain simultaneous possession of the ball, and the referee stops play. Also, the game starts with a jump ball called a "tip off."

jump hook   A hook shot taken while jumping.

jump shot   An attempted field goal in which a player jumps in the air prior to taking the shot. Sometimes referred to as simply a J.

lane   Painted area near each basket between the end line and the free-throw line. The side farthest from the basket defines the line for free throws. A player shooting a free throw must stand outside the lane.

loose-ball foul   Foul committed while neither team has possession of the ball.

lottery   Process that determines the order of player selection in a draft

low post   Area at the base of the foul lane to either side of the basket.

man-to-man defense   As the term would imply, individual members of the team on defense are assigned to guard individual members of the team on offense. In contrast with a zone defense.

NBA   National Basketball Association founded in 1946 and based in New York City. The primary professional basketball league in the United States. Currently composed of thirty teams, fifteen in an Eastern Conference and fifteen in a Western Conference.

NBPA   The National Basketball Players Association. The union that represents the players of the NBA.

net   15- to 18-inch long netted cord that hangs from the rim of the basket.

open shot   Another term for an uncontested shot. No defender is close to the player taking the shot.

outlet pass   A pass thrown to a teammate after getting a rebound.

over the limit (penalty situation)   After a certain number of fouls (the limit) has been reached, the team committing the fouls is said to be "over the limit," and the other team is given free throws after subsequent fouls. The limit is four fouls per quarter.

overtime   A five-minute extra period that is played when the game is tied after four quarters. If a game remains tied following the initial overtime period, another is played, and another until there is a winner. There are no ties in NBA games, whether during the regular season or playoffs.

pace factor (pace of play)   A measure of the number of ball possessions per unit of time. Thought to be predictive of basketball team performance, with faster pace being a positively related to points scored.

pick (set a pick)   Occurs when an offensive player frees a teammate for a shot by establishing a stationary position, preventing a defensive player from guarding the shooter. An offensive foul can be called if the player who is setting a pick is not stationary and contact is made with a defender. This type of foul results in loss of possession by the team setting the pick (team on offense).

pick-and-roll   A play in which an offensive player sets a pick, takes a pass, and then heads toward the basket to take a shot.

pivot   The area near the basket, generally where the center operates. The term also refers to the act of changing directions by keeping one foot planted on the ground while stepping in one or more directions with the other foot.

player control foul   Another term for charging.

point guard   Team's primary ball handler, the player who sets up the team's offense.

power forward   The larger of a team's two forwards. His primary duties include rebounding as much as scoring.

possessions   Measure representing both the number of times the team has the ball and the number of times the opposing team has the ball.

press   When the players of one team as a group guard players on the team with the ball very closely, the team without the ball is said to be "putting on the press."

quarter (period)   One of four twelve-minute divisions of the game.

quadruple-double   Achievement in which a player accumulates double figures in four of the following categories in the same game: points, rebounds, assists, steals and blocked shots.

rebound   To gain control of a missed shot. The number of defensive rebounds (DRB) and the defensive rebound percentage ($DRB\%$) are measures of defensive prowess. The number of offensive rebounds (ORB) and the offensive rebound percentage ($ORB\%$) are measures of offensive prowess.

rejection   Another term for a blocked shot.

sag   A defensive tactic in which a player drops off or moves away from the offensive player he is assigned to defend (in a man-to-man defense) in order to double-team another player on offense.

salary cap   The maximum amount each team may pay in salaries during an NBA season. Defined by the collective bargaining agreement between the NBA and its players (represented by the NBPA).

screen   Occurs when the offensive player who stands between a teammate and a defender, giving his teammate a chance to take an open or uncontested shot.

set-shot   A shot taken while a player has both feet on the floor in a set position, as opposed to a jump shot.

shot clock   The 24-second clock used to time possessions. A team must attempt a shot that hits the rim within 24 seconds or lose possession of the ball.

SRS   Simple rating system is a rating that takes into account average point differential and strength of schedule. The rating is denominated in points above/below average, where zero is average.

steal percentage   Calculated using the formula: 100 * (STL * (Tm MP / 5)) / (MP * Opp Poss). Steal Percentage is an estimate of the percentage of opponent possessions that end with a steal.

strength of schedule   A rating of strength of a team's schedule based on the strength of the teams that it plays. The rating may be denominated in points above or below average, where zero is average.

sixth man   A team's primary reserve, the first substitute to enter a game.

sky-hook   A hook shot in which the ball is released while the shooter's hand is at the top of the arc. Due to the height and angle of the shot, it is difficult to block.

skywalk   Moving laterally (when jumping) while in the air.

squaring up   Occurs when a player's shoulders are facing the basket as he releases the ball for a shot; considered good shooting position.

stutter   A short, choppy step used to slow body momentum.

switch   Occurs when teammates exchange defensive assignments during play.

team fouls   Occurs when a team goes over the limit, its opponent is awarded free throw opportunities.

technical foul   A rules violation involving unsportsmanlike conduct, such as abusive language or fighting.

three-point shot   A shot taken from beyond an arc that is twenty-two feet from the basket. It is worth three points.

three-point attempts   Shots made outside the three-point line, attempting to make a field goal. Represented by $3PA$.

three-point field goals   Field goals made from outside the three-point line. Represented by $3P$.

three-point field goal percentage   Called a percentage, but actually a proportion. Proportion of three-point shots that result in field goals. Represented by $3P\%$.

three-sixty (360)   Eluding a defender by making a 360-degree turn.

three-second violation   An offensive player may not stand in the lane for more than three seconds.

tip-in   To tip a missed shot into the basket.

tip-off   The start of a basketball game, with the ball being tossed up between two players, one from each team.

trailer   An offensive player who trails on a fast break and gets himself in a good position to score.

transition   The movement from offense to defense, or vice versa.

traveling   A rule violation that involves taking too many steps without dribbling the ball.

triple-double   Achievement in which a player accumulates double figures in three of the following categories in the same game: points, rebounds, assists, steals and blocked shots.

turnover   Occurs when the offense loses possession through its own fault by passing the basketball out of bounds or committing a floor violation.

two-point attempts   Shots made inside the three-point line, attempting to make a field goal. Represented by $2PA$.

two-point field goals   Field goals from inside the three-point line. Represented by $2P$. These field goals are worth two points.

two-point field goal percentage   Called a percentage, but actually a proportion. Proportion of two-point shots that result in field goals. Represented by $2P\%$.

veteran free agent   A player who completes his contractual obligation to his team and becomes free to sign with an NBA team. Defined by the collective bargaining agreement between the NBA and NBPA.

weakside   A position that is more than one pass away from the ball because of distance or another player obstructing the direct passing lane. Also the side of the lane opposite the ball.

wing   A perimeter position on the side of the basket outside the free throw line.

zone defense   A defensive tactic in which players guard areas of the court, rather than specific players (as with a man-to-man defense).

Baseball Glossary

All Star Game   In Major League Baseball, a game played toward the middle of the baseball season with players selected from various teams for their exceptional skills.

American League   In Major League Baseball, one of two leagues composed of fifteen teams, five in each of three divisions. The American League allows the designated hitter. See *National League*.

around the horn   Baseball slang for throwing the ball around the infield after completing a play with no one on base.

at bats (AB)   Batting appearance in which the batter does not receive a base-on-balls (walk), is not hit by a pitch, and does not sacrifice (by bunt of sacrifice fly). The total at bats is used as the denominator in computing a player's batting average. A subset of plate appearances.

bailing out   Baseball slang for a batter who's foot closest to the pitcher moves away from home plate when swinging at the ball. May happen to a batter regardless of his batting stance (closed or open). Also, known as *stepping in the bucket*.

ball   A pitch outside the strike zone and is not hit by the batter. Any ball that touches the ground prior to reaching home plate.

base   One of four points that a runner must touch to score a run: first base, second base, third base, and home base (home plate).

base on balls (BB)   The batter is awarded first base without hitting the ball because he receives four balls before getting three strikes.

Developed in conjunction with Miller (2016), this is a guide to terms used by baseball players, managers, analysts, and fans. It provides an introduction to the language of the game as it has evolved over more than two hundred years of play in the United States. Official definitions of terms are provided by Major League Baseball (2015). Hample (2007) reviews baseball slang. Ripken and Ripken (2004, 2007) explain baseball fundamentals for players and coaches. Additional useful resources are Dickson (2009), the MLB.com website, and the Wikipedia (2015) *Glossary of Baseball*.

---

base runner   Offensive player on base (first, second, or third base).

bases loaded   Baseball slang for having runners on first, second, and third base.

base coach   Team member in uniform designated by the manager to help with advising runners on the base paths. The first base coach advises runners on first about running to second base. The third base coach advises runners about running to home base.

base hit   A hit in which the batter reaches as far as first base. See *single (1B)*.

baserunner   Offensive player who has reached one of the bases safely and remains on-base until the inning is over.

baserunning error   An offensive player runs outside the base path or fails to touch a base. Counts as an out for the batting team, but is not recorded as an error in the box score for the team. Recorded errors are for the fielding team only.

batter   Initial role of offensive player. Uses bat to hit the ball thrown by the pitcher. Stands in the batter's box. Also called hitter.

batter in the hole   Offensive player in the dugout set to be the batter after the batter on deck.

batter on deck   Offensive player due next in the batter's box. That is, the player set to follow the batter currently at bat. There is a special area called the *next batter's box* where the batter on deck is supposed to stand or kneel.

batter's box   Area in which batter must stand while at bat.

battery   The pitcher and catcher as a unit.

batting average (BA, AVG)   Hits divided by at bats (with walks and sacrifices not counted in at bats):

$$BA = \frac{Hits}{At\ Bats}$$

A batting average above 0.300 is highly valued. Batting below 0.200 (sometimes called the *Mendoza Line*) is tolerated only for pitchers and exceptionally good catchers and infielders. The average regular-season BA across the thirty MLB teams in the 2014 season was 0.251 (Sports Reference LLC 2015). A rule of thumb in selecting batters is to look for BA values above 0.250—that is, we look for batters who get a hit about one in every four at bats. Hitters batting above 0.300 are rare.

batting stance   A batter's position in the batter's box relative to home plate prior to the pitcher's throwing the ball. Also see *closed batting stance* and *open batting stance*.

batting (team)   The team on offense, as opposed to the team on defense (on the field).

behind in the count   From the batter's point of view, a situation in which he has more strikes than balls. Also called *down in the count* or *in the hole*. Opposite of *ahead in the count*.

bench   Seating area for a team. Also called the *dugout*. Players not in the line-up are referred to as *sitting on the bench*. A team with talented players not in the line-up is said to have *bench strength* or a *deep bench*.

big leagues   Major League Baseball. Affectionately called "the bigs" or "the show."

bloop single   Term used for a ball that falls for a hit between the infielders and the outfielders. Also called a "Texas Leaguer."

bunt   Batting strategy that involves holding the bat in a fixed position, rather than swinging the bat. With two strikes, a bunted foul ball results in a third strike.

call   As a verb, the umpire calls plays (calls a pitch a ball or strike, calls a hit ball fair or foul, and calls a runner safe or out). As a noun, the umpire makes calls.

called game   A game canceled or postponed by the umpire. Prior to lighted stadiums, a game might have been called due to darkness. Currently, games are commonly called due to inclement weather.

catcher   Defensive player who crouches behind home plate and catches balls thrown by the pitcher. The only player on the fielding team positioned in foul territory.

caught looking   The batter is called out on strikes without swinging the bat.

caught off base   A base runner is permitted to step off base but may be tagged out by a defensive player when off base.

caught stealing (CS)   On an attempted steal, a base runner is tagged out prior to reaching the next base.

center fielder   Defensive player who plays in the middle of the outfield, between the left fielder and right fielder.

Championship Series   At the end of the regular season, following the Wild Card Game, there are two Division Series playoffs in each league. The winners of these Division Series play each other in a best-of-seven series known as a Championship Series, one in the American League and one in the National League.

changeup   An off-speed pitch (MLB speeds 70–85 mph). Speed, rather than movement, is what distinguishes this pitch from a fastball. Comes in various forms, including the circle changeup, three-finger changeup, and four-finger changeup.

check swing   A batter begins to swing at a pitched ball, but not far enough to be called a strike. Whether a batter's swing is a check swing or a strike swinging is a matter of judgment. The call can be made by the home plate umpire, with possible appeal to the first base umpire for a right-handed batter or to the third base umpire for a left-handed batter.

choking up   Holding the bat with hands away from the bottom (bat handle end) of the bat. A technique used by singles hitters who take shorter swings and have more control of the bat.

chop single   Base hit in which the batter intentionally hits the ball down toward the ground so that it bounces high and is hard to catch in time to throw the batter out at first base.

closed batting stance   A batter's position in the batter's box in which the foot closest to the pitcher is closer to home plate than the foot farthest from the pitcher.

closer   Relief pitcher who ends a game.

clutch hitter   A hitter who does well with runners on base and/or when the game is coming to an end.

coach   Team member in uniform designated by the manager to help with coaching duties such as acting as a base coach.

command   A pitcher with command can throw strikes when he needs to throw strikes. Also see *control*.

control   A pitcher with control can throws strikes much more often than balls. Also see *command*.

cover the bases   A player on the fielding team covers a base by standing close to the base. By being close to the base the fielder is ready to execute a tag out or a force out. Having a defensive player on every base is covering the bases.

crowd the plate   Batter stands in the batter's box very close to home plate.

curveball (curve)   A breaking ball much slower than a fastball (MLB speed 65–80 mph). With a right-handed pitcher throwing to a right-handed hitter or with a left-handed pitcher throwing to a left-handed hitter, a curve ball breaks away from the hitter. The standard curveball is the overhand curveball, affectionately known as *Uncle Charlie* or *the hook*. Some pitchers throw what is known as a *knuckle curveball*.

cut fastball (cutter)   Also called a *cut fastball*. A fastball with movement.

cut-off position   A position on the field of play between an outfielder and home plate. With a runner rounding the bases and heading for home, the outfielder can throw a ball toward home plate using a low trajectory, so an infielder in the cut-off position can intercept the ball and throw to another base, usually second base, to prevent another runner from advancing around the bases. Alternatively, the infielder cutting off the ball from the outfield can decide to throw the ball home enabling the catcher to tag the runner out. Because the infielder is closer to home base than the outfielder, the infielder's throw is likely to be more accurate than the outfielder's. Many outfielders do not have strong throws to home base, so throwing to the player in the cut-off position is essential.

defense   Team on the field, as opposed to the team that is up to bat (offense).

defensive indifference   A runner on base attempts to take the next base, and the team on the field allows it. The situation occurs late in a game when the team on the field has a lead of more than one run, so an additional run by the hitting team will not win the game. When the official scorer rules defensive indifference, the runner's act of taking the next base is not recorded as a stolen base.

designated hitter (DH)   A player who has a place in the batting order but does not play a position in the field. This player hits in place of the weakest hitting player who takes the field (usually the pitcher). In Major League Baseball, the designated hitter role may be used in the American League, but not the National League.

diamond   Another word for the baseball field of play. Gets its name from the square/diamond shape of the infield defined by the four bases.

dig in   Batter uses spikes on shoes to make a hole in the batter's box.

Division Series   After the end of the regular season, a best-of-five series of playoff games within a league between winners of the three divisions and/or the Wild Card Game. There are two division series within each league.

double (2B)   A hit in which the batter reaches as far as second base. Also called a *two-bagger*.

double-header   Two games played the same day. A standard double-header has two games with a short break between them. A *day-night double-header* has a number of hours between the games.

double play   Getting two outs on one play. Various double plays are designated by player position numbers. For example, a 4-6-3 double play involves a throw from the second baseman to the shortstop, followed by a throw from the shortstop to the first baseman. An *unassisted double play* is a double play executed by one player alone.

double-switch   Player substitution involving two players. Often used to substitute a position player along with a relief pitcher, with the position player (usually a better hitter) placed in the line-up so that he hits before the pitcher (usually a poorer hitter).

dugout   Seating area for a team. Also called the *bench*.

earned run average (ERA)   Index of pitching performance. The number of runs allowed (not due to errors) per nine innings of play. Also see *WHIP*.

expected runs   Computed for any half-inning state or game situation, the number of runs the hitting team can expect to earn through the end of the half-inning. The computation is based on historical play-by-play data for the state or game situation. Expected runs are especially useful in the evaluation of alternative playing strategies, such as whether to use the sacrifice bunt or whether to attempt a stolen base.

extra-base hit   Hit greater than a single. That is, a double, triple, or home run.

fair ball   Ball hit inside the foul lines.

fair territory   Region inside the foul lines.

fan   Short for "fanatic" or "fancier." Another earlier term was "crank." A consumer of the sport, someone who loves the game and/or a particular team.

fantasy baseball   Fans of baseball pretend to manage a Major League Baseball team by assembling a team of players. Enables fans to make decisions as if they were owners of teams.

fastball   Faster than any other type of pitch, has MLB speeds 80–100 mph. Comes in various forms defined by the pitcher's grip on the ball, including the *four-seam fastball*, *two-seem fastball*, *cut fastball* (also called a *cutter*), and a *split-finger fastball* (also called a *splitter*). The four-seam fastball is faster but has less movement than other fastballs.

fielder   Player on defense.

fielder's choice   Batter arrives at first base because a fielder elects to get a runner out in place of the batter. Batter is not awarded a hit.

fielding error   A defensive play that should have resulted in an out, but does not. Due to catching, not throwing. Also see *throwing error*.

first base   The base a batter/hitter must touch first in order to get a hit.

first baseman   Defensive player and infielder who plays closest to first base.

five-tool player   A player with strong baseball skills for running, fielding, throwing, hitting, and hitting with power.

fly ball   Ball hit in the air, as opposed to a ground ball, but not hit low in the air, as opposed to a line drive.

fly out   Ball hit in the air and caught in the air, resulting in an out. May be in fair or foul territory. Also called a *fly ball out*. Different from a *ground out*.

forfeited game   Game ended by the umpire-in-chief in favor of a team that is leading by a score of nine to nothing or for violation of the rules of the game.

force out   As opposed to a *tag out*, an out recorded when a defensive player with ball in hand or glove touches the base that a runner must advance toward because previous bases are occupied or about to be occupied. Also called a *force play*. Also see *neighborhood play*.

foul ball   Ball hit out of play, outside the foul lines.

foul territory   Region outside the foul lines.

foul tip   A foul ball that comes directly off the batter's bat and into the catcher's glove or hand. It counts as a strike, including a third strike.

frame (a pitch)   Catcher's attempt to catch a ball thrown by a pitcher in a way that appears to be within the strike zone even if it does not fall within the strike zone.

free agent   Player not under contract to any specific team and eligible to sign with any team.

full count   Three balls and two strikes on the batter.

game (G)   A baseball game or appearance in a game.

grand slam   A home run with the bases loaded.

ground ball   Ball hit on the ground, as opposed to a line drive or fly ball.

ground out   Batter is thrown out at first base after hitting a ground ball to one of the fielders. As opposed to a *fly out*.

ground-rule double   When a hit bounces over a fence, leaving the field of play, the batter is awarded second base (a double).

hit (H)   Batter hits the ball and reaches a base safely without the aid of an error, fielder's choice, walk, or hit-by-pitch. Includes singles, doubles, triples, and home runs.

hitter   Another term for batter.

hitting slump   A batter is having trouble hitting for a number of games in a row, either having no hits or having very few hits.

hitting streak   A batter is doing exceptionally well at the plate. Usually assessed by the number of games in a row with at least one hit. Joe DiMaggio holds the record, hitting safely in 56 consecutive games.

hitting for power   Hitting home runs.

holding runner on base   Activity of the first baseman, standing close to first base when a runner is at first base, so that the runner will take stay closer to the base (take less of a lead) to avoid being tagged out if the pitcher were to throw the ball to the first baseman. This is done so that the runner is less likely to steal second base.

home plate   Flat rubber marker with a square shape facing toward the pitcher and a triangular side facing away from the pitcher. Catchers work in a crouched position behind home plate. When batting, players stand beside home plate in the batter's box. And after running around the bases, they must touch home plate to score a run. Also called *home base*.

home run (HR)   A hit in which the batter reaches as far as home plate. Also called a *homer* or the *long ball*. Usually obtained by hitting the ball over the fences. For an *inside-the-part home run*, the ball stays in the field of play while the batter runs around the bases, touching home plate safely.

illegal pitch   A pitch delivered by the pitcher without his pivot foot on the pitcher's plate, a quick pitch, or a balk.

infielder   Defensive player who plays close to the bases.

inning   Unit of play in a baseball game. An inning consists of three outs. A full inning consists of the visiting team batting, followed by the home team batting. The top of the inning is the portion of the inning in which the visiting team is batting. The bottom of the inning is the portion of the inning with the home team batting.

intentional base on balls   The pitcher gives a batter a base on balls without trying to throw strikes. Used as baseball strategy to avoid pitching to the hitter (who may be a good hitter) or to put a runner on first base so that force-outs are possible.

interference   Offensive interference occurs when the batting team interferes with, obstructs, impedes, or confuses any fielder attempting to make a play. For example, a runner hit by the ball while running interferes with the fielder trying to catch the ball. This is referred to as being *soaked*, and the runner is called out. Defensive interference occurs when the catcher's glove touches the bat, affecting the batter's swing or preventing him from hitting the ball. There can also be umpire interference and spectator/fan interference.

in the hole   From the batter's point of view, a situation in which he has more strikes than balls. Also called *down in the count*.

knuckleball   A very slow pitch (MLB speeds 55–70 mph) with little spin that moves in an unpredictable manner. Also called a *knuckler*.

lead-off hitter   The first hitter in the line-up, selected to begin the team's hitting because he has a good chance of getting on base.

leave the yard (go yard)   Baseball slang for hitting a home run.

left fielder (LF)   Defensive player who plays on the left side of the outfield where "left side" is defined by looking at the field from home plate.

left on base (LOB)   Player on base while the team reaches three outs, ending that batting team's half-inning.

lefty   Player who bats or throws left-handed.

line drive   Ball hit in the air, as opposed to a ground ball, but not hit high in the air, as opposed to a fly ball.

lineup   The order of players/hitters for a team submitted to the home plate umpire at the beginning of the game, with changes reported to the umpire during the game.

live ball   A ball that is in play.

live ball era   After 1920 there was a requirement to use a new white ball in Major League Baseball.

making the turn   A runner running to first base is permitted to run beyond the base and toward foul territory. If instead of running toward foul territory, the runner begins on the path to second base, he is referred to as making the turn and may be tagged out by a fielder.

manager   Person responsible for a team's actions on the field. May be one of the players.

manufactured run   Run generated by a "small ball" strategy of getting runners on base and advancing them one base at a time by singles, walks, and stolen bases, as opposed to extra-base hits.

men on base   Batting team's runners on first, second, and/or third base.

middle reliever   Pitcher who enters a game after the start of the game and before the end of the game. Distinct from the starting pitcher and the closer.

middle infielder   Second baseman or shortstop. See *up the middle*.

MLB   Major League Baseball. Professional baseball organization in the United States. Currently composed of thirty teams in two leagues, fifteen in the American League and fifteen in the National League.

National League   In Major League Baseball, one of two leagues composed of fifteen teams, five in each of three divisions. The National League does not allow the designated hitter. See *American League*.

neighborhood play   When there is a close play at second base with the runner sliding into the base, a force out may be recorded even if the second baseman does not keep his foot on the base. As long as the second baseman's foot is in the neighborhood of second base, the force out is recorded. This is to avoid injuries to the players who are wearing spikes on their shoes. See *force out*.

no hitter   Pitcher pitches nine innings without allowing a hit, although batters may reach base through walks or errors. Also see *perfect game*.

no-no   Baseball slang for a no hitter. Think in terms of no hits and no runs scored by the other team. Also see *perfect game*.

obstruction   A fielder impeding the progress of a runner while not in possession of the ball.

offense   Team up to bat, as opposed to the team that in the field (defense).

official scorer   Person designated to keep records of the game and make decisions about hits versus fielding errors.

on the field (team)   The team on the field is the team playing defense, as opposed to the batting team.

on-base percentage (OBP)   Proportion of plate appearances in which a batter reaches base through a hit, walk, or hit by pitch. Does not include reaching base by a fielding error, fielder's choice, dropped/uncaught third strike, fielder's obstruction, or catcher's interference. Also called on-base average (OBA). Usually presented as a proportion, not a percentage. Popularized by the Lewis (2003) book *Moneyball* and the subsequent movie by the same name, OBP is seen as a better index of offensive performance than batting average. Computed as

$$OBP = \frac{(Hits + Walks + Hit\ by\ Pitch)}{(At\ Bats + Walks + Hit\ by\ Pitch + Sacrifices)}$$

Getting a walk or being hit by a pitch has the same effect as a base hit for the batter himself—they move the batter to first base without an out being recorded. The average regular-season OBP across the thirty MLB teams in the 2014 season was 0.314 (Sports Reference LLC 2015). A rule of thumb in selecting good batters is to look for OBP values above 0.333—that is, we look for batters who get on base about one in every three plate appearances.

on-base percentage plus slugging (OPS)   Measure of overall hitting prowess.

$$OPS = OBP + SLG$$

The average regular-season OPS across the thirty MLB teams in the 2014 season was 0.700 (Sports Reference LLC 2015).

open batting stance   A batter's position in the batter's box in which the foot closest to the pitcher is further away from home plate than the foot farthest from the pitcher.

out   One of three units of play for the batting team. That is, there are three outs in a half-inning.

"out"   Umpire call indicating that an out is to be recorded.

outfielder   Defensive player who plays far away from the bases.

overslide   At second or third base, a runner can, after touching the base, go beyond the base and lose contact with the base. When the player loses contact with the base, he may be tagged out by a fielder. An overslide can occur at second and third base. An overslide is not relevant at first base where running beyond the base and toward foul territory is permitted. An overslide is not relevant at home base, where running beyond home base after scoring a run completes the runner's path around the bases.

pace of play   Also called *pace of game*. Major League Baseball has been experimenting with ways to speed up the game, focusing on unnecessary delays by pitchers or batters. This is controversial because the leisurely pace and lack of a time clock are attractions of baseball. The introduction of video replay affects pace of play, making games longer.

passed ball   Pitch that gets past the catcher that is the fault of the catcher, as opposed to a wild pitch, which is the fault of the pitcher.

PECOTA   A measurement and prediction system that uses player-comparable age curves as its base data. The name refers to Bill Pecota, a Kansas City Royals infielder from the 1980s.

perfect game   Pitcher pitches nine innings without allowing a runner to reach base—no hits, no walks, no errors. Twenty-seven batters come to the plate, and they all make outs.

pick off assignment   Designation of the fielder responsible for covering the bag for a pick off play. Relevant to pick offs at second base, where either the second baseman or the shortstop could cover the bag.

pick off play   A pitcher throws to first, second, or third base in an attempt to catch a runner off base. The fielder receiving the ball must tag the runner out before the runner touches a base. Most commonly executed with a runner at first base.

pinch hitter   Player batting for another player, replacing the original player in the lineup. The original player may not return to the game.

pinch runner   Player running for another player who happens to be on base, replacing the original player in the lineup. The original player may not return to the game.

pitch   Ball delivered by the pitcher to the batter.

pitch count   The number of pitches (balls plus strikes) thrown by a pitcher after his entry into a game. This number is watched carefully by managers. A starting pitcher's pitch count of one hundred is seen as a warning signal by many managers. With higher pitch counts, pitchers are more susceptible to injuries. At higher pitch counts, a pitcher's fastball velocity is reduced. The pitcher is less effective in getting outs. Pitch count also refers to the number of pitches that a batter has faced in a given at-bat. The offensive team may employ a high-pitch-count strategy, attempting to take more pitches (balls and strikes) to drive up the starting pitcher's pitch count, thus forcing that pitcher out of the game. This was one of the strategies popularized by the Lewis (2003) book *Moneyball* and the subsequent movie by the same name.

pitcher (P)   Defensive player responsible for throwing the ball to the batter.

pitcher's duel   A game in which two dominant pitches are pitching, with very few runs being scored.

pitcher's park   Parks such as U.S. Cellular Field in Chicago and AT&T Park in San Francisco are known to be favorable to pitchers, yielding lower expected runs across all in-game states. As opposed to a *hitter's park*.

pitcher's plate   A rectangular hard rubber platform near the middle of the pitcher's mound. The pitcher's pivot foot must be on the pitcher's plate prior to delivering the ball to the batter. Also called the *rubber*.

pitching from the stretch   Instead of using a full windup, the pitcher uses a partial windup, coming to a full stop before throwing. Typically used when there is a runner on base.

pitching depth   Number of pitchers a team has available for a game.

pitching mound   Raised circular area from which the pitcher pitches.

pitching rotation   The ordered set of four or five players that a team uses as its starting pitchers. Across games in the regular season, starting pitchers usually have a fixed sequence of appearance so that each pitcher has three or four days rest between starts.

pivot foot   Pitcher's foot that must be in contact with the pitcher's plate when delivering the ball to the batter.

place hitter   Hitter who controls the bat so well as to place the ball where no fielders can get to it, while keeping the ball in the park.

plate   Baseball slang verb for scoring a run. Comes from the term "home plate." So "they plate two" means "they score two runs."

plate appearance   Sum of at bats, walks, hit by pitches and sacrifices.

$$Plate\ Apperances = At\ Bats + Walks + Hit\ by\ Pitch + Sacrifices$$

platooning   A managerial strategy in which different lineups are used when facing right-handed versus left-handed pitchers. For example, the lineup may include more right-handed hitters when the starting pitcher of the opposing team is left-handed and more left-handed hitters when the starting pitcher of the opposing team is right-handed. This is done because right-handed hitters are expected to be less effective against right-handed pitchers and left-handed hitters are expected to be less effective against left-handed pitchers. These differences in effectiveness are due to the fact that a curve ball breaks away from a like-handed hitter, making it harder to hit.

"play ball"   Umpire-in-chief's order to begin the game.

pop-up   Ball hit in the air that does not travel far. Usually caught by an infielder, catcher, or pitcher.

position number   Number associated with field position and used for official scoring: (1) pitcher, (2) catcher, (3) first baseman, (4) second baseman, (5) third baseman, (6) shortstop, (7) left fielder, (8) center fielder, and (9) right fielder.

position player   Player other than the pitcher. That is, an infielder, outfielder, or catcher.

power hitter   Baseball player who hits home runs.

productive at bat   An at bat that advances a runner in some way, including a hit, sacrifice bunt, sacrifice fly, or hitting behind a runner to advance the runner. Also called a *productive out*, with the opposite being an *unproductive out*.

pull hitter   A right-handed batter who usually hits the ball between second and third base or to left field. Alternatively, a left-handed batter who usually hits the ball between first and second base or to right field. In response to pull hitters, some fielding teams put on a shift, moving players away from their normal positions.

pull the string   Baseball slang for fooling a batter with a pitch, usually a curveball.

quick pitch   A pitch delivered by the pitcher without giving the batter sufficient time to get situated in the batter's box. Also called a *quick return*.

reaching for the fences   Baseball player who tries to hit home runs.

regulation game   Game that counts as an official completed game. Some games are canceled. Others are postponed without being complete and must be completed at a later time or date.

relief pitcher   Pitcher who enters the game after the starting pitcher has been removed from the game.

replay review   A subset of umpire calls is subject to video replay review by umpires located in a remote location. These *reviewable calls* include potential home run calls, non-home-run boundary calls, specified fair/foul ball calls, force out/tag out calls, catches in the outfield, hit-by-pitch calls, collisions at home plate, tag-up calls, and various force-out/tag-out calls. Balls and strikes called by the home plate umpire are not reviewable.

retouch   Runner returning to base after passing a base. Runner must be touching the base to avoid being tagged out by a fielder.

reverse curve   A breaking ball that moves in the opposite direction from a curveball. Also called a *screwball* or *fall-away*.

right fielder (RF)   Defensive player who plays on the right side of the outfield where "right side" is defined by looking at the field from home plate.

rounding the bases   Baseball slang for running around the bases, from first to second, to third, to home.

run   Unit of scoring in baseball. Also called a *score*. Analogous to a point in football or basketball.

run batted in (RBI)   When a runner scores as a result of a batter's hit, sacrifice, or fielder's choice out, the batter gets an RBI.

run down   A runner caught between bases may be tagged out by a fielder. Often two or more fielders are involved in this activity, throwing the ball back and forth in an attempt to tag the runner out.

runner   Offensive player no longer at bat, but on the base paths.

sacrifice bunt   A bunt that successfully advances a baserunner.

sacrifice fly   A line drive or fly ball that successfully advances a baserunner. The baserunner must tag the current base and advance to the next base without being tagged out.

"safe"   Umpire call, awarding a base to a runner.

scoring position   A runner on second or third base is referred to as a runner in scoring position because a single is usually enough to get that runner home.

screwball   A breaking ball that moves in the opposite direction from a curveball. Also called a *reverse curve* or *fall-away*.

season   In Major League Baseball, a baseball season consists of 162 games, 81 away games and 81 home games.

second base   Base in the middle of the infield, between first and third bases. Also called the *keystone sack*.

second baseman   Defensive player, infielder who plays closest to second base.

secondary lead   A baserunner takes his initial lead off the base while the pitcher is in his windup. But after the pitcher throws the ball, the baserunner moves further away from the base. This additional distance from the base is known as a secondary lead.

semi-intentional walk   A walk in which the pitcher pitches to the batter with the intention of walking him but without the catcher signaling an intentional walk. The event is recorded as a walk, rather than an intentional walk.

shadow ball   Baseball pantomime or playing with an imaginary ball to entertain fans. Popularized in the black baseball teams during the depression.

shift   On-the-field players playing out of position to adjust to the particular strengths of the hitter. For a right-handed pull hitter, for example, a shift may involve the second baseman playing between second base and third base, instead of in his normal position between second base and first base. The use of the shift is controversial. Fielders playing away from their normal positions may be less proficient in making double plays, executing pick offs, and taking cut-off positions. The shift also affects the integrity of baseball data. Suppose a third baseman is in a shift, playing between first base and second base with a left-handed pull hitter at bat. When that third baseman fields a ground ball between first and second base, throwing the batter out at first, the play is recorded as a 5-3 put out, implying that the ball was hit toward third base.

shine ball   The pitcher rubs the ball clean on one side using his uniform, while applying dirt or powder on the other side. Employed to affect the ball's trajectory.

shutout   A complete nine-inning game thrown by one pitcher not allowing the opposing team to score any runs.

shortstop   Defensive player, infielder who, like the third baseman, plays between second base and third base. But the shortstop is further from third base than the third baseman.

side-arm delivery   Pitching delivery in between a common overhand delivery and an underhand delivery (as in softball).

single (1B)   A hit in which the batter reaches as far as first base. Also called a *base hit*.

slider   A ball gripped like a two-seam fastball, but slightly off-center. With MLB speeds 70–85 mph, it is not as fast as a fastball but breaks in the same direction as a curveball.

slugging percentage (SLG)   Measure of hitting power. Babe Ruth's slugging percentage was 0.690, the MLB all-time record. The maximum value possible is 4.0, implying that a player hits a home run in every at bat. Computed as

$$SLG = \frac{(Singles + (2 \times Doubles) + (3 \times Triples) + (4 \times Home\ Runs)}{At\ Bats}$$

The average regular-season SLG across the thirty MLB teams in the 2014 season was 0.386 (Sports Reference LLC 2015).

small ball   Baseball strategy based on base hits, walks, and stolen bases. That is, runs are scored by advancing by one base at a time—manufactured runs. Also called an *inside game*, suggesting that the action is inside the base paths.

spin rate   The rate of a pitched ball's spin on its way from the pitcher's hand to home plate. Fastballs with the same speed in miles per hour may have very different spin rates. Fastballs with low spin rates (fewer than 2,000 revolutions per minute) are sometimes called "heavy." They appear to sink. Fastballs with high spin rates (more than 2,500 revolutions per minute) have more movement.

spitball   Also called a *spitter*. The pitcher applies saliva or some foreign substance to the ball, which may affect the ball's trajectory. Spitballs are not allowed in Major League Baseball, although some pitchers have been suspected of throwing spitballs.

squeeze play   A batter bunts with a runner on third and fewer than two outs, trying to bring the runner home. With a *suicide squeeze*, the runner on third begins running home as the pitcher begins to throw the ball. With a *safety squeeze*, the runner on third begins running after the batter bunts the ball.

starting pitcher   The pitcher who is in the starting line-up for a game, as opposed to a relief pitcher.

steal (stolen base, SB)   Advancing from first to second base, second to third, or third to home without the assistance of a hit, passed ball, or wild pitch. The MLB success rate in stolen bases since 1990 is around 70 percent (Baumer and Zimbalist 2014).

stepping in the bucket   Baseball slang for a batter whose foot closest to the pitcher moves away from home plate when swinging at the ball. May happen to a batter regardless of his batting stance (closed or open). Also, known as *bailing out*.

strike   For a *called strike*, a pitched ball within the strike zone that the batter does not swing at on any strike. Or a ball that the batter hits foul on a first or second strike. For a *strike swinging*, a ball that the batter swings at but does not hit on any strike. Or, on a third strike, a ball that the batter swings at and hits foul directly into the catcher's glove or hand, which is also known as a *foul tip*. Or, on an attempted bunt on the third strike, a bunt that is hit outside the foul lines is a strike swinging. For keeping a complete record of balls and strikes, any ball that is put into play (regardless of its position in the strike zone) is counted as a strike.

strikeout (K)   A batter gets three strikes before getting four balls. Can be a *strikeout looking* or *called strike three* with the batter not swinging at the ball or a *strikeout swinging*. The symbol *K* represents a strikeout and may be thought of as coming from the word "knockout" or from the letter "k" in "strikeout." The *K* is sometimes written backwards to indicate a strikeout looking. If first base is unoccupied by a runner and the catcher fails to catch the third strike, then the batter can be granted first base if he reaches that base before being forced out. The symbol *SO* is used to represent a strikeout or the number of strikeouts by a batter.

strike zone   Rectangular region with its base width and depth defined by the area of home plate and its height defined by reference to the batter, extending from the batter's kneecap to approximately three baseballs above the batter's belt. Formerly, the upper range of the strike zone was the batter's shoulders. The effective strike zone varies from one umpire to the next. A smaller or narrow strike zone favors the batter. A larger or wide strike zone favors the pitcher. Baseball analysts measure the size of the strike zone by area in square feet.

suspended game   A called game to be completed at a later time/date.

sweep   Baseball slang for winning all games in a short series (usually three or four games) with another team. Also known as a "clean sweep."

switch hitter   Batter who can hit either from the left or right side.

switch pitcher   Pitcher who can throw with either hand. Extremely rare player.

tagging up   When there are fewer than three outs, a runner may keep his foot on a base, wait until a fly ball is caught, and then run to the next base. Upon tagging up in this way, the runner will be granted the next base if he is not tagged out by a fielder prior to touching the next base.

tag out   As opposed to a *force out*, an out recorded for a runner by tagging him with the ball or glove containing the ball before the runner can touch the base. Also called a *tag play*.

take a lead (off base)   A runner moves away from the base he is positioned at and in the direction of the next base in order to get a head start in running to or stealing the next base. See *holding runner on base*.

take a pitcher deep   Baseball slang for hitting a home run.

Texas Leaguer   Term used for a ball that falls for a hit between the infielders and the outfielders. Also called a "bloop single." The Texas League is a Double-A minor league baseball league, but there is no evidence that this type of hit is any more prevalent in that league than in any other league.

third base   The base after first and second base that a runner must touch on his way to home plate to score a run.

third baseman   Defensive player, infielder who plays closest to third base.

three-bagger   A hit in which the batter reaches as far as third base. Also called a *triple*.

throw   Any act of throwing the ball in play other than pitching to the batter.

throwing error   A defensive play that should have resulted in an out, but does not. Due to throwing, not catching. Also see fielding error.

tie game   Regulation game called with home and away teams having the same number of runs. Rare event in baseball.

tip a pitch   An action by the pitcher that reveals the type of pitch that is being thrown. This could be the pitcher's position on the pitcher's plate (rubber), arm angle, or release point. If any of these varies with the type of pitch, an astute batter may be able to make an inference about the type of pitch being thrown. Knowing the type of pitch that is being thrown gives the batter an advantage in hitting.

total bases (TB)   The number of bases a player gains as a result of hits. That is, the number of singles, plus two times the number of doubles, three times the number of triples, and four times the number of home runs.

triple (3B)   A hit in which the batter reaches as far as third base. Also called a *three-bagger*.

triple crown   Batter across the regular season who leads the league in batting average, home runs, and runs batted in.

triple-play   Getting three outs on one play. Various triple plays are designated by player position numbers. For example, a 5-4-3 triple-play involves a throw from the third baseman to the second baseman, followed by a throw from the second baseman to the first baseman. An *unassisted triple-play* is a triple-play performed by one player alone.

two-bagger   A hit in which the batter reaches as far as second base. Also called a *double (2B)*.

umpire   Person enforcing the official rules of Major League Baseball, calling safe or out on the base paths, fair or foul balls, and balls or strikes at home base. Four umpires are set for regular season games, associated with each of the bases and with the umpire at home base calling balls and strikes. In playoff games two additional umpires are added, one for the right field line and one for the left field line.

umpire-in-chief   Lead umpire of the umpiring crew.

up the middle   Sound defense up the middle refers to the play of the middle infielders (second baseman and shortstop) and the center fielder. Many teams put their best fielders in these positions because so many balls are hit toward the middle of the field (up the middle).

up to bat (team)   The batting team or team on offense, as opposed to the fielding team.

VORP   A player's value over a replacement player of average ability at the same position. Expressed in units of runs per game. A summary performance measure similar to *WAR*.

walk   Batter awarded first base because four balls are called before three strikes. Also called a *base on balls (BB)*.

walk-off balk   A pitcher's balk that brings a runner on third home to win a game in the bottom of the ninth inning. A very rare event. Could also be called a *balk-off win*.

walk-off hit   A hit that scores a run for the home team in the bottom of the ninth inning, winning the game.

walk-off home run   A home run for the home team in the bottom of the ninth inning, winning the game.

WAR (WARP)   Wins above replacement (player) across an entire season. A player's value over a replacement player of average ability at the same position. A WAR value of 5, say, means that the team will win five fewer runs across the entire season if it has to replace the player. Expressed in units of wins across the season, with ten runs being equivalent to one win. Various proprietary versions of this measure exist, one variation being wins above replacement player (WARP). WAR is a summary performance measure similar to *VORP*. The measure *openWAR* represents an open-source measure of WAR, which permits calculation from public-domain data sources.

WHIP   Walks and hits allowed per inning pitched. Like earned run average (ERA), a summary measure of pitching performance.

Wild Card Game   After the end of the regular season, a one-game playoff game between two wildcard teams, which are the teams with the best records without having won their divisions.

wild pitch   Pitch that gets past the catcher that is the fault of the pitcher, as opposed to a passed ball, which is the fault of the catcher. A wild pitch is viewed as uncatchable.

windup position   Legal pitching position usually used when there are no offensive players on base. In the windup position, the pitcher does not come to a complete stop prior to throwing the ball. The other legal position is the *set position*.

World Series   Best-of-seven game playoff at the end of the Major League Baseball season, featuring the winner of the American League Championship Series (pennant) against the winner of the National League Championship Series (pennant). Played every year since 1903, with the exception of 1904 and 1994.

Soccer Glossary

added time   The span of time added at the end of each half of a soccer game to compensate for stoppages during a game. This is also called injury or stoppage time.

advantage rule   A clause in soccer which states that a referee should not stop play for a foul if it will benefit the offending team.

against the run of play   Describes a situation that happens against the dominant flow of the game; for example, if team A has been having possession and scoring chances throughout the game but it was team B that scored.

aggregate score   The overall number of goals a team has scored; in tournaments where teams play each other twice (home and away), aggregate score is used to determine which team advances to the next phase.

anchorman   A midfield player positioned in front of the center-backs, whose primarily responsibility is to break up the opponent's attacks; also known as defensive midfielder, holding midfielder, midfield anchor.

angle of the pass   Direction of a pass in relation to defender, attacker.

angle of the run   The direction of the run from a supporting player.

angling   A technique by which goalkeepers make themselves closer to an attacker to narrow the angle of shooting to the net.

arc (penalty arch)   A curved line on top of the penalty box. A player fouled in this part of the soccer field is awarded a penalty kick.

area chica   Spanish slang for the six-yard box in front of the goal, known in English as the goal box.

Definitions in this glossary draw on published *Laws of the Game* available from the Fédération Internationale de Football Association (2015). The word "soccer" is used in this book to distinguish the sport from football in the United States. Outside the U.S., soccer is called "football."

---

assist   A pass in a soccer game which leads directly to a goal.

assistant referee   Flag-bearing officials positioned along the sideline; formerly called soccer linesman.

attacker   Player whose main responsibility is to score goal or any member of the team in offense.

attacking half   The half of the soccer field which contains the opposing team's goal.

attacking midfielder   A midfielder in a more advanced position, whose task is to assist in scoring.

attacking team   Team that has possession of the ball.

auto goal   Goal scored by a player in his or her own net, also know as "own goal" or "autogol".

away   Game played in the opponent's stadium or used when a command is given by the coach to the defender, telling him or her to kick the ball away from his or her goal.

away goal   A goal scored by a visiting team on the home team's stadium.

away goals rule   A method of tie-breaking in soccer tournaments where teams play each other twice, once at each team's home stadium. The away goals rule states that the team that has scored more goals away from home will win if scores are equal at the end of a stage.

AYSO   American Youth Soccer Organization, a non-profit group in the United States which provides nationwide training and development to children between 4 to 19 years of age.

B team   The reserve team of a club or national team.

back   Players who make up the defensive line of a team.

back and face   Instruction usually given after a turnover, telling players to drop back and defend.

back four   When a team plays with four defenders.

back header   A header in soccer that involves using the back of the head.

back heel   The technique of kicking the ball using the back of the heel.

back pass (pass back)   When a player passes the ball back to their own goalkeeper. A tactic often used to consume time and to preserve possession of the ball.

back pass rule   Prohibits goalkeepers from touching the ball with their hands if it has been passed back to them deliberately by a teammate.

back tackle   Tackling the ball carrier from behind.

ball watching   Tendency of player to be unaware of surroundings and become too focused on the ball instead of the game and the movement of other players.

banana kick   A special kick in soccer which causes the ball to take a curved path.

bench   Substitute players of a team.

bend   When the soccer ball curves in midair.

booking   When the referee writes a player's number on his or her notebook after giving a yellow or red card.

box   A short term for the penalty box, the area where a goalkeeper can handle the ball, the 18-yard box where strikers do the damage.

box-to-box midfielder   A midfielder who possess exceptional skills and stamina which allows him or her to play both in offense and defense; called such because he or she plays from one penalty box to the other.

break   A run that penetrates the opponent's defense.

breakaway   To run clear of all the defending players; typically used in situations when an attacker has run free from all the defenders and is in a one-on-one situation with the goalkeeper.

burn   The act of passing an opponent using speed, agility, and/or dribbling skill.

captain   Official leader of a team recognizable by the wearing of an armband.

cards   Used to punish unsportsmanlike behavior. When a yellow card is given, it is a warning, while a red card signifies ejection from the game.

center   The middle part of the soccer field.

center back (central defender)   Player that is positioned in the center of the defensive line, in between the fullbacks.

center circle   The big circle on the middle most part of the field.

center forward   Player whose main job is on the offense, usually a major goal scorer.

center half (center back)   A defender positioned at the center of the field.

center line   The horizontal line on the middle part of the soccer field.

center midfielder   This position carries a lot of responsibility and plays both offense and defense. Considered the strategist of the game.

challenge   Attempt by a defender to take the ball away from an attacker.

channels   Area approximately fifteen yards away from the touchline.

charge   A shoulder-to-shoulder contact, made by a defender to steal possession from an attacker.

chest (chest trap)   Controlling the ball in flight using the upper torso.

chilena   A term commonly used in South America for the bicycle kick.

chip   A short lofted pass or shot that gets the ball in the air.

chip pass   A pass that gets the ball high in the air.

clear   To kick the ball away from one's goal.

cleats   Shoe designed for playing soccer.

closing down   When the player advances to an opponent with the ball in an attempt to stall play or win back possession.

club   Playing in a league, used to avoid confusion with a "team," which typically refers to playing in a national team.

combination play   A play which involves two or more basic moves.

commit   Getting your opponent to commit to a planned course of action.

conditioned play   Training condition where game time is simulated, forcing players to perform a specific skill, technique, or tactic.

Confederations Cup   A soccer tournament competed by national teams every four years that is organized by FIFA.

control (the ball)   Bring the ball under control by cushioning its arrival with a surface on the body.

control   Play possession of the ball throughout the soccer game.

corner   Restart situation where a player touches the ball last and it travels over their own goal line.

cover   Occurs when an additional player provides cover to another player to support a teammate marking an attacker by going behind or beside him or her; the second or third players who mark the same attacker.

cross   A long pass often in the air that is played diagonally from the channels into the box. A ball kicked from the side of the field in or near the penalty area. There are various forms of the cross. An *inswinging cross* arcs from the center of the pitch to the goal area. An *outswinging cross* arcs from the by line out to the center of the soccer pitch. A *far post* is a long cross from a corner that misses out the penalty box and aims for the farthest post. A *near post* is a short cross aimed at the nearest post.

corner arc   A white arc drawn at each corner part of the soccer field.

corner ball   Alternate term for the corner kick in soccer, a free kick made by an attacker if the ball goes over the goal line and a defender was the last to touch it.

corner flag   The flags at each of corner of the soccer pitch.

corner kick   A kick made by an attacker if the ball goes over the goal line and a defender was the last to touch it.

corridor of uncertainty   A cross or pass that travels between the goalkeeper and the last defender; called such because it is uncertain which player will play the ball and which one will leave it to the other.

counterattack   Quickly attacking right after retrieving the ball in defense.

crossbar   The horizontal bar on top of the goal which connects the two goalposts, also called simply the bar.

cul-de-sac   Used to describe a player who carries the ball to a part of the field where it can have little effect on the game.

cup-tied   A term used to describe a player who can no longer play in a cup competition after transferring from another club during that same season; a player can only play for one team during an entire cup's length.

danger zone   The inside of the penalty area, where most goals are scored.

decoy run   Occurs when a soccer player executes a run to draw attention from the intended play. Also known as creating space.

defend deep   A command given to a defending team to stay on their defensive half.

defender (defenseman)   Player whose position in soccer requires him or her to deny the opponents ball possession and scoring opportunities.

defensive half   The half of the soccer field where a team's goal is located.

defensive midfielder   A midfield player whose primary task is to defend.

deflection   A ball that bounced off a player; defenders deflect the ball to prevent goal-scoring or to cut a pass.

diamond   A diamond-shaped formation of players on the midfield: created when two players are assigned as wingers, one as an attacking midfielder, and another one as a defensive midfielder; typically used in the 4-4-2 formation.

direct free kick   A type of free kick in which a player can score a goal directly; its opposite is the indirect free kick, in which another player must touch the ball before a goal can be attempted.

disallow   To declare that a goal is invalid because of a rule violation; a goal can also be disallowed if the referee thinks the ball has not completely crossed the goal line.

dive To pretend to have been fouled by a defender in order to get a penalty or free kick: diving in soccer is punishable with a yellow card; also called simulation.

diving header A way of heading the soccer ball by jumping parallel to the ground; often made when the ball is too high to be kicked or too low for a standing header.

draw (D) A game that ended with a tied score.

dribble To move and control the ball with the feet while it remains on the ground.

dribbling The art of close control while moving with the soccer ball at the feet.

drop back An expression given to defenders encouraging them to go to their defensive half and play defense.

dummy Any trick, technique, or skill that unbalances or confuses an opponent to gain an advantage.

early ball Soccer play in which an immediate pass is played to a teammate at the earliest opportunity, often to exploit space.

El Clasico Refers to the rivalry between Real Madrid and Barcelona, the two most popular clubs in Spain. Recognized as one of the most-watched sporting events in the world.

European Champions League The most prestigious club tournament in the whole world where the top clubs of Europe compete each year. Also called "Champs League" or "Champions League."

extra time Occurs when the score is tied at the end of regulation, typically given extra 15 minutes to play on each side for a total of 30 minutes or until either time scores a goal in the extra time.

equalizer A goal which brings the score into a tie.

expulsion To be disallowed to continue a match because of a serious, or consistent, violation of the game rules. Players under expulsion are not allowed to stay on the side of the pitch or on the team's bench.

end line Alternate term for the goal line, the marking at each end of the soccer field.

eighteen-yard line A short reference to the penalty box; called such because its length from the goal line is 18 yards.

FA The oldest English soccer association, credited for formulating the basic game rules of soccer. Associated with the Football Association Challenge Cup.

fair charging A shoulder-to-shoulder contact made against an opponent to gain advantage over the ball; it is "fair charging" if it is not too forceful or does not put the opponent in danger; also called *shoulder charge*.

fair play   Occurs when the scores of two teams are tied and there is no way of breaking the tie; the team which incurred the least number of yellow and red cards advance to the next round.

fake (feint)   A dribbling move in soccer that deceives or tricks an opponent.

fakeover   A technique in which a player looks as if they are to take the ball from their teammate who is in possession but they don't and just run past each other.

FC   An abbreviation for "football club," often found as suffix to American and English football club names.

FIFA   Fédération Internationale de Football Association, the world's highest governing body for soccer (football). Established in 1904 and based in Switzerland. Responsible for setting the *Laws of the Game* as they apply to both men's and women's soccer in international competitions, including the World Cup.

FIFA Ballon d'Or   An award given by FIFA annually to the player considered the best of the year; also called Footballer of the Year.

FIFA World Cup   The biggest soccer competition in the world, held every four years. Being a World Cup champion is the highest prestige a team, nation, or player can achieve.

final whistle   An idiom in soccer referring to the end of a match. Although the length of a soccer game is defined, it is the referee who decides when to blow the final whistle.

first half   The first period of a soccer match; a game is divided into two halves of forty-five minutes each.

first team   The set of players in a club that participates in competitions; the players not included in the first team are called reserves.

first touch   The first contact a player makes with the ball; a good first touch makes a player control the ball well or shoot it accurately.

fist (boxing)   A technique for goalkeepers—punching a high-flighted ball that is difficult to control.

fixture   A soccer game of regulation length (ninety minutes).

flat four   A defensive line made up of two central defenders and two fullbacks; called such because they often form a flat line; also called flat back four.

flick pass   Quick pass made with the outside of the foot; usually done by attackers in front of the goal in order to beat the keeper.

footwork   Skillful movements with the feet used to evade opponents or dribble the ball.

formation   The arrangement of players on the soccer field; modern soccer formations often place a balanced number of players on the defensive and offensive halves.

forward   The players positioned nearest to the opponents goal; their primarily responsibility is to score.

forward line   The player or set of players nearest to the opponents' goal; for example, in a 3-5-2 formation, the forward line is made up of the front two players.

foul   An act that is unfair, dangerous, or against the game rules. Fouls in soccer are enumerated in the FIFA's *Laws of the Game*.

free agent   A player who is not affiliated with any club for the time being.

free kick   Occurs when play has been stopped by the referee for an infringement of the laws of the game.

front block tackle   A tackle made with a solid contact to the ball while facing the opponent.

front header   A header made with the front of the forehead.

front tackle   To approach an attacking opponent face-to-face and attempt kick the ball away from him or her.

full time   The end of a soccer match.

full back   A defender who is the first line of defense.

Futebol   Football or soccer.

Galácticos   A term used to describe Real Madrid players who were purchased at high cost—a record transfer of forty-six million pounds in 2001.

give and go (one-two pass, wall pass)   Soccer technique in which a player passes the ball to a teammate who touches the ball and passes the ball back quickly to the teammate.

goal   A score in soccer, happens when the ball crosses the goal line between the goal posts and the crossbar; the structure where the ball must be shot at to score a goal. The soccer goal's measurement is 8 feet by 24 feet.

goal area (penalty box)   The part of the soccer field where a goalkeeper can legally handle the ball, demarcated by a big rectangular box: measures 18 yards by 44 yards.

goal average   Average number of goals a player or team scores over a season or tournament.

goal kick   The method of restarting play after the ball goes out of bounds over the goal line and an attacking player was the last to touch it.

goal line   Line found at each end of the soccer field; a goal is awarded when the ball crosses the goal line between the two goal posts.

goal posts   The two vertical posts of a goal, measuring eight feet tall each.

goal side   Area between the goal and the ball.

goalaso   A Spanish interjection when an amazing goal is made.

goalie (goalkeeper, keeper)   The only required soccer position according to the rules. Also the only player allowed to touch the ball with his or her hands while in the penalty box around the defending team's goal.

golden goal   A former rule which states that the first team to score in extra time wins the match; the game is ended immediately after the golden goal is made.

ground ball   A pass or shot that travels on the ground.

hacking   The act of kicking an opponent's legs; a serious offense punishable by a yellow or red card.

half   Any of the two 45-minute playing periods of a soccer match.

halfback   The players positioned between the forwards and the defenders.

half-time (interval, break)   The period between the first and second halves, typically 15 minutes long; it is a time for players to recuperate and for coaches to give motivational or tactical speeches.

halfway line   The bold line in the middle of the football pitch which divides its length into two equal parts.

half volley   Occurs when a player volleys (using their laces) an upward bouncing ball that has just landed in front of them, kicking a soccer ball in mid-air after it bounces off the ground.

hand ball   A contact with the ball with the hands; a handball is punishable by a booking if the referee deems it deliberate but play may go on without an infraction called if the referee thinks it is accidental; also called hands.

hat-trick   Scoring three goals in a single match by one player.

head   (also termed header or heading) To strike the ball with the head; heading skills in football are very crucial when the game is played near the goal.

head coach   The person in charged of running a team or club. Duties include selecting the lineup and strategies in matches, buying or selling players, and scouting for new talent. He or she is found on a team's bench during a game, shouting instruction to players. In Britain, the head coach is called the "manager."

high press   Tactical deployment of the soccer team where all players apply immediate pressure to the opponents when possession is conceded, often in opponent's half.

hits the post   Describes when the ball hits either of the goalposts and does not go inside.

holding the line   Defenders keeping an imaginary line to catch opponents offside.

holding midfielder   A midfield player whose primary task is to break up the opponent's attack; also called defensive midfielder, anchorman, midfield anchor.

horseshoe formation   The 4-5-1 formation, called such because its shape on the blackboard resembles a horseshoe.

indirect kick   A free kick in which another player (aside from the taker) must touch the ball before a shot toward the goal can be made.

injury time   Time added at the end of each half to make up for time not played during the match because of fouls, injuries, time-wasting, or technical issues.

intercept   To block or cut a pass between opponents.

jockeying   The act of limiting an attacker's movement without attempting to tackle him or her delaying and holding up play, not diving in with a tackle but staying up right and preventing the advancement of the opponent.

kick-off   The method of starting a football match or restarting it after a goal is scored; it is done by placing the ball at the centermost part of the football pitch and kicking it to a teammate nearby.

last defender   The last field player nearest to the goal.

Laws of the Game   The rules of soccer (football) that are followed internationally. See Fédération Internationale de Football Association 2015.

league   A competition format in which the team that earns the most number of points at the end wins; in a league, a win is rewarded with three points, a draw is worth one point, and none for a loss; also called, division, table, championship.

League Cup   Officially, the Football League Cup: a knockout tournament played among professional teams in England and Wales; typically held from June to February.

left back   A defensive player positioned on the left-hand side of his goalkeeper.

left winger   A midfield player who plays along the left-hand side of the pitch.

line of recovery   Occurs when a player is beaten, this is the line on which they retreat back toward their own goal to get goal side of the attack.

linesman   A former term for the assistant football referee; in football games there are two linesmen who monitor offsides and throw-ins and help the head referee in decision-making.

lineup   Short reference to the starting line up, the set of players that start a football match and are expected to play most of the match.

lofted pass   A high pass executed by kicking the bottom half of the ball sending it into the air.

long ball   A long pass, such as ones made by a defender to a striker.

long shot   A shot toward the goal that is taken from a long distance.

man-on   An interjection used to warn a teammate in possession that an opposing player is nearby.

man short   A term used to describe a team that plays with one less player after a send-off.

manager   British term for head coach.

mark (marking)   To cover a player who may or may not have the ball, preventing that player from receiving the ball. When a defender covers an offensive player without the ball.

match   A regulation football game; used interchangeably with game, fixture, clash.

match officials   The persons in charged of regulating a football match, often made up of one head referee and two assistant referees or linesmen. In professional leagues, a fourth football official is present to administer player substitutions and other technical matters.

measured ball   A well-calculated pass that reaches its desired target; also called measured shot.

metodo system   Classic formation 2-3-2-3.

midfield   The middle third of the football field; for tactical reasons, the playing field is divided into three parts: the back or defensive third, the midfield, and the attacking third.

midfield anchor   A midfield player positioned at the middle with the primary task is of breaking the attacks of opponents.

midfielder   Player positioned on the middle part of the pitch, between the forwards and the defenders.

mistimed tackle   A tackle made before an opponent receives the ball or after he or she passes it; a dangerous move that is punishable by a red card or yellow card.

multiball system   A football match where many balls are used to save time; when a ball goes out of bounds, the playing ball is replaced by a reserved ball thereby reducing the time spent on retrieving the ball.

Mundial   A short reference to the FIFA World Cup, the biggest international football tournament.

narrowing the angle   Closing down a player so that the angle they have to shoot or pass is reduced significantly.

netting   The act of finishing, to score or attempt to score a goal after a pass is made.

obstruction   Getting in the way of an attacker without trying to win the ball; this act is considered a foul in football.

offensive player   Any player who attempts to score or goes forward to help in the attack.

official caution   Alternate term for the yellow card.

off-season   The period before the start of a regular season.

offside   A penalty called when an attacking player is in front of the ball, but behind all the defenders but one (usually the goalie).

off the ball   Movement of players, to create space and provide options.

olympic goal   A very difficult way of scoring a goal: happens when a player scores a goal directly from a corner kick without the ball being touched by anybody else.

on offense   A term that refers to the team in possession of the ball.

one-touch   Playing the ball after only one touch, as in passing or shooting it right after reception.

one-touch pass   Occurs when a player is able to play the ball with one touch after a pass. Some passes are badly placed or too strong, which is why recipients may have to do two or more touches to control the ball.

one-touch soccer   An offensive football tactic where players distribute the ball quickly after receiving it.

one-two   An offensive technique in which a player passes the ball to teammate then receives it after going past defenders; also called wall pass, give-and-go.

open space   The space between an attacker and the goal when there are no defenders on it.

out of bounds (out of play)   Another term for out of play, when the whole of the ball goes beyond the touchline or goal line.

overtime   Two fifteen-minute periods played if the score is tied after the regular ninety-minute game; also called extra time.

pace   The speed of a player or ball.

pass   Technique to move the ball from one player to another. Various techniques apply, including the chip, half volley, push, and lofted pass.

pass and move   A strategy of offensive soccer. Means that players should always be moving and should be ready to pass or dribble the soccer ball as soon as they get it. Also, pass and move is a strategy used by a player to an open space as soon as he or she has passed the ball.

pass back (back pass)   When a player passes the ball back to their own goalkeeper, a tactic often used to consume time and to preserve possession of the ball.

penalty area   An area or box near the goal. Penalties in this area may result in a penalty kick.

penalty kick   A type of free kick that is taken from twelve yards out from goal and with only the goalkeeper of the defending team between the kicker and the goal.

penetration   A phase of play where a team breaks through the opponent's defense.

peripheral vision   Ability to see wider than what is directly in front.

play maker   A designated player who has good vision, excellent passing ability, who can open up defensive lines and create opportunities.

plyometrics   Drills and exercises that develop explosiveness in players.

pressure training   Method of training that requires rapid repetition for a limited time.

receiving   Technique required to control an incoming ball.

running with the ball   A player in possession exploits space by carrying the ball quickly and efficiently, as opposed to dribbling.

save   Occurs when the goalkeeper or defender prevents a goal.

shadow play   Playing without opponents.

shielding   Keeping possession and control of the ball by using the body to come between the ball and the opponent.

show   Occurs when a player makes himself or herself available.

sliding tackle   Occurs when a defending player goes to ground and uses an extended leg to win the ball.

soccer ball   Spherical object that the game revolves around.

support play   Occurs when teammates move into and create space and options for the player in possession.

sweeper   A soccer player position. This player is a defender who roams the area behind the other defenders looking to "sweep up" any passes that get through.

switching play   Changing the angle of attack.

tackle   A challenge to win the ball off an opponent.

tackling   A defensive move that steals the ball, but does not contact the offensive player. Often resulting in the offensive player falling down.

taking a player on   Occurs when a player in possession runs at a defending player with the aim of going past them.

target man   A striker/attacker (often big and able to shields the ball well) who should always be available for a pass from the midfield who can then hold up the play until reinforcements arrive.

through pass   A pass which is played between two defenders for an attacker to run onto.

throw-in   A throw from the sidelines when the opposing team was the last to touch the soccer ball prior to the ball crossing over the side line.

trials   Term used to describe a process of evaluation on a player's ability and suitability for a team. For example, a manager might say, "We are holding trials to bring in new players."

turning an opponent   Occurs when running at an opponent, the use of feints and fakes to trick the opponent into turning or by pushing the ball past them and causing them to turn.

volley   Striking the ball before it lands, difficult skill to master but very powerful.

Tennis Glossary

ace A shot that derives from a serve and is a winner.

ad court The left side of the court for each player.

advantage When a player wins the deuce point and is one point away from obtaining the game.

all Refers to the situation when players have the same number of points, games, or sets.

all-court player A player who can play from all positions on the court: baseline, transition, and/or the net.

alley The side area on the outside of the singles courts, used to play doubles.

alternate A player who is on wait-list and may replace another player in a tournament due to injury/withdrawal.

angles Shot used to force the opponent wide off the court.

approach shot Shot that is used when a player wants to transition from baseline to the net.

ATP Association of Tennis Professionals recognized as the governing body of the men's professional tennis world tour.

Australian Formation Doubles formation strategy where the net player positions themselves at center of the net while his or her partner serves.

backhand Tennis stroke originating from the player's non-dominant hand.

backswing Part of the stroke when the player takes their racquet back in order to begin their swing.

Definitions in this glossary draw on the *2015 Rules of Tennis* (International Tennis Federation 2015).

bagel   A term used to refer to the situation when a player wins a set without dropping a game.

ballperson   A person who picks up tennis ball during a tennis match and provides the ball to the player during their service game.

backhand   A tennis stroke originating from the player's non-dominant hand.

ball toss   Important component of the serve—the ball is tossed into the air prior to being struck by the racquet.

baseline   The two inch wide boundary mark at the rear of the court that distinguishes what is in and what is out. It is a line that is parallel to the net.

baseliner   A player that prefers to stand at the baseline and use their groundstrokes to win points, games, sets, and matches.

break   When a player wins a game on their opponent's serve.

breakpoint   The point that gives a player the opportunity to win the game on their opponent's serve.

bye   Allows a player to advance to the next round of a tournament without having to face an opponent; a bye is usually awarded to the top seeds in the tournament.

call   A term used by the linesman (lines judge and tennis player themselves until pro level) to determine if the ball was in or out.

center line   The line in the direct center of the baseline.

challenge   Request made by the player to an official regarding the accuracy of line call using Hawk-Eye in order to determine whether the ball landed in or out.

Challenger Tour   Tournament level comprised of players who are one step below the ATP Tour. Players who do well on the Challenger Tour may gain ranking points in order to earn entry to the ATP Tour.

change-over   Consists of 120 seconds of a rest period when players switch sides of the court (mostly when the sums of games being played equal an odd number).

chip and charge   Strategy that consists of a player hitting a chip and then rushing to the net.

clip the line   A shot for which some part of the ball lands on the line.

code violation   Occurs when a player commits a violation of the rules/regulations including the throwing of a racquet or verbal obscenities.

counterpuncher   A defensive minded baseliner who waits for his or her opponent to make mistakes and can consistently return many shots inside the court.

court   Area used for playing tennis.

crosscourt   Occurs when you hit the ball diagonally across the court whether it is coming from the backhand or forehand side, used very often in conservative play during groundstroke rallies.

Davis Cup   An international competition where male players of the same nation represent their country in a team format against other nations.

deep   Refers to a ball that lands near the back of the court close to the baseline.

deuce   The right side of the court of each player when the score is tied at 40-40 or also termed 40-all and when two points are needed to win the game.

double bagel   Occurs when a player wins a match without losing a game; the score of a double bagel is 6-0, 6-0.

double fault   Occurs when the server misses two consecutive serves and consequently results in a point deduction.

doubles   Game played with four players, two teams of two players on a larger surface area that includes the alleys of the tennis court.

drop shot   A shot that is intentionally left short on the court and barely makes it over the net.

down the line   Refers to balls that are hit straight ahead rather than across the court.

Entry System   Method used to select players to compete in a tournament, usually based on ranking or number of points.

fault   A serve that lands outside the service area or hits the net.

Fed Cup   An international competition (Davis Cup) in which female players are selected to represent their nations and compete against other countries in a team format.

flat   A shot that has been hit with little to no spin.

follow-through   Describes the ending part of a groundstroke.

foot fault   Occurs when the server steps on the baseline during the process of serving the ball (technically, the player steps on the baseline and then immediately hits the ball).

forced error   Occurs when a player hits a difficult shot that causes the other player to miss their shot (in essence the error is forced).

forehand   Tennis stroke originating from the player's dominant hand.

Futures   A series of tournaments one level below the Challenger circuit and two levels below the Pro Tour.

game   Term used in tennis for scoring; a game consists of a player winning at least four points (0, 15, 30, 45, Game). There are six games in each set, and play continues until a player wins two out of three sets (except for some tournaments, which may continue until a player wins three out of five sets).

Golden Slam   Winning all four Grand Slam tournaments (the Australian Open, Wimbledon, French Open, and the U.S. Open) along with winning an Olympic Gold Medal, in a single calendar year.

Grand Slam   Winning all four Grand Slam tournaments (the Australian Open, Wimbledon, French Open, and the U.S. Open) within a lifetime.

groundstroke   Tennis strokes hit from the baseline, usually a forehand or backhand.

Hawk-Eye   A computer system that is currently being used on the ATP and WTA tour to determine if a ball landed in or not; currently used when players challenge a call.

hold   When the player serving wins the game they serve.

I-Formation   A doubles strategy that consist of the server and net player positioning themselves on the same side of the court before the server begins the point.

inside out   A singles strategy that consists of a player running around his or her non-dominant (usually his or her backhand) to hit a forehand crosscourt.

ITF   International Tennis Federation, the governing body of tennis.

let   Permitted when the player's serve touches the net and continues on its travelled path and lands inside its designated court area. When this happens, it is considered proper etiquette to "do over" the serve. In the case that a neighboring ball (other people playing on another tennis court hit a ball into your court for example, you can call a let, and replay the point).

linesmen (line judge)   Official who calls the balls in or out, they judge whether the shot landed in or out of the court.

lob   Tennis stroke that has a high arc and still lands inside the court, usually hit with lots of topspin.

love   In tennis love means nothing (zero). It is used to state that you have zero points when you say the score and it is first in the order. For example if you say, Love-40, it means you have 0 points and your opponent has three and is one point away from winning the game.

Match Point   The point at which there is an opportunity to win the match if the point is won.

mixed doubles   A doubles team consisting of one female and one male player.

miss-hit   When a player fails to hit the ball on the sweet spot of the racquet or hits the ball with the frame instead of the strings.

natural gut   Type of string made from cow and/or sheep intestines.

net The net divides the tennis court into halves. It is an object stretched across the middle of the court with a height of 3.6 feet on the ends and 3 feet in the center. To remain in play, the ball must go over the net.

no man's land Area of the court between the baseline and the service line. This area is called "no man's land" because it has been thought of as an area where a strong defensive or offensive play cannot occur.

NTRP Rating The National Tennis Rating Program which is used to rate players based on a ranking scale (from 1.0 to 7.0).

out When the ball lands outside the designated area of play.

overhead (smash) A shot you hit over your head during a rally.

overrule The overturning of a linesman's call by the umpire.

passing shot Occurs when the opponent is at the net and the other player hits a passing shot from the baseline, thereby passing the player at the net.

racquet Equipment used in tennis to hit the ball, consisting of a frame, hitting surface area encapsulated by string with a handle. Racquets vary in composition—titanium, graphite, carbon fiber, or wood.

racquet head Part of the racquet that contains the strings.

rally Series of shots exchanged between players. Usually a rally takes place when players are hitting their groundstrokes.

receiver The player not serving who receives the serve.

referee A person in charge of enforcing the rules in a tournament.

return Used to describe the shot that the receiver hit (that is, a good return).

second serve The serve after the first attempt fails to land in the opponent's service box. If this serve is missed, a double fault is called, and the point is awarded to the receiver.

serve The stroke that begins every tennis point.

set The culmination of six games. The first player to reach six games and win by two games is said to have won a set. It is customary for a player to win two out of three sets to win a tennis match (except for some tournaments, which require a player to win three out of five sets to win a match).

set point The point prior to winning a set.

singles The tennis game played with one player on each side of the court.

slice Tennis stroke that is usually hit from high to low which generates underspin (backspin).

spin   The effect that is placed on the ball by the type of stroke a player hits. The ball can have sidespin, topspin, or underspin depending on how the ball was hit.

split step   Footwork technique performed by split stepping and then jumping an inch or two off the ground and landing shoulder width apart with the knees slightly bent.

stance   Position of the body prior to hitting the ball.

stroke   Technique used to swing at the ball.

T   Refers to the intersection of the center line and service line.

tiebreaker   A playoff when players are tied, thus the term tiebreaker. The first player to reach seven points and win by two is said to have won the tiebreaker.

tennis ball   Air-filled rubber ball coated in a yellow synthetic fur and used in the game of tennis.

Tennis Hall of Fame   Refers to the Tennis Hall of Fame located in Newport, Rhode Island, where many great tennis players are honored.

topspin   A forward rotation on the ball, usually generated from a ball being hit from low to high.

umpire (official)   Person in charge of the scoring and line calls of the tennis match.

underspin   A backward rotation on the ball, usually generated from a ball being hit from high to low.

unforced error   An error made due to the player's own lack of judgement and/or carelessness.

volley   Tennis stroke in which the ball is hit in the air before it bounces. Technically, a short stroke.

Wildcard   A tournament entry given to player who has not officially qualified. Some tournaments reserve several wildcard slots in the tournament draw and generally award them to players from the same country where the tournament is being played or other specified criteria.

winner   A shot that is too good; the opponent cannot return the ball, completely missed the ball, and/or their racquet did not touch the ball.

WTA   WTA is the Women's Tennis Association, the women's professional tour.

Bibliography

Abdelkrim, N. B., A. Chaouachi, K. Chamari, M. Chtara, and C. Castagna 2010. Positional role and competitive-level differences in elite-level men's basketball players. *Journal of Strength & Conditioning Research* 24(5):1346–1355.

Abe, T., K. Kumagai, and W. F. Brechue 2000. Fascicle length of leg muscles is greater in sprinters than distance runners. *Medicine and Science in Sports and Exercise* 32(6): 1125–1129.

Achten, J., M. Gleeson, A. E. Jeukendrup, and others 2002. Determination of the exercise intensity that elicits maximal fat oxidation. *Medicine and Science in Sports and Exercise* 34(1):92–97.

Ackland, T. 1999. Talent identification: What makes a champion swimmer? In *Applied Proceedings of the XVII International Symposium of Biomechanics in Sports*, Volume 17, pp. 67–74.

Ackland, T. R., B. Elliott, and J. Bloomfield 2009. *Applied Anatomy and Biomechanics in Sport*. Human Kinetics.

Ackland, T. R., A. B. Schreiner, and D. A. Kerr 1997. Absolute size and proportionality characteristics of world championship female basketball players. *Journal of Sports Sciences* 15(5):485–490.

Agresti, A. and M. Kateri 2011. *Categorical Data Analysis*. Springer.

Alemdaroğlu, U. 2012. The relationship between muscle strength, anaerobic performance, agility, sprint ability and vertical jump performance in professional basketball players. *Journal of Human Kinetics* 31:149–158.

Alexander, C. C. 1991. *Our Game: An American Baseball History*. Macmillan.

Alexander, C. C. 2002. *Breaking the Slump: Baseball in the Depression Era*. Columbia University Press.

Alexander, M. J. 1976. The relationship of somatotype and selected anthropometric measures to basketball performance in highly skilled females. *Research Quarterly. American Alliance for Health, Physical Education and Recreation* 47(4):575–585.

Alexander, R. M. 2013. *The Human Machine*. Columbia University Press.

Alston, W. E. and D. C. Weiskopf 1972. *The Complete Baseball Handbook: Strategies and Techniques for Winning*. Allyn & Bacon.

Altman, D. G., J. M. Bland, and others 2005. Standard Deviations and Standard Errors. *BMJ* 331(7521):903.

Alwin, D. F. and J. A. Krosnick 1985. The measurement of values in surveys: A comparison of ratings and rankings. *Public Opinion Quarterly* 49(4):535–552.

American College of Sports Medicine 2013a. *ACSM's Guidelines for Exercise Testing and Prescription*. Lippincott Williams Wilkins. 19, 23, 32, 35, 40

American College of Sports Medicine 2013b. *ACSM's Health-related Physical Fitness Assessment Manual*. Lippincott Williams Wilkins.

Andersen, M. B. and J. M. Williams 1988. A model of stress and athletic injury: Prediction and prevention. *Journal of Sport and Exercise Psychology* 10(3):294–306.

Anderson, C. and D. Sally 2013. *The numbers game: Why everything you know about soccer is wrong*. New York: Penguin. 144

Anderson, D. 1988. *The Story of Basketball*. William Morrow.

Anderson, D., D. Sweeney, T. Williams, J. Camm, and J. Cochran 2015. *An Introduction to Management Science: Quantitative Approaches to Decision Making*. Cengage Learning.

Anderson, M. J. 2001. A new method for non-parametric multivariate analysis of variance. *Austral Ecology* 26(1):32–46.

Anderson, T. and J. T. Kearney 1982. Effects of three resistance training programs on muscular strength and absolute and relative endurance. *Research Quarterly for Exercise and Sport* 53(1):1–7.

Andrew, D. P., P. M. Pedersen, and C. D. McEvoy 2011. *Research Methods and Design in Sport Management*. Human Kinetics.

Andrews, D. L. 1999. Whither the NBA, whither America? *Peace Review* 11(4):505–510.

Andrews, D. L. 2001. The fact(s) of Michael Jordan's blackness: Excavating a floating racial signifier. *Michael Jordan, Inc.: Corporate Sport, Media Culture, and Late-modern America*:107–153.

Angyan, L., T. Teczely, Z. Zalay, and I. Karsai 2003. Relationship of anthropometrical, physiological and motor attributes to sport-specific skills. *Acta Physiologica Hungarica* 90(3):225–231.

Appaneal, R. N., B. R. Levine, F. M. Perna, J. L. Roh, and others 2009. Measuring postinjury depression among male and female competitive athletes. *Journal of Sport & Exercise Psychology* 31(1):60–76.

Apple, A. 1983. Offensive rebounding. *Journal of Physical Education, Recreation & Dance* 54 (1):45–45.

Appleton, D. R. 1995. May the best man win? *The Statistician* 44(4):529–538.

Arnason, A., S. B. Sigurdsson, A. Gudmundsson, I. Holme, L. Engebretsen, and R. Bahr 2004. Physical fitness, injuries, and team performance in soccer. *Medicine & Science in Sports & Exercise* 36(2):278–285.

Association, A. F. C. 2000. *Offensive Football Strategies*. Human Kinetics.

Association, N. B. C. and others 2009. *NBA Coaches Playbook: Techniques, Tactics, and Teaching Points*. Human Kinetics.

Åstrand, P.-O. 2003. *Textbook of Work Physiology: Physiological bases of exercise*. Human Kinetics.

Atkinson, G. and A. M. Nevill 1998. Statistical methods for assessing measurement error (reliability) in variables relevant to sports medicine. *Sports Medicine* 26(4):217–238.

Atkinson, G. and A. M. Nevill 2001. Selected issues in the design and analysis of sport performance research. *Journal of Sports Sciences* 19(10):811–827.

Atmosukarto, I., B. Ghanem, S. Ahuja, K. Muthuswamy, and N. Ahuja 2013. Automatic recognition of offensive team formation in American football plays. In *IEEE Conference on Computer Vision and Pattern Recognition Workshops (CVPRW)*, pp. 991–998.

Aunola, S., J. Marniemi, E. Alanen, M. Mäntylä, M. Saraste, and H. Rusko 1988. Muscle metabolic profile and oxygen transport capacity as determinants of aerobic and anaerobic thresholds. *European Journal of Applied Physiology and occupational physiology* 57(6):726–734.

Backman, S. E. 2002. NFL players fight for their freedom: The history of free agency in the NFL. *Sports Law Journal* 9:1.

Baechle, T. R. and R. W. Earle (eds.) 2008. *Essentials of Strength Training and Conditioning* (third ed.). Champaign, Ill.: Human Kinetics. National Strength and Conditioning Association. 13, 20

Bal, B. S., S. Singh, and N. Singh 2008. Analysis of the personality traits of medalist and non medalist athletes. *Shield-Research Journal of Physical Education Sports Science.* 3.

Banerjee, A. N. and J. F. Swinnen 2004. Does a sudden death liven up the game? Rules, incentives, and strategy in football. *Economic Theory* 23(2):411–421.

Bangsbo, J. 1993. The physiology of soccer–with special reference to intense intermittent exercise. *Acta Physiologica Scandinavica. Supplementum* 619:1–155.

Bangsbo, J. and B. Peitersen 2000. *Soccer Systems and Strategies*. Human Kinetics.

Banzer, W., C. Thiel, A. Rosenhagen, and L. Vogt 2008. Tennis ranking related to exercise capacity. *British Journal of Sports Medicine* 42(2):152–154.

Bard, K. A. 2015. *An Introduction to the Archaeology of Ancient Egypt*. John Wiley & Sons.

Barros, R. M., M. S. Misuta, R. P. Menezes, P. J. Figueroa, F. A. Moura, S. A. Cunha, R. Anido, and N. J. Leite 2007. Analysis of the distances covered by first division Brazilian soccer players obtained with an automatic tracking method. *Journal of Sports Science & Medicine* 6(2):233.

Bauer, D. J. and P. J. Curran 2003. Distributional assumptions of growth mixture models: implications for overextraction of latent trajectory classes. *Psychological Methods* 8(3):338.

Baumer, B. and A. Zimbalist 2014. *The Sabermetric Revolution: Assessing the Growth of Analytics in Baseball*. Philadelphia: University of Pennsylvania Press. 223

Beck, A. T. and R. A. Steer 1990. *BAI, Beck Anxiety Inventory*. Psychological Corporation.

Becker, C. 2007. The Cincinnati football Reds: A franchise in failure. *Ohio History* 114(1):7–27.

Beilock, S. L. and Gray, R. 2007. Why do athletes choke under pressure? In G. Tenenbaum and B. Eklund (eds.), Handbook of Sport Psychology, pp. 425-444. New York: Wiley.

Beise, D. and V. Peaseley 1937. The relation of reaction time, speed, and agility of big muscle groups to certain sport skills. *Research Quarterly. American Physical Education Association* 8(1):133–142.

Bell, D. R., K. M. Guskiewicz, M. A. Clark, and D. A. Padua 2011. Systematic review of the Balance Error Scoring System. *Sports Health: A Multidisciplinary Approach* 3(3): 287–295.

Bell, W. and G. Rhodes 1975. The morphological characteristics of the Association Football player. *British Journal of Sports Medicine* 9(4):196.

Berg, K. and R. W. Latin 1995. Comparison of physical and performance characteristics of NCAA Division I basketball and football players. *Journal of Strength & Conditioning Research* 9(1):22–26.

Berger, T. 2015. *Pau Gasol 121 Success Secrets-121 Most Asked Questions On Pau Gasol— What You Need To Know*. Emereo Publishing.

Berri, D. J. 1999. Who is 'most valuable'? Measuring the player's production of wins in the National Basketball Association. *Managerial and Decision Economics* 20(8):411–427.

Berri, D. J., S. L. Brook, and A. J. Fenn 2011. From college to the pros: Predicting the NBA amateur player draft. *Journal of Productivity Analysis* 35(1):25–35.

Berri, D. J. and R. Simmons 2011. Catching a draft: On the process of selecting quarterbacks in the National Football League amateur draft. *Journal of Productivity Analysis* 35(1):37–49.

Berry, R. C., W. B. Gould, and P. D. Staudohar 1986. *Labor Relations in Professional Sports*. Greenwood Publishing Group.

Berry, W. D. 1993. *Understanding Regression Assumptions*, Volume 92. Sage Publications.

Beynnon, B. D., D. F. Murphy, and D. M. Alosa 2002. Predictive factors for lateral ankle sprains: a literature review. *Journal of Athletic Training* 37(4):376.

Bigliani, L. U., T. P. Codd, P. M. Connor, W. N. Levine, M. A. Littlefield, and S. J. Hershon 1997, Sep-Oct. Shoulder motion and laxity in the professional baseball player. *The American Journal of Sports Medicine* 25(5):609–613.

Billat, V., D. Hill, J. Pinoteau, B. Petit, and J.-P. Koralsztein 1996. Effect of protocol on determination of velocity at VO_2 max and on its time to exhaustion. *Archives of Physiology and Biochemistry* 104(3):313–321.

Bishop, G. 2015, July 6. Brett Favre. *Sports Illustrated* 123(1):15–26.

Bishop, T. and E. G. McFarland 1993. Sport-specific: In-season strength program for baseball players. *Strength & Conditioning Journal* 15(4):42–45.

Black, K. 2011. *Business Statistics: For Contemporary Decision Making*. John Wiley & Sons.

Blackburn, M. L. 2013. Ranking the performance of tennis players: An application to women's professional tennis. *Journal of Quantitative Analysis in Sports* 9(4):367–378. 174

Blackwood, T. 2008. Bushidō baseball? Three 'fathers' and the invention of a tradition. *Social Science Japan Journal* 11(2):223–240.

Bloomfield, J., R. Polman, and P. O'Donoghue 2007. Physical demands of different positions in FA Premier League soccer. *Journal of Sports Science & Medicine* 6(1):63.

Boone, J., R. Vaeyens, A. Steyaert, L. V. Bossche, and J. Bourgois 2012. Physical fitness of elite Belgian soccer players by player position. *Journal of Strength & Conditioning Research* 26(8):2051–2057.

Bosco, C., P. Luhtanen, and P. V. Komi 1983. A simple method for measurement of mechanical power in jumping. *European Journal of Applied Physiology and Occupational Physiology* 50(2):273–282. 29

Brand, R., P. Heck, and M. Ziegler 2014. Illegal performance-enhancing drugs and doping in sport: A picture-based brief Implicit Association Test for measuring athletes' attitudes. *Substance Abuse Treatment, Prevention, and Policy* 9(7).

Brand, R., M. Melzer, and N. Hagemann 2011. Towards an Implicit Association Test (IAT) for measuring doping attitudes in sports. Data-based recommendations developed from two recently published tests. *Psychology of Sport and Exercise* 12(3):250–256.

Bredemeier, B. 1975. The assessment of reactive and instrumental athletic aggression. *Psychology of Sport and Motor Behaviour-II*:71–83.

Bressel, E., J. C. Yonker, J. Kras, and E. M. Heath 2007. Comparison of static and dynamic balance in female collegiate soccer, basketball, and gymnastics athletes. *Journal of Athletic Training* 42(1):42.

Brevers, D., B. Dan, X. Noel, and F. Nils 2011. Sport superstition: Mediation of psychological tension on non-professional sportsmen's superstitious rituals. *Journal of Sport Behavior* 34(1):3–24.

Broglio, S. P., J. J. Sosnoff, K. S. Rosengren, and K. McShane 2009. A comparison of balance performance: Computerized dynamic posturography and a random motion platform. *Archives of Physical Medicine and Rehabilitation* 90(1):145–150.

Brown, L. and V. Ferrigno 2014. *Training for Speed, Agility, and Quickness, 3E*. Human Kinetics.

Brown, L. E. and J. P. Weir 2001. ASEP procedures recommendation I: Accurate assessment of muscular strength and power. *Professionalization of Exercise Physiology* 4(11).

Brown, L. P., S. L. Niehues, A. Harrah, P. Yavorsky, H. P. Hirshman, and others 1988. Upper extremity range of motion and isokinetic strength of the internal and external shoulder rotators in Major League Baseball players. *American Journal of Sports Medicine* 16(6):577–585.

Brown, M. T. and others 2003. An analysis on online marketing in the sport industry: User activity, communication objectives, and perceived benefits. *Sport Marketing Quarterly* 12(1):48–55.

Brownell, S. 2008. *The 1904 anthropology days and Olympic games: Sport, race, and American imperialism*. University of Nebraska Press.

Burgos, A. 2007. *Playing America's Game: Baseball, Latinos, and the Color Line*, Volume 23. University of California Press.

Burpee, R. H. and W. Stroll 1936. Measuring reaction time of athletes. *Research Quarterly. American Physical Education Association* 7(1):110–118.

Cale, K. 2010. How well they play the game. *The Hardball Times*.

Campbell, F. G. 2014. *An Insider's Guide to Basketball*. The Rosen Publishing Group.

Campomar, A. 2014. *Golazo!: The Beautiful Game from the Aztecs to the World Cup: the Complete History of how Soccer Shaped Latin America*. Penguin.

Cantwell, J. D. 2004. The physician who invented basketball. *The American journal of cardiology* 93(8):1075–1077.

Carda, R. and M. Looney 1994. Differences in physical characteristics in collegiate base-ball players: A descriptive position by position analysis. *Journal of Sports Medicine and Physical Fitness* 34(4):370–376.

Carlin, B. P. 1996, February. Improved NCAA basketball tournament modeling via point spread and team strength information. *The American Statistician* 50(1):39–43.

Carling, C. 2011. Influence of opposition team formation on physical and skill-related performance in a professional soccer team. *European Journal of Sport Science* 11(3): 155–164.

Carling, C., A. M. Williams, and T. Reilly 2005. *Handbook of Soccer Match Analysis: A Systematic Approach to Improving Performance*. Psychology Press.

Carney, G. 2006. *Burying the Black Sox: How Baseball's Cover-Up of the 1919 World Series Fix Almost Succeeded*. Potomac Books, Inc.

Carroll, B. 1999. *Total Football II: The Official Encyclopedia of the National Football League*. Harper Collins.

Carroll, L. 1989. A comparative study of narcissism, gender, and sex-role orientation among bodybuilders, athletes, and psychology students. *Psychological Reports* 64(3): 999–1006.

Carron, A. V. 2002. Cohesion and performance in sport. *Journal of Sport & Exercise Psychology* 24:168–188.

Carron, A. V. and L. R. Brawley 2000. Cohesion conceptual and measurement issues. *Small Group Research* 31(1):89–106.

Carron, A. V., W. N. Widmeyer, and L. R. Brawley 1985. The development of an instrument to assess cohesion in sport teams: The Group Environment Questionnaire. *Journal of Sport Psychology* 7(3):244–266.

Carvajal, W., A. Ríos, I. Echevarría, M. Martínez, J. Miñoso, D. Rodríguez, and others 2009. Body type and performance of elite Cuban baseball players. *MEDICC Rev* 11 (2):15–20.

Casajús, J. A. 2001. Seasonal variation in fitness variables in professional soccer players. *Journal of Sports Medicine and Physical Fitness* 41(4):463–469.

Casey, S. 2001. *Cautious Crusade: Franklin D. Roosevelt, American Public Opinion, and the War Against Nazi Germany*. Oxford University Press.

Castlebury, F. D., M. J. Hilsenroth, L. Handler, and T. W. Durham 1997. Use of the MMPI-2 personality disorder scales in the assessment of DSM-IV antisocial, borderline, and narcissistic personality disorders. *Assessment* 4(2):155–168.

Cattell, R. B., H. W. Eber, and M. M. Tatsuoka 1970. *Handbook for the Sixteen Personality Factor Questionnaire (16 PF): In Clinical, Educational, Industrial, and Research Psychology, for Use with All Forms of the Test*. Institute for Personality and Ability Testing. 47, 52

Cervone, D., A. D'Amour, L. Bornn, and K. Goldsberry 2014. Pointwise: Predicting points and valuing decisions in real time with NBA optical tracking data. *Proceedings MIT Sloan Sports Analytics*. 37

Chamari, K., A. Chaouachi, M. Hambli, F. Kaouech, U. Wisløff, and C. Castagna 2008. The five-jump test for distance as a field test to assess lower limb explosive power in soccer players. *Journal of Strength & Conditioning Research* 22(3):–950.

Chambers, C. 2006. *Goal!: How Football Conquered the World*. Black Dog Books.

Charnock, B. L., M. W. Wiliams, E. L. Sims, W. E. Garrett, and R. M. Queen 2007. Proprio 5000: A New Method for Assessing Dynamic Balance.

Chartrand, J. M., D. P. Jowdy, and S. J. Danish 1992. The Psychological Skills Inventory for Sports: Psychometric characteristics and applied implications. *Journal of Sport and Exercise Psychology* 14:405–405.

Chi, E. H. 2008. Sensors and ubiquitous computing technologies in sports. *Computers in Sport* 68:249–268. 37, 40

Chin, E. R., E. N. Olson, J. A. Richardson, Q. Yang, C. Humphries, J. M. Shelton, H. Wu, W. Zhu, R. Bassel-Duby, and R. S. Williams 1998. A calcineurin-dependent transcriptional pathway controls skeletal muscle fiber type. *Genes & Development* 12(16):2499–2509.

Clark, J. F., J. K. Ellis, J. Bench, J. Khoury, and P. Graman 2012. High-performance vision training improves batting statistics for University of Cincinnati baseball players. *PloS ONE* 7(1):1–6.

Clark, M., S. Lucett, and D. T. Kirkendall 2010. *NASM's essentials of sports performance training*. Lippincott Williams & Wilkins.

Clarke, K. and R. Warwick 2001. An approach to statistical analysis and interpretation. *Change in Marine Communities* 2.

Clarke, S. R. and D. Dyte 2000. Using official ratings to simulate major tennis tournaments. *International Transactions in Operational Research* 7(6):585–594. 174

Clarkson, H. M. 2000. *Musculoskeletal Assessment: Joint Range of Motion and Manual Muscle Strength*. Lippincott Williams & Wilkins.

Classé, J. G., L. P. Semes, K. M. Daum, R. Nowakowski, L. J. Alexander, J. Wisniewski, J. A. Beisel, K. Mann, R. Rutstein, M. Smith, and others 1997. Association between visual reaction time and batting, fielding, and earned run averages among players of the southern baseball league. *Journal of the American Optometric Association* 68(1): 43–49.

Coate, D. and D. Robbins 2001. The tournament careers of top-ranked men and women tennis professionals: Are the gentlemen more committed than the ladies? *Journal of Labor Research* 22(1):185–193.

Coleman, A. E. and L. M. Lasky 1992. Assessing running speed and body composition in professional baseball players. *Journal of Strength & Conditioning Research* 6(4):207–213.

Coleman, L. 1995. *Fundamental Soccer*. Lerner Publications.

Conn, C. A. and L. Kravitz 2003. The remarkable calorie. *IDEA Personal Trainer* 14:28–35.

Conn, D. 2010. *The Beautiful Game?: Searching for the Soul of Football*. Random House.

Connor-Linton, J. 2003. Chi square tutorial. *Retrieved October* 20:2005.

Constant, C. and A. Murley 1987. A clinical method of functional assessment of the shoulder. *Clinical Orthopaedics and Related Research* 214:160–164.

Constant, C. R., C. Gerber, R. J. Emery, J. O. Søjbjerg, F. Gohlke, and P. Boileau 2008. A review of the constant score: Modifications and guidelines for its use. *Journal of Shoulder and Elbow Surgery* 17(2):355–361.

Cornelissen, S. 2010. Football's tsars: Proprietorship, corporatism and politics in the 2010 FIFA World Cup. *Soccer & Society* 11(1-2):131–143.

Corry, N., R. D. Merritt, S. Mrug, and B. Pamp 2008. The factor structure of the Narcissistic Personality Inventory. *Journal of Personality Assessment* 90(6):593–600.

Costa, G. B., M. R. Huber, and J. T. Saccoman 2007. *Understanding Sabermetrics: An Introduction to the Science of Baseball Statistics*. McFarland.

Costa, G. B., M. R. Huber, and J. T. Saccoman 2009. *Practicing Sabermetrics: Putting the Science of Baseball Statistics to Work*. McFarland.

Covassin, T. and S. Pero 2004. The relationship between self-confidence, mood state, and anxiety among collegiate tennis players. *Journal of Sport Behavior* 27(3):230–242.

Cox, R. H. and others 1998. *Sport Psychology: Concepts and Applications*. (fourth ed.). McGraw-Hill.

Cox, R. H., M. P. Martens, W. D. Russell, and others 2003. Measuring anxiety in athletics: The revised Competitive State Anxiety Inventory-2. *Journal of Sport and Exercise Psychology* 25(4):519–533.

Cox, R. H., W. D. Russell, and R. Marshall 1998. Development of a CSAI-2 short form for assessing competitive state anxiety during and immediately prior to competition. *Journal of Sport Behavior* 21(1):30.

Coyle, E. F., M. E. Feltner, S. A. Kautz, M. T. Hamilton, S. J. Montain, A. M. Baylor, L. D. Abraham, and G. W. Petrek 1991. Physiological and biomechanical factors associated with elite endurance cycling performance. *Medicine and Science in Sports and Exercise* 23(1):93–107.

Craats, R. 2001a. *Baseball*. Weigl Publishers.

Craats, R. 2001b. *Basketball*. Weigl Publishers.

Craft, L. L., T. M. Magyar, B. J. Becker, and D. L. Feltz 2003. The relationship between the Competitive State Anxiety Inventory-2 and sport performance: A meta-analysis. *Journal of Sport & Exercise Psychology*:44–65.

Crawford, J. R. and D. C. Howell 1998. Comparing an individual's test score against norms derived from small samples. *Clinical Neuropsychologist* 12(4):482–486.

Crawley, M. J. 2014. *Statistics: An Introduction Using R*. John Wiley & Sons.

Creighton, D. W., I. Shrier, R. Shultz, W. H. Meeuwisse, and G. O. Matheson 2010. Return-to-play in sport: A decision-based model. *Clinical Journal of Sport Medicine* 20(5):379–385.

Crepeau, R. C. 2014. *NFL Football: A History of America's New National Pastime*. University of Illinois Press.

Crespo, M., M. Reid, D. Miley, and F. Atienza 2003. The relationship between professional tournament structure on the national level and success in men's professional tennis. *Journal of Science and Medicine in Sport* 6(1):3–13. 174

Crespo, M., M. Reid, and A. Quinn 2006. *Tennis psychology: 200+ practical drills and the latest research*. International Tennis Federation.

Cronin, J. B. and K. T. Hansen 2005. Strength and power predictors of sports speed. *Journal of Strength & Conditioning Research* 19(2):349–357.

Cross, D. 2009. Moneyball. *Journal of Revenue & Pricing Management* 8:107–108.

Crossman, J. 1997. Psychological rehabilitation from sports injuries. *Sports Medicine* 23(5):333–339.

Crotin, R. L. and D. K. Ramsey 2012. Stride length compensations and their impacts on brace-transfer ground forces in baseball pitchers. *Proceedings of the 36th Annual American Society of Biomechanics. American Society of Biomechanics*:243–244.

Crowder, M. J. and D. J. Hand 1990. *Analysis of Repeated Measures*. CRC Press.

Crowther, N. B. 2007. *Sport in Ancient Times*. Greenwood Publishing Group.

Csikszentmihalyi, M. 1991. *Flow: The Psychology of Optimal Experience*. HarperPerennial. 46

Cunningham, C. 2006. *American Hoops: The History of United States Olympic Basketball from Berlin to Barcelona*. ProQuest.

Curran, P. J., D. J. Bauer, and M. T. Willoughby 2004. Testing main effects and interactions in latent curve analysis. *Psychological Methods* 9(2):220.

Currey, J. D. 2002. *Bones: structure and mechanics*. Princeton University Press.

Curry, G. 2002. The trinity connection: An analysis of the role of members of Cambridge University in the development of football in the mid-nineteenth century. *Sports Historian* 22(2):46–73.

Curry, G. and E. Dunning 2015. *Association Football: A Study in Figurational Sociology*. Routledge.

Dadebo, B., J. White, and K. P. George 2004, Aug. A survey of flexibility training protocols and hamstring strains in professional football clubs in England. *British Journal of Sports Medicine* 38(4):388–394.

Daly, C. and A. Sachare 1992. *America's Dream Team: The Quest for Olympic Gold*. Turner Pub.

Daneshvar, D. H., C. M. Baugh, C. J. Nowinski, A. C. McKee, R. A. Stern, and R. C. Cantu 2011. Helmets and mouth guards: The role of personal equipment in preventing sport-related concussions. *Clinics in Sports Medicine* 30(1):145–163.

Davenport, T. H. 2006. Competing on analytics. *Harvard Business Review* 84(1):98.

Davis, C. S. 2002. *Statistical Methods for the Analysis of Repeated Measurements*. Springer Science & Business Media.

Davis, P. A. and W. E. Sime 2005. Toward a psychophysiology of performance: Sport psychology principles dealing with anxiety. *International Journal of Stress Management* 12(4):363.

Dawson, P., S. Dobson, and B. Gerrard 2000. Estimating coaching efficiency in professional team sports: Evidence from English Association football. *Scottish Journal of Political Economy* 47(4):399–421.

Dayton, C. M. 1992. Logistic regression analysis. *Stat*:474–574.

De Francisco Palacios, C. M. 2015. Versin reducida del Athlete Burnout Questionnaire (ABQ). In *Revista de psicologa del deporte*, Volume 24, pp. 0177–183.

De Houwer, J. 2002. The Implicit Association Test as a tool for studying dysfunctional associations in psychopathology: Strengths and limitations. *Journal of Behavior Therapy and Experimental Psychiatry* 33(2):115–133.

Dean, H. L., D. Martí, E. Tsui, J. Rinzel, and B. Pesaran 2011. Reaction time correlations during eye–hand coordination: Behavior and modeling. *Journal of Neuroscience* 31(7): 2399–2412.

Delgado, F. 1999. Sport and politics Major League Soccer, constitution, and (the) Latino audience(s). *Journal of Sport & Social Issues* 23(1):41–54.

Dellaserra, C. L., Y. Gao, and L. Ransdell 2014. Use of integrated technology in team sports: A review of opportunities, challenges, and future directions for athletes. *Journal of Strength & Conditioning Research* 28(2):556–573. 37, 40

Delp, M. D. and C. Duan 1996. Composition and size of type I, IIa, IId/x, and IIb fibers and citrate synthase activity of rat muscle. *Journal of Applied Physiology* 80(1):261–270.

DeMaris, A. 1995. A tutorial in logistic regression. *Journal of Marriage and the Family*:956–968.

Deurenberg, P., J. A. Weststrate, and J. C. Seidell 1991. Body Mass Index as a measure of body fatness: Age-and sex-specific prediction formulas. *British Journal of Nutrition* 65 (02):105–114.

Dežman, B., S. Trninić, and D. Dizdar 2001. Expert model of decision-making system for efficient orientation of basketball players to positions and roles in the game—empirical verification. *Collegium Antropologicum* 25(1):141–152.

Diamant, L., J. H. Byrd, and M. J. Himelein 1991. Personality traits and athletic performance. *Mind-body maturity: Psychological approaches to sports, exercise, and fitness*: 227–236.

Dickson, P. 2009. *The Dickson Baseball Dictionary* (third ed.). New York: W.W. Norton & Company.

Didehbani, N., C. M. Cullum, S. Mansinghani, H. Conover, and J. Hart 2013. Depressive symptoms and concussions in aging retired NFL players. *Archives of Clinical Neuropsychology* 28(5):418–424.

Dirks, K. T. 2000. Trust in leadership and team performance: Evidence from NCAA basketball. *Journal of Applied Psychology* 85(6):1004.

Dixon, W. J., F. J. Massey, and others 1969. *Introduction to Statistical Analysis*, Volume 344. McGraw-Hill New York.

Domínguez-Almendros, S., N. Benítez-Parejo, and A. Gonzalez-Ramirez 2011. Logistic regression models. *Allergologia et Immunopathologia* 39(5):295–305.

Donatelli, R., T. S. Ellenbecker, S. R. Ekedahl, J. S. Wilkes, K. Kocher, and J. Adam 2000. Assessment of shoulder strength in professional baseball pitchers. *Journal of Orthopaedic Sports Physical Therapy* 30(9):544–551.

Draper, N. R., H. Smith, and E. Pownell 1966. *Applied Regression Analysis*. Wiley New York.

Drinkwater, E. J., D. B. Pyne, and M. J. McKenna 2008. Design and interpretation of anthropometric and fitness testing of basketball players. *Sports Medicine* 38(7):565–578.

Dufek, J. S. and B. T. Bates 1991. Biomechanical factors associated with injury during landing in jump sports. *Sports Medicine* 12(5):326–337.

Duncan, T. E., S. C. Duncan, and L. A. Strycker 2013. *An Introduction to Latent Variable Growth Curve Modeling: Concepts, Issues, and Application*. Routledge Academic. 67

Dunmore, T. 2011. *Historical Dictionary of Soccer*. Scarecrow Press.

Durall, C. J., R. C. Manske, and G. J. Davies 2001. Avoiding shoulder injury from resistance training. *Strength & Conditioning Journal* 23(5):10.

Ebben, W. P., M. J. Hintz, and C. J. Simenz 2005. Strength and conditioning practices of Major League Baseball strength and conditioning coaches. *Journal of Strength & Conditioning Research* 19(3):538–546.

Edgerton, V. R., J. Smith, and D. Simpson 1975. Muscle fibre type populations of human leg muscles. *Histochemical Journal* 7(3):259–266.

Edwards, T., L. Hardy, and others 1996. The interactive effects of intensity and direction of cognitive and somatic anxiety and self-confidence upon performance. *Journal of Sport and Exercise Psychology* 18:296–312.

Egloff, B. and S. C. Schmukle 2002. Predictive validity of an Implicit Association Test for assessing anxiety. *Journal of Personality and Social Psychology* 83(6):1441.

Einolf, K. W. 2004. Is winning everything? A data envelopment analysis of Major League Baseball and the National Football League. *Journal of Sports Economics* 5(2):127–151. 177

Elliott, A. C. and W. A. Woodward 2007. *Statistical Analysis Quick Reference Guidebook: With SPSS Examples*. Sage.

Elman, W. F. and S. J. McKelvie 2003. Narcissism in football players: Stereotype or reality. *Athletic Insight* 5(1).

Engström, B. K. and P. A. Renström 1998. How can injuries be prevented in the World Cup soccer athlete? *Clinics in Sports Medicine* 17(4):755–768.

Ermes, M., J. Parkka, J. Mantyjarvi, and I. Korhonen 2008. Detection of daily activities and sports with wearable sensors in controlled and uncontrolled conditions. *IEEE Transactions on Information Technology in Biomedicine* 12(1):20–26.

Eschker, E., S. J. Perez, and M. V. Siegler 2004. The NBA and the influx of international basketball players. *Applied Economics* 36(10):1009–1020.

Falla, J., R. Lester, D. M. Nelson, R. Schmidt, J. L. Shulman, W. G. Bowen, R. A. Smith, and J. S. Watterson 2015. Football, professional. *Sports in America from Colonial Times to the Twenty-First Century: An Encyclopedia*:361.

Fanning, M. 2014. A study of predictive measures of winning percentage in Major League Baseball over the past decade.

Faubert, J. 2013. Professional athletes have extraordinary skills for rapidly learning complex and neutral dynamic visual scenes. *Scientific Reports* 3.

Fay, M. P. and M. A. Proschan 2010. Wilcoxon-Mann-Whitney or *t*-test? On assumptions for hypothesis tests and multiple interpretations of decision rules. *Statistics Surveys* 4:1.

Fazey, J. and L. Hardy 1988. *The Inverted-U Hypothesis: A Catastrophe for Sport Psychology*. British Association of Sports Sciences.

Fédération Internationale de Football Association 2015. *Laws of the Game*. Retrieved from the World Wide Web, December 11, 2015 at `http://www.FIFA.com/about-FIFA/official-documents/law-regulations/index.html#lawsOfTheGame`. 236

Feir-Walsh, B. J. and L. E. Toothaker 1974. An empirical comparison of the ANOVA *F*-test, normal scores test and Kruskal-Wallis test under violation of assumptions. *Educational and Psychological Measurement* 34(4):789–799.

Feltz, D. and M. Chase 1998. The measurement of self-efficacy and confidence in sport. *Advances in Sport and Exercise Psychology Measurement*:65–80.

Feltz, D., S. Short, and P. Sullivan 2008. Self efficacy in sport: Research and strategies for working with athletes, teams and coaches. *International Journal of Sports Science and Coaching* 3(2):293–295.

Ferraro, T. and S. Rush 2000. Why athletes resist sport psychology. *Athletic Insight* 2(3): 9–14.

FIBA-Fédération Internationale 2000. Official basketball rules for men and women–as adopted by the central board of FIBA on 5th May 2000, Munich, Germany. *Web: http://www. fiba. com.*

Fichman, M. and M. A. Fichman 2012. From Darwin to the diamond: How baseball and Billy Beane arrived at Moneyball. *Available at SSRN 2112109.*

Field, A. 2009. *Discovering Statistics Using SPSS.* Sage publications.

Figueroa, P., N. Leite, R. M. Barros, I. Cohen, and G. Medioni 2004. Tracking soccer players using the graph representation. In *Proceedings of the 17th International Conference on Pattern Recognition, 2004. ICPR 2004.*, Volume 4, pp. 787–790.

Filaire, E., X. Bernain, M. Sagnol, and G. Lac 2001. Preliminary results on mood state, salivary testosterone: Cortisol ratio and team performance in a professional soccer team. *European Journal of Applied Physiology* 86(2):179–184.

Filipčič, T., A. Filipčič, and T. Berendijaš 2008. Comparison of game characteristics of male and female tennis players at Roland Garros 2005. *Acta Univ Palacki Olomuc. Gymnica* 38(3):21–28.

Finnoff, J. T., V. J. Peterson, J. H. Hollman, and J. Smith 2009. Intrarater and interrater reliability of the Balance Error Scoring System (BESS). *PM&R* 1(1):50–54.

Fischer, B. and L. Rogal 1986. Eye-hand-coordination in man: A reaction time study. *Biological Cybernetics* 55(4):253–261.

Fischer, D. 2015. *The Super Bowl: The First Fifty Years of America's Greatest Game.* Skyhorse Publishing, Inc.

Fischman, M. G. and T. Schneider 1985. Skill level, vision, and proprioception in simple one-hand catching. *Journal of Motor Behavior* 17(2):219–229.

Fisher, R. and J. E. Katz 2008. Social-desirability bias and the validity of self-reported values. 17:105–120.

Fisher, R. and K. Wakefield 1998. Factors leading to group identification: A field study of winners and losers. *Psychology & Marketing* 15(1):23–40.

Fitts, R. H. and J. J. Widrick 1995. Muscle mechanics: Adaptations with exercise-training. *Exercise and Sport Sciences Reviews* 24:427–473.

Fitts, R. K. 2012. *Banzai Babe Ruth: Baseball, Espionage, & Assassination During the 1934 Tour of Japan.* University of Nebraska Press.

Fitzpatrick, R. 2012. *El Clasico: Barcelona V Real Madrid: Football's Greatest Rivalry.* Bloomsbury Publishing.

Flake, C. R., M. J. Dufur, and E. L. Moore 2013. Advantage men: The sex pay gap in professional tennis. *International Review for the Sociology of Sport* 48(3):366–376.

Fleishman, E. A. 1964. *Structure and Measurement of Physical Fitness.* Prentice-Hall.

Fleishman, E. A. and G. D. Ellison 1962. A factor analysis of fine manipulative tests. *Journal of Applied Psychology* 46(2):96.

Fleishman, E. A., E. J. Kremer, and G. W. Shoup 1961. The Dimensions of Physical Fitness: A Factor Analysis of Speed, Flexibility, Balance, and Coordination Tests. Technical Report, DTIC Document.

Formosa, D. and P. Hamburger 2009. *Baseball Field Guide: An In-depth Illustrated Guide to the Complete Rules of Baseball.* Da Capo Press.

Fortenbaugh, D., G. Fleisig, and B. Bolt 2010. Coming down: Throwing mechanics of baseball catchers. In *ISBS-Conference Proceedings Archive*, Volume 1 (1).

Fox, E. L., R. W. Bowers, M. L. Foss, and others 1993. *The Physiological Basis for Exercise and Sport.* Brown & Benchmark.

Fox, J. 2005. Getting started with the R Commander: A basic-statistics graphical user interface to R. *Journal of Statistical Software* 14(9):1–42.

Francis, S. R., M. B. Andersen, and P. Maley 2000. Physiotherapists' and male professional athletes' views on psychological skills for rehabilitation. *Journal of Science and Medicine in Sport* 3(1):17–29.

Frank, K. A. 2000. Impact of a confounding variable on a regression coefficient. *Sociological Methods & Research* 29(2):147–194.

Fredricks, G. A. and R. B. Nelsen 2007. On the relationship between Spearman's rho and Kendall's tau for pairs of continuous random variables. *Journal of Statistical Planning and Inference* 137(7):2143–2150.

Fredricks, J. A. and J. S. Eccles 2005. Sport psychology. *Journal of Sport & Exercise Psychology* 27:3–31.

Freedman, L. 2010. *The Day All the Stars Came Out: Major League Baseball's First All-Star Game, 1933.* McFarland.

Friend, J., A. Leunes, and others 1990. Predicting baseball player performance. *Journal of Sport Behavior* 13(2):73–86.

Fry, A. C. and W. J. Kraemer 1991. Physical performance characteristics of American collegiate football players. *Journal of Strength & Conditioning Research* 5(3):126–138.

Fry, R. W., A. R. Morton, and D. Keast 1991. Overtraining in athletes. *Sports Medicine* 12 (1):32–65.

Fry, T. R., G. Galanos, and A. Posso 2014. Let's get Messi? Top-scorer productivity in the European Champions League. *Scottish Journal of Political Economy* 61(3):261–279. 177

Furst, D. M. and J. S. Hardman 1988. The iceberg profile and young competitive swimmers. *Perceptual and Motor Skills* 67(2):478–478.

Fydrich, T., D. Dowdall, and D. L. Chambless 1992. Reliability and validity of the Beck Anxiety Inventory. *Journal of Anxiety Disorders* 6(1):55–61.

Gallego, J. H. 2013. El Fútbol Británico antes de la International Board,(1863-1886). *Cuadernos de Fútbol: Primera revista de historia del fútbol Español* 42(1):10–11.

Galli, N., R. S. Vealey, and others 2008. Bouncing back from adversity: Athletes experiences of resilience. *The Sport Psychologist* 22(3):316–335.

Gandolfi, G. (ed.) 2009. *NBA Coaches Playbook: Techniques, Tactics, and Teaching Points.* Champaign, Ill.: Human Kinetics.

Gardner, F. L. 2001. Applied sport psychology in professional sports: The team psychologist. *Professional Psychology: Research and Practice* 32(1):34.

Garstecki, M. A., R. W. Latin, and M. M. Cuppett 2004. Comparison of selected physical fitness and performance variables between NCAA Division I and II football players. *Journal of Strength & Conditioning Research* 18(2):292–297.

Gartner, L. 1996. The Rookie Primer. *Radcliffe Rugby Football Club*.

Gastin, P. B. 2001. Energy system interaction and relative contribution during maximal exercise. *Sports Medicine* 31(10):725–741.

Gelman, A. and J. Hill 2006. *Data Analysis Using Regression and Multilevel/Hierarchical Models*. Cambridge University Press.

Gibbons, J. D. and S. Chakraborti 2011. *Nonparametric Statistical Inference*. Springer.

Gifford, C. 2008. *Soccer*. The Rosen Publishing Group.

Gifford, C. 2009. *American Football*. Evans Brothers.

Gil, S. M., J. Gil, F. Ruiz, A. Irazusta, and J. Irazusta 2007. Physiological and anthropometric characteristics of young soccer players according to their playing position: Relevance for the selection process. *Journal of Strength & Conditioning Research* 21(2):438–445.

Ginsburg, D. E. 2004. *The fix is in: A History of Baseball Gambling and Game Fixing Scandals*. McFarland.

Giossos, Y., A. Sotiropoulos, A. Souglis, and G. Dafopoulou 2011. Reconsidering on the early types of football. *Baltic Journal of Health and Physical Activity* 3(2):129–134.

Girden, E. R. 1992. *ANOVA: Repeated Measures*. Number 84. Sage.

Giulianotti, R. 2012. *Football*. Wiley Online Library.

Glazer, D. D. 2009, Mar-Apr. Development and preliminary validation of the Injury-Psychological Readiness to Return to Sport (I-PRRS) scale. *Journal of Athletic Training* 44(2):185–189.

Gobbi, A. and R. Francisco 2006. Factors affecting return to sports after anterior cruciate ligament reconstruction with patellar tendon and hamstring graft: A prospective clinical investigation. *Knee Surgery, Sports Traumatology, Arthroscopy* 14(10):1021–1028.

Goff, B. L., W. F. S. II, and R. D. Tollison 1997. Batter up! Moral hazard and the effects of the designated hitter rule on hit batsmen. *Economic Inquiry* 35(3):555–561.

Goldblatt, D. 2008. *The Ball is Round: A Global History of Soccer*. Penguin.

Goldstein, W. 2014. *Playing for Keeps: A History of Early Baseball*. Cornell University Press.

Gollnick, P., K. Piehl, C. Saubert, R. Armstrong, and B. Saltin 1972. Diet, exercise, and glycogen changes in human muscle fibers. *Journal of Applied Physiology* 33(4):421–425.

Gollnick, P. D., R. Armstrong, B. Saltin, C. Saubert, W. L. Sembrowich, and R. E. Shepherd 1973. Effect of training on enzyme activity and fiber composition of human skeletal muscle. *Journal of Applied Physiology* 34(1):107–111.

Goplerud III, C. P. 1997. Collective bargaining in the National Football League: A historical and comparative analysis. *Villanova Sports & Entertainment Law Journal* 4:13.

Gotwals, J. K., J. G. Dunn, and H. A. Wayment 2003. An examination of perfectionism and self-esteem in intercollegiate athletes. *Journal of Sport Behavior* 26(1):17. 48, 52

Grabiner, D. and S. P. Sabermetrics 2006. Do clutch hitters exist? In *SABRBoston Presents Sabermetrics Conference*.

Gray, R. 2004. Attending to the execution of a complex sensorimotor skill: Expertise differences, choking, and slumps. *Journal of Experimental Psychology: Applied* 10(1): 42.

Gray-Little, B., V. S. Williams, and T. D. Hancock 1997. An item response theory analysis of the Rosenberg Self-Esteem Scale. *Personality and Social Psychology Bulletin* 23(5): 443–451. 48, 52

Green, S. L. and R. S. Weinberg 2001. Relationships among athletic identity, coping skills, social support, and the psychological impact of injury in recreational participants. *Journal of Applied Sport Psychology* 13(1):40–59.

Greenwald, A. G., D. E. McGhee, and J. L. Schwartz 1998. Measuring individual differences in implicit cognition: The Implicit Association Test. *Journal of Personality and Social Psychology* 74(6):1464.

Gribble, P. A. and J. Hertel 2003. Considerations for normalizing measures of the Star Excursion Balance Test. *Measurement in Physical Education and Exercise science* 7(2): 89–100. 29

Grimm, L. G. and P. R. Yarnold 1995. *Reading and Understanding Multivariate Statistics.* American Psychological Association.

Gripentrog, J. 2010. The transnational pastime: Baseball and American perceptions of Japan in the 1930s. *Diplomatic History* 34(2):247–273.

Groeneveld, R. A. 1990, November. Ranking teams in a league with two divisions of t teams. *The American Statistician* 44(4):277–281.

Guay, F., R. J. Vallerand, and C. Blanchard 2000. On the assessment of situational intrinsic and extrinsic motivation: The Situational Motivation Scale (SIMS). *Motivation and Emotion* 24(3):175–213. 42

Guskiewicz, K. M. and D. H. Perrin 1996. Research and clinical applications of assessing balance. *Journal of Sport Rehabilitation* 5:45–63.

Guthrie-Shimizu, S. 2004. For love of the game: Baseball in early US-Japanese encounters and the rise of a transnational sporting fraternity. *Diplomatic History* 28(5):637–662.

Guthrie-Shimizu, S. 2008. Baseball in US-Japanese Relations. *Soft power superpowers: Cultural and national assets of Japan and the United States*:154.

Gutman, B. 1979. *Modern Soccer Superstars.* Putnam Pub Group.

Guttmann, A. 2002. *The Olympics, A History of the Modern Games.* University of Illinois Press.

Haas, D. J. 2003. Technical efficiency in the Major League Soccer. *Journal of Sports Economics* 4(3):203–215.

Haff, G. G. and C. Dumke 2012. *Laboratory Manual for Exercise Physiology.* Human Kinetics. 13, 18, 30, 32, 33, 40

Hample, Z. 2007. *Watching Baseball Smarter: A Professional Fan's Guide for Beginners, Semi-experts, and Deeply Serious Geeks* (Revised and Updated ed.). New York: Vintage/Random House.

Hand, D. J. 2012. Who's # 1? The Science of Rating and Ranking. *Journal of Applied Statistics* 39(10):2309–2310.

Hanin, Y. L. 1995. Individual Zones of Optimal Functioning (IZOF) model: An idiographic approach to performance anxiety. *Sport Psychology: An Analysis of Athlete behavior* 3:103–119.

Hanin, Y. L. 1997. Emotions and athletic performance: Individual Zones of Optimal Functioning model. *European Yearbook of Sport Psychology* 1:29–72.

Hanin, Y. L. 2000. Individual Zones of Optimal Functioning (IZOF) model. *Emotions in Sport*:65–89.

Hanin, Y. L. 2004. Emotions in sport: An individualized approach. *Encyclopedia of Applied Psychology* 1:739–750.

Hanlon, T. W. 2009. *The Sports Rules Book*. Human Kinetics.

Hardy, L. 1996. A test of catastrophe models of anxiety and sports performance against multidimensional anxiety theory models using the method of dynamic differences. *Anxiety, Stress, and Coping* 9(1):69–86.

Hardy, L. 1996. Testing the predictions of the cusp catastrophe model of anxiety and performance. *Sport Psychologist* 10:140–156.

Hardy, L. and G. Parfitt 1991. A catastrophe model of anxiety and performance. *British Journal of Psychology* 82(2):163–178.

Härtel, T. and A. Schleichardt 2008. Evaluation of start techniques in sports swimming by dynamics simulation (P18). In *The Engineering of Sport 7*, pp. 89–96. Springer.

Hastie, T., R. Tibshirani, and J. Friedman 2009. *The Elements of Statistical Learning: Data Mining, Inference, and Prediction* (second ed.). New York: Springer. 67

Haupt, H. A. 2001. Upper extremity injuries associated with strength training. *Clinics in Sports Medicine* 20(3):481–490.

Hausman, J. A. and G. K. Leonard 1997. Superstars in the National Basketball Association: Economic value and policy. *Journal of Labor Economics* 15(4):586–624.

Heil, J. 1993. *Psychology of Sport Injury*. Champaign, Ill.: Human Kinetics.

Herman, M. 2009. *The Complete Guide to Kickology*. (third ed.). Footballguys. `http://www.footballguys.com/cdcheck/kickologylite.pdf`.

Hetzler, R. K., B. L. Schroeder, J. J. Wages, C. D. Stickley, and I. F. Kimura 2010, Jun. Anthropometry increases 1 Repetition Maximum predictive ability of NFL-225 test for Division IA college football players. *Journal of Strength and Conditioning Research* 24(6):1429–1439.

Heyward, V. H., D. R. Wagner, and others 2004. *Applied Body Composition Assessment*. Human Kinetics. 19

Hibbs, A. E., K. G. Thompson, D. French, A. Wrigley, and I. Spears 2008. Optimizing performance by improving core stability and core strength. *Sports Medicine* 38(12):995–1008.

Hickey, K. C., C. E. Quatman, G. D. Myer, K. R. Ford, J. A. Brosky, and T. E. Hewett 2009, Dec. Methodological report: dynamic field tests used in an NFL Combine setting to identify lower-extremity functional asymmetries. *Journal of Strength and Conditioning Research* 23(9):2500–2506.

Hill, D. M., S. Hanton, S. Fleming, and N. Matthews 2009. A re-examination of choking in sport. *European Journal of Sport Science* 9(4):203–212.

Hill, D. M., S. Hanton, N. Matthews, and S. Fleming 2010. Choking in sport: A review. *International Review of Sport and Exercise Psychology* 3(1):24–39.

Hill, J. R. and W. Spellman 1983. Professional baseball: The reserve clause and salary structure. *Industrial Relations: A Journal of Economy and Society* 22(1):1–19.

Hill, L. 2010. Football as code: The social diffusion of "soccer" in South Africa. *Soccer & Society* 11(1-2):12–28.

Ho, R. 2006. *Handbook of Univariate and Multivariate Data Analysis and Interpretation with SPSS*. CRC Press.

Hochbaum, D. S. 2015. *Ranking Sports Teams and The Inverse Equal Paths Problem*. http://ieor.berkeley.edu/People/Faculty/hochbaum.htm.

Hoffman, J. 2006. *Norms for Fitness, Performance, and Health*. Human Kinetics. 29

Hoffman, J., C. Association, and others 2012. *NSCA's Guide to Program Design*. Human Kinetics.

Hoffman, J., M. Bar-Eli, and G. Tenenbaum 1999. An examination of mood changes and performance in a professional basketball team. *Journal of Sports Medicine and Physical Fitness* 39(1):74.

Hoffman, J. R., S. Epstein, M. Einbinder, and Y. Weinstein 2000. A comparison between the Wingate anaerobic power test to both vertical jump and line drill tests in basketball players. *Journal of Strength & Conditioning Research* 14(3):261–264.

Hoffman, J. R., J. Vazquez, N. Pichardo, and G. Tenenbaum 2009. Anthropometric and performance comparisons in professional baseball players. *Journal of Strength & Conditioning Research* 23(8):2173–2178.

Hoffmann, F., G. Falk, and M. J. Manning 2013. *Football and American Identity*. Routledge.

Hofmann, W., B. Gawronski, T. Gschwendner, H. Le, and M. Schmitt 2005. A meta-analysis on the correlation between the Implicit Association Test and explicit self-report measures. *Personality and Social Psychology Bulletin* 31(10):1369–1385.

Hopwood, C. J., K. M. Thomas, K. E. Markon, A. G. Wright, and R. F. Krueger 2012. DSM-5 personality traits and DSM–IV personality disorders. *Journal of Abnormal Psychology* 121(2):424.

Horn, T. S. 2008. *Advances in Sport Psychology*. Champaign, Ill.: Human Kinetics.

Hosmer, D. W., T. Hosmer, S. Le Cessie, S. Lemeshow, and others 1997. A comparison of goodness-of-fit tests for the logistic regression model. *Statistics in Medicine* 16(9): 965–980.

Hosmer, D. W., S. Taber, and S. Lemeshow 1991. The importance of assessing the fit of logistic regression models: A case study. *American Journal of Public Health* 81(12): 1630–1635.

Hsu, H. and P. A. Lachenbruch 2008. Paired *t*-test. *Wiley Encyclopedia of Clinical Trials*.

Hughes, S., M. Shank, and others 2005. Defining scandal in sports: Media and corporate sponsor perspectives. *Sport Marketing Quarterly* 14(4):207. 175

Hurley, B. F. 1995, Nov. Age, gender, and muscular strength. *The Journals of Gerontology. Series A, Biological Sciences and Medical Sciences* 50 Spec No:41–44.

Hyman, R. 1953. Stimulus information as a determinant of reaction time. *Journal of Experimental Psychology* 45(3):188.

International Tennis Federation 2015. *2015 Rules of Tennis*. Available in English, French, and Spanish. Retrieved from the World Wide Web, December 11, 2015 at http://www.itftennis.com/officiating/rulebooks/rules-of-tennis.aspx. 241

Isberg, L. 2000. Anger, aggressive behavior, and athletic performance. *Emotions in Sport* 1:13–33.

Iwase, S. and H. Saito 2004. Parallel tracking of all soccer players by integrating detected positions in multiple view images. In *Proceedings of the 17th International Conference on Pattern Recognition, 2004. ICPR 2004.*, Volume 4, pp. 751–754.

Izenman, A. J. 2008. *Modern Multivariate Statistical Techniques: Regression, Classification, and Manifold Learning*. New York: Springer. 67

Izquierdo, M., K. Häkkinen, J. J. Gonzalez-Badillo, J. Ibanez, and E. M. Gorostiaga 2002. Effects of long-term training specificity on maximal strength and power of the upper and lower extremities in athletes from different sports. *European Journal of Applied Physiology* 87(3):264–271.

Jackson, A. S. and M. L. Pollock 1978. Generalized equations for predicting body density of men. *British Journal of Nutrition* 40(03):497–504.

Jackson, S. A., P. R. Thomas, H. W. Marsh, and C. J. Smethurst 2001. Relationships between flow, self-concept, psychological skills, and performance. *Journal of Applied Sport Psychology* 13(2):129–153.

James, B. 2014. *The Bill James' Guide to Baseball Managers*. Diversion Books.

Jarmey, C. 2013. *The Concise Book of Muscles*. North Atlantic Books.

Jeličić, M., M. Trninić, and I. Jelaska 2010. Differences between three types of basketball players on the basis of situation-related efficiency. *Acta Kinesiologica* 1:82–89.

Jenkinson, B. 2007. *The Year Babe Ruth Hit 104 Home Runs: Recrowning Baseball's Greatest Slugger*. Da Capo Press.

Jiménez, I. P. and M. T. Pain 2008. Relative age effect in Spanish Association Football: Its extent and implications for wasted potential. *Journal of Sports Sciences* 26(10):995–1003.

Johnson, D. 2013. *The Complete Guide to Pitching*. Human Kinetics.

Johnson, L. 1992. Patterns of shoulder flexibility among college baseball players. *Journal of Athletic Training* 27(1):44–49.

Johnson, M., J. Winkin, J. Leggett, and P. McMahon 2001. *Baseball Skills and Drills*. Human Kinetics.

Johnson, R. A., D. W. Wichern, and others 1992. *Applied Multivariate Statistical Analysis*, Volume 4. Prentice hall Englewood Cliffs, NJ.

Johnston, D. and J. Gigliotti 2005. *Watching Football: Discovering the Game within the Game*. Globe Pequot.

Jones, G., S. Hanton, and A. Swain 1994. Intensity and interpretation of anxiety symptoms in elite and non-elite sports performers. *Personality and Individual Differences* 17(5):657–663.

Jones, G. and A. Swain 1992. Intensity and direction as dimensions of competitive state anxiety and relationships with competitiveness. *Perceptual and Motor Skills* 74(2):467–472.

Jones, R. and T. Tranter 1999. *Soccer Strategies: Defensive and Attacking Tactics*. Reedswain Inc.

Jordet, G., E. Hartman, C. Visscher, and K. A. Lemmink 2007. Kicks from the penalty mark in soccer: The roles of stress, skill, and fatigue for kick outcomes. *Journal of Sports Sciences* 25(2):121–129.

Jowett, S. and I. Cockerill 2003. Olympic medallists' perspective of the althlete–coach relationship. *Psychology of Sport and Exercise* 4(4):313–331.

Jukić, I., G. Sporiš, and D. Vuleta 2010. Fitness Profiling in Soccer: Physical and Physiologic Characteristics of Elite Players. In *The Second World Conference on Science and Soccer*.

Kahn, L. M. 1991. Discrimination in professional sports: A survey of the literature. *Industrial & Labor Relations Review* 44(3):395–418.

Karpinski, A. 2004. Measuring self-esteem using the Implicit Association Test: The role of the other. *Personality and Social Psychology Bulletin* 30(1):22–34.

Karpinski, A. and J. L. Hilton 2001. Attitudes and the Implicit Association Test. *Journal of Personality and Social Psychology* 81(5):774.

Katch, F., E. D. Michael, and S. M. Horvath 1967. Estimation of body volume by underwater weighing: Description of a simple method. *Journal of Applied Physiology* 23(5): 811–813.

Kayali, F. 2013. Playing ball. *Sports Videogames*:197.

Keith, T. Z. 2014. *Multiple Regression and Beyond: An Introduction to Multiple Regression and Structural Equation Modeling*. Routledge. 64

Kelly, B. T., W. R. Kadrmas, and K. P. Speer 1996. The manual muscle examination for rotator cuff strength an electromyographic investigation. *American Journal of Sports Medicine* 24(5):581–588.

Kennedy, J. 2008. 'El Primer Crack'of Argentine basketball: Oscar Furlong. *Sporting Traditions in Ireland and Latin America*:49.

Kenney, W. L., J. Wilmore, and D. Costill 2015. *Physiology of Sport and Exercise, 6th Edition*. Human Kinetics.

Kenny, D. A., L. Mannetti, A. Pierro, S. Livi, and D. A. Kashy 2002. The statistical analysis of data from small groups. *Journal of Personality and Social Psychology* 83(1):126.

Kerr, J. 1985. The experience of arousal: A new basis for studying arousal effects in sport. *Journal of Sports Sciences* 3(3):169–179.

Kerr, J. H. and others 1999. The role of aggression and violence in sport: A rejoinder to the ISSP position stand. *Sport Psychologist* 13(1):83–88.

Keselman, H., and others 1998. Statistical practices of educational researchers: An analysis of their ANOVA, MANOVA, and ANCOVA analyses. *Review of Educational Research* 68(3):350–386.

Kibler, W. B., T. J. Chandler, B. P. Livingston, and E. P. Roetert 1996, May-Jun. Shoulder range of motion in elite tennis players: Effect of age and years of tournament play. *American Journal of Sports Medicine* 24(3):279–285.

King, D. 2006. Hold-up in the NFL:Team specific investment in the National Football League. Ph.D. thesis, Department of Economics-Simon Fraser University.

Kinzey, S. J. and C. W. Armstrong 1998. The reliability of the Star Excursion [Balance] Test in assessing dynamic balance. *Journal of Orthopaedic & Sports Physical Therapy* 27 (5):356–360. 29

Klaassen, F. and J. R. Magnus 2014. *Analyzing Wimbledon: The Power of Statistics*. Oxford University Press. 174

Klaassen, F. J. and J. R. Magnus 1998. *On the Independence and Identical Distribution of Points in Tennis*. Tilburg University.

Klaassen, F. J. and J. R. Magnus 2003. Forecasting the winner of a tennis match. *European Journal of Operational Research* 148(2):257–267.

Kleine, D. 1990. Anxiety and sport performance: A meta-analysis. *Anxiety Research* 2(2): 113–131.

Kloke, J. and J. W. McKean 2014. *Nonparametric Statistical Methods Using R*. Boca Raton, Fla.: Chapman and Hall/CRC. 67

Kolber, M. J., K. S. Beekhuizen, M.-S. S. Cheng, and M. A. Hellman 2010. Shoulder injuries attributed to resistance training: A brief review. *Journal of Strength & Conditioning Research* 24(6):1696–1704.

Komi, P. V. and C. Bosco 1978. Muscles by men and women. *Medicine and Science in Sports* 10(4):261–265.

Korch, R. 1990. *The Official Pro Football Hall of Fame Play Book*. Simon & Schuster.

Korhonen, M. T., A. Cristea, M. Alén, K. Häkkinen, S. Sipilä, A. Mero, J. T. Viitasalo, L. Larsson, and H. Suominen 2006. Aging, muscle fiber type, and contractile function in sprint-trained athletes. *Journal of Applied Physiology* 101(3):906–917.

Kornspan, A. S. 2014. A historical analysis of the Chicago Cubs' use of statistics to analyze baseball performance. *NINE: A Journal of Baseball History and Culture* 23(1):17–40.

Kovacs, M. M. S. 2007. Tennis physiology. *Sports Medicine* 37(3):189–198.

Kraemer, W. J. 1997. A series of studies-the physiological basis for strength training in American football: Fact over philosophy. *Journal of Strength & Conditioning Research* 11(3):131–142.

Kraemer, W. J. and N. A. Ratamess 2004. Fundamentals of resistance training: progression and exercise prescription. *Medicine and Science in Sports and Exercise* 36(4):674–688.

Kraemer, W. J., J. C. Torine, R. Silvestre, D. N. French, N. A. Ratamess, B. A. Spiering, D. L. Hatfield, J. L. Vingren, and J. S. Volek 2005. Body size and composition of National Football League players. *Journal of Strength & Conditioning Research* 19(3):485–489.

Krane, V. 1992. Conceptual and methodological considerations in sport anxiety research: From the inverted-U hypothesis to catastrophe theory. *Quest* 44(1):72–87.

Krane, V. and J. M. Williams 1994. Cognitive anxiety, somatic anxiety, and confidence in track and field athletes: The impact of gender, competitive level and task characteristics. *International Journal of Sport Psychology*.

Krause, J., D. Meyer, and J. Meyer 2008. *Basketball Skills and Drills*. Human Kinetics.

Krautmann, A., P. Von Allmen, and D. J. Berri 2009. The underpayment of restricted players in north American sports leagues. *International Journal of Sport Finance* 4(3): 161–175.

Krohne, H. W. and C. Hindel 1988. Trait anxiety, state anxiety, and coping behavior as predictors of athletic performance. *Anxiety Research* 1(3):225–234.

Krumer, A., T. Shavit, and M. Rosenboim 2011. Why do professional athletes have different time preferences than non-athletes? *Judgment and Decision Making* 6(6):542–551.

Kuhn, G. 2011. *Soccer vs. the State: Tackling Football and Radical Politics*. PM Press.

Kuzmits, F. E. and A. J. Adams 2008, Nov. The NFL Combine: Does it predict performance in the National Football League? *Journal of Strength and Conditioning Research* 22(6):1721–1727.

Kwak, D. H., G. E. Clavio, A. N. Eagleman, and K. T. Kim 2010. Exploring the antecedents and consequences of personalizing sport video game experiences. *Sport Marketing Quarterly* 19(4):217–225.

Laby, D. M., J. L. Davidson, L. J. Rosenbaum, C. Strasser, M. F. Mellman, A. L. Rosenbaum, and D. G. Kirschen 1996. The visual function of professional baseball players. *American Journal of Ophthalmology* 122(4):476–485.

Lago, C. and R. Martín 2007. Determinants of possession of the ball in soccer. *Journal of Sports Sciences* 25(9):969–974.

Lago-Peñas, C., L. Casais, A. Dellal, E. Rey, and E. Domínguez 2011. Anthropometric and physiological characteristics of young soccer players according to their playing positions: Relevance for competition success. *Journal of Strength & Conditioning Research* 25(12):3358–3367.

Lago-Peñas, C. and A. Dellal 2010. Ball possession strategies in elite soccer according to the evolution of the match-score: The influence of situational variables. *Journal of Human Kinetics* 25:93–100.

Lancaster, H. O. 1969. *Chi-Square Distribution*. Wiley Online Library.

Lane, A. M., D. F. Sewell, P. C. Terry, D. Bartram, and M. S. Nesti 1999. Confirmatory factor analysis of the Competitive State Anxiety Inventory-2. *Journal of Sports Sciences* 17(6):505–512.

Lane, D. C. 2004. From Mao to Yao: New game plan for China in the era of basketball globalization. *Pac. Rim L. & Pol'y J.* 13:127.

Langville, A. N. and C. D. Meyer 2012. *Who's #1? The Science of Rating and Ranking.* Princeton, N.J.: Princeton University Press. 176

Lapinski, M., E. Berkson, T. Gill, M. Reinold, J. Paradiso, and others 2009. A distributed wearable, wireless sensor system for evaluating professional baseball pitchers and batters. In *International Symposium on Wearable Computers, 2009. ISWC'09*, pp. 131–138. 37

Larsson, L., G. Grimby, and J. Karlsson 1979. Muscle strength and speed of movement in relation to age and muscle morphology. *Journal of Applied Physiology* 46(3):451–456.

Latin, R. W., K. Berg, and T. Baechle 1994. Physical and performance characteristics of NCAA Division I male basketball players. *Journal of Strength & Conditioning Research* 8(4):214–218.

Laviers, K., G. Sukthankar, D. W. Aha, M. Molineaux, C. Darken, and others 2009. Improving Offensive Performance through Opponent Modeling. In *AIIDE*.

Leddy, M. H., M. J. Lambert, and B. M. Ogles 1994. Psychological consequences of athletic injury among high-level competitors. *Research Quarterly for Exercise and Sport* 65(4): 347–354.

Leeds, M. A. and S. Kowalewski 2001. Winner take all in the NFL the effect of the salary cap and free agency on the compensation of skill position players. *Journal of Sports Economics* 2(3):244–256.

Lehman, G., E. J. Drinkwater, and D. G. Behm 2013. Correlation of throwing velocity to the results of lower-body field tests in male college baseball players. *Journal of Strength & Conditioning Research* 27(4):902–908.

Lemyre, P.N., D. C. Treasure, and G. C. Roberts 2006. Sport psychology. *Journal of Sport & Exercise Psychology* 28:32–48.

Levinger, I., C. Goodman, D. L. Hare, G. Jerums, D. Toia, and S. Selig 2009. The reliability of the 1RM strength test for untrained middle-aged individuals. *Journal of Science and Medicine in Sport* 12(2):310–316.

Lewis, M. 2003. *Moneyball: The Art of Winning an Unfair Game*. New York: W. W. Norton & Company. 175

Light, R. J. and B. H. Margolin 1971. An analysis of variance for categorical data. *Journal of the American Statistical Association* 66(335):534–544.

Lin, C.C., V. Chen, C.C. Yu, and Y.C. Lin 2006. A schema to determine basketball defense strategies using a fuzzy expert system. In *Proceedings of the 7th WSEAS International Conference on Fuzzy Systems*, pp. 49–54. World Scientific and Engineering Academy and Society (WSEAS).

Little, R. J. and D. B. Rubin 2014. *Statistical Analysis with Missing Data*. John Wiley & Sons.

Little, T. and A. G. Williams 2005. Specificity of acceleration, maximum speed, and agility in professional soccer players. *Journal of Strength & Conditioning Research* 19(1):76–78. 35

Lix, L. M., J. C. Keselman, and H. Keselman 1996. Consequences of assumption violations revisited: A quantitative review of alternatives to the one-way analysis of variance F-test. *Review of Educational Research* 66(4):579–619.

Lopez, S. T. 2012. Special issue on heroes, icons, legends: Legacies of great men in world soccer. *Soccer & Society* 13(4).

Lotz, S. and N. Hagemann 2007. Using the Implicit Association Test to measure athlete's attitude toward doping. *Journal of Sport & Exercise Psychology* 29.

Loveday, A., L. B. Sherar, J. P. Sanders, P. W. Sanderson, and D. W. Esliger 2015. Technologies that assess the location of physical activity and sedentary behavior: A systematic review. *Journal of Medical Internet Research* 17(8):e192.

Lowe, S. 2014. *Fear and Loathing in La Liga: Barcelona, Real Madrid, and the World's Greatest Sports Rivalry*. Nation Books.

Lucey, P., A. Bialkowski, P. Carr, Y. Yue, and I. Matthews 2014. How to get an open shot: Analyzing team movement in basketball using tracking data. MIT Sloan Sports Analytics Conference.

Lukaski, H. C., P. E. Johnson, W. W. Bolonchuk, and G. I. Lykken 1985, Apr. Assessment of fat-free mass using bioelectrical impedance measurements of the human body. *American Journal of Clinical Nutrition* 41(4):810–817.

Lutz, D. 2012. A cluster analysis of NBA players. MIT Sloan Sports Analytics Conf., Boston, MA.

Luxbacher, J. 2005. *Soccer: Steps to Success*. Human Kinetics.

Lynch, C. J., Y. Xu, A. Hajnal, A. C. Salzberg, and Y. I. Kawasawa 2015. RNA sequencing reveals a slow to fast muscle fiber type transition after olanzapine infusion in rats. *PloS ONE* 10(4).

Lyons, B. D., B. J. Hoffman, and J. W. Michel 2009. Not much more than G? An examination of the impact of intelligence on NFL performance. *Human Performance* 22(3): 225–245.

MacDougall, D. and D. Sale 2014. *Physiology of Training for High Performance.* Oxford University Press.

Macy, S. 1993. *A Whole New Ball Game: The Story of the All-American Girls Professional Baseball League.* Macmillan.

Magnusen, M. 2007. *Assessing Differences in Strength and Conditioning Coach Self-perceptions of Leadership Style at the NBA, Division I, and Division II Level.* ProQuest.

Major League Baseball 2015. *Official Rules of Major League Baseball.* Chicago: Triumph Books.

Mall, F. P. 1908. On the teaching of anatomy. *Anatomical Record* 2(8):313–335.

Mallett, C., M. Kawabata, P. Newcombe, A. Otero-Forero, and S. Jackson 2007. Sport Motivation Scale-6 (SMS-6): A revised six-factor Sport Motivation Scale. *Psychology of Sport and Exercise* 8(5):600–614.

Mangine, G. T., J. R. Hoffman, M. S. Fragala, J. Vazquez, M. C. Krause, J. Gillett, and N. Pichardo 2013. Effect of age on anthropometric and physical performance measures in professional baseball players. *Journal of Strength & Conditioning Research* 27 (2):375–381.

Mangine, G. T., J. R. Hoffman, J. Vazquez, N. Pichardo, M. S. Fragala, and J. R. Stout 2013. Predictors of fielding performance in professional baseball players. *International Journal of Sports Physiology and Performance.*

Manzi, V., S. D'Ottavio, F. M. Impellizzeri, A. Chaouachi, K. Chamari, and C. Castagna 2010, May. Profile of weekly training load in elite male professional basketball players. *Journal of strength and conditioning research* 24(5):1399–1406.

Marchi, M. and J. Albert 2014. *Analyzing Baseball Data with R.* Boca Raton, Fla.: Chapman & Hall/CRC.

Marcos, F. M. L., P. A. S. Miguel, D. S. Oliva, and T. G. Calvo 2010. Interactive effects of team cohesion on perceived efficacy in semi-professional sport. *Journal of Sports Science & Medicine* 9(2):320.

Margaria, R., P. Aghemo, and E. Rovelli 1966, Sep. Measurement of muscular power (anaerobic) in man. *Journal of Applied Physiology* 21(5):1662–1664. 29

Marks, S. C. and S. N. Popoff 1988. Bone cell biology: The regulation of development, structure, and function in the skeleton. *American Journal of Anatomy* 183(1):1–44.

Marple, D. 1983. Tournament earnings and performance differentials between the sexes in professional golf and tennis. *Journal of Sport & Social Issues* 7(1):1–14.

Martens, R. 1971. Anxiety and motor behavior: A review. *Journal of Motor Behavior* 3(2): 151–179.

Martens, R. and D. M. Landers 1970. Motor performance under stress: A test of the inverted-U hypothesis. *Journal of Personality and Social Psychology* 16(1):29.

Martin, J. J. and D. L. Gill 1991. The relationships among competitive orientation, sport-confidence, self-efficacy, anxiety, and performance.

Martin, L. 2013. Improving Exercise Adherence and Physical Measures in Latina Women. Doctoral dissertation, University of Miami, Coral Gables.

Martin, L. 2015. Is socioeconomic status a contributing factor to tennis players' success? *Journal of Medicine and Science in Tennis* 20(3):116–121. 163

Martin, L. and T. W. Miller 2016. *A Model for Measurement in Sports.* Manhattan Beach, Calif.: Research Publishers. `http://www.research-publishers.com/`. 52

Martin, L., J. F. Signorile, B. E. Kahn, A. W. Perkins, S. Ahn, and A. C. Perry 2015. Improving exercise adherence and physical measures in English-speaking Latina women. *Journal of Racial and Ethnic Health Disparities*:1–10.

Martin, R. and K. Davids 1995. The effects of group development techniques on a professional athletic team. *Journal of Social Psychology* 135(4):533–535.

Martin-Krumm, C. P., P. G. Sarrazin, C. Peterson, and J.-P. Famose 2003. Explanatory style and resilience after sports failure. *Personality and individual differences* 35(7): 1685–1695.

Masters, R. S. 1992. Knowledge, nerves and know-how: The role of explicit versus implicit knowledge in the breakdown of a complex motor skill under pressure. *British Journal of Psychology* 83(3):343–358.

Maud, P. J. and C. Foster 2006. *Physiological Assessment of Human Fitness.* Human Kinetics.

Maxwell, J., R. Masters, and J. Poolton 2006. Performance breakdown in sport: The roles of reinvestment and verbal knowledge. *Research Quarterly for Exercise and Sport* 77(2): 271–276.

Maxwell, J. and E. Moores 2007. The development of a short scale measuring aggressiveness and anger in competitive athletes. *Psychology of Sport and Exercise* 8(2):179–193. 47

Mayhew, J., K. Hancock, L. Rollison, T. Ball, and J. Bowen 2001. Contributions of strength and body composition to the gender difference in anaerobic power. *Journal of Sports Medicine and Physical Fitness* 41(1):33.

Mayhew, J., J. J. Houser, B. B. Briney, T. B. Williams, F. C. Piper, and W. F. Brechue 2010, Feb. Comparison between hand and electronic timing of 40-yd dash performance in college football players. *Journal of Strength and Conditioning Research* 24(2):447–451.

Mayhew, J., F. Piper, T. Schwegler, and T. Ball 1989. Contributions of speed, agility and body composition to anaerobic power measurement in college football players. *Journal of Strength Conditioning Research* 3(4):101–106.

Mayhew, J. and P. C. Salm 1990. Gender differences in anaerobic power tests. *European Journal of Applied Physiology and Occupational Physiology* 60(2):133–138.

Mayhew, J., J. S. Ware, M. G. Bemben, B. Wilk, T. E. Ward, B. Farris, J. Juraszek, and J. P. Slovak 1999. The NFL-225 test as a measure of bench press strength in college football players. *Journal of Strength & Conditioning Research* 13(2):130–134.

McArdle, W. D., F. I. Katch, and V. L. Katch 2006. *Essentials of Exercise Physiology.* Lippincott Williams & Wilkins.

McArdle, W. D., F. I. Katch, and V. L. Katch 2010. *Exercise Physiology: Nutrition, Energy, and Human Performance.* Lippincott Williams & Wilkins.

McCann, J. and D. Bryson 2009. *Smart Clothes and Wearable Technology.* Elsevier.

McComas, A. J. 1996. *Skeletal Muscle: Form and Function.* Champaign, Ill.: Human Kinetics.

McFarland, S. G. and Z. Crouch 2002. A cognitive skill confound on the Implicit Association Test. *Social Cognition* 20(6):483–510. 49

McGee, K. J. and L. N. Burkett 2003. The National Football League Combine: A reliable predictor of draft status? *Journal of Strength & Conditioning Research* 17(1):6–11. 74

McGinn, B. 2009. *The Ultimate Super Bowl Book*. MVP Books.

McGuine, T. A., J. J. Greene, T. Best, and G. Leverson 2000. Balance as a predictor of ankle injuries in high school basketball players. *Clinical Journal of Sport Medicine* 10 (4):239–244.

McGuire, F. 1958. *Offensive Basketball*. Englewood Cliffs, N.J.: Prentice Hall.

McGuire, F. 1960. *Defensive Basketball*. Englewood Cliffs, N.J.: Prentice Hall.

McHale, I. and S. Davies 2007. Statistical analysis of the effectiveness of the FIFA world rankings. *Statistical Thinking in Sports*:77–90. 175

McHale, I. and A. Morton 2011. A Bradley-Terry type model for forecasting tennis match results. *International Journal of Forecasting* 27(2):619–630. 174

McHale, I. G., P. A. Scarf, and D. E. Folker 2012. On the development of a soccer player performance rating system for the English Premier League. *Interfaces* 42(4):339–351. 175

McIntosh, J. 2014. *Soccer*. Mason Crest.

McKelvey, G. R. 2001. *For It's One, Two, Three, Four Strikes You're Out at the Owners' Ball Game: Players Versus Management in Baseball*. McFarland.

McLester, J. and P. S. Pierre 2007. *Applied Biomechanics: Concepts and Connections*. Cengage Learning. 26

McMorris, T. 2014. *Acquisition and Performance of Sports Skills*. New York: John Wiley & Sons.

McMurray, R. G., J. Driskell, I. Wolinsky, and others 2002. Laboratory methods for determining energy expenditure of athletes. *Nutritional Assessment of Athletes*:203–224.

Mead, W. B. and P. Dickson 1997. *Baseball: The Presidents' Game*. Bloomsbury Publishing USA.

Medoff, M. H. 1977. Positional segregation and professional baseball. *International Review for the Sociology of Sport* 12(1):49–56.

Menard, S. 2002. *Applied Logistic Regression Analysis*, Volume 106. Sage.

Meng, X.L., R. Rosenthal, and D. B. Rubin 1992. Comparing correlated correlation coefficients. *Psychological Bulletin* 111(1):172.

Messner, M. A. 1988. Sports and male domination: The female athlete as contested ideological terrain. *Sociology of Sport Journal* 5(3):197–211.

Metaxas, T. I., N. Koutlianos, T. Sendelides, and A. Mandroukas 2009. Preseason physiological profile of soccer and basketball players in different divisions. *Journal of Strength & Conditioning Research* 23(6):1704–1713.

Meyers, M. C., J. C. Sterling, S. Treadwell, A. E. Bourgeois, and A. LeUnes 1994. Mood and psychological skills of world-ranked female tennis players. *Journal of Sport Behavior* 17(3):156.

Mielke, D. 2003. *Soccer fundamentals*. Human Kinetics.

Mierke, J. and K. C. Klauer 2001. Implicit association measurement with the IAT: Evidence for effects of executive control porcesses. *Zeitschrift fÃ1/4r Experimentelle Psychologie*.

Miladinovic, M. 2008. Improving the Ranking System for Women's Professional Tennis. Ph.D. thesis, Stetson University. 174

Miller, S. and R. Bartlett 1996. The relationship between basketball shooting kinematics, distance and playing position. *Journal of Sports Sciences* 14(3):243–253.

Miller, T. W. 2015a. *Marketing Data Science: Modeling Techniques in Predictive Analytics with R and Python*. Old Tappan, N.J.: Pearson Education.

Miller, T. W. 2015b. *Modeling Techniques in Predictive Analytics with Python and R: A Guide to Data Science*. Upper Saddle River, N.J.: Pearson Education.

Miller, T. W. 2015c. *Modeling Techniques in Predictive Analytics: Business Problems and Solutions with R* (revised and expanded ed.). Upper Saddle River, N.J.: Pearson Education.

Miller, T. W. 2015d. *Web and Network Data Science: Modeling Techniques in Predictive Analytics with Python and R*. Upper Saddle River, N.J.: Pearson Education.

Miller, T. W. 2016. *Sports Analytics and Data Science: Winning the Game with Methods and Models*. Old Tappan, N.J.: Pearson Education. Data sets and programs available at http://www.ftpress.com/miller/ and https://github.com/mtpa/. 176

Mitchell, J. E. 2003. Realignment in the National Football League: Did they do it right? *Naval Research Logistics (NRL)* 50(7):683–701.

Mochizuki, K., D. Lee, and R. Gonzalez 1993. *Baseball Saved Us*. Lee & Low.

Montville, L. 2007. *The Big Bam: The Life and Times of Babe Ruth*. Anchor Books.

Moorad, J. S. 1997. Major League Baseball's labor turmoil: The failure of the counter-revolution. *Villanova Sports & Entertainment Law Journal* 4:53.

Moran, A. 2004. *Sport and exercise psychology: A critical introduction*. Routledge.

Morgan, W. 1980. Test of champions: The iceberg profile. *Psychology Today* 14(2):92.

Morgan, W. P. 1985. Selected psychological factors limiting performance: A mental health model. *Limits of Human Performance*:70–80.

Moritz, S. E., D. L. Feltz, K. R. Fahrbach, and D. E. Mack 2000. The relation of self-efficacy measures to sport performance: A meta-analytic review. *Research Quarterly for Exercise and Sport* 71(3):280–294.

Morris, G., T. Engelland, and B. Jones 1976. *Basketball Basics*. Prentice-Hall.

Morrow, H. E. 2003. The wide world of sports is getting wider: A look at drafting foreign players into US professional sports. *Houston Journal of International Law* 26:649.

Morrow, J. R. 2011. *Measurement and Evaluation in Human Performance*. Human Kinetics.

Motulsky, H. 2013. *Intuitive Biostatistics: A Nonmathematical Guide to Statistical Thinking*. Oxford University Press, USA.

Mullins, L. S. and R. E. Kopelman 1988. Toward an assessment of the construct validity of four measures of narcissism. *Journal of Personality Assessment* 52(4):610–625.

Murphy, K. P. 2012. *Machine Learning: A Probabilistic Perspective*. Cambridge, Mass.: MIT Press. 67

Murray, B. and W. J. Murray 1998. *The World's Game: A History of Soccer*. University of Illinois Press.

Muscolino, J. E. 2005. *The Muscular System Manual: The Skeletal Muscles of the Human Body*. Mosby.

Muscolino, J. E. 2014. *Kinesiology: The Skeletal System and Muscle Function*. Elsevier Health Sciences.

Naismith, J. 1914. Basket ball. *American Physical Education Review* 19(5):339–351.

Naismith, J. 1941. *Basketball: Its Origin and Development*. University of Nebraska Press.

Naismith, J. 1983. *Rules for Basket Ball*. [Springfield, Mass.: Triangle Publishing Company], 1892 (Springfield, Mass.: Springfield Print. and Binding Company).

National Basketball Association 2015a. *A Glossary of NBA Terms*. Retrieved from the World Wide Web, December 12, 2015 at `http://www.nba.com/analysis/00422966.html`.

National Basketball Association 2015b. *Official Rules of the National Basketball Association 2015–2016*. Retrieved from the World Wide Web, December 12, 2015 at `https://turnernbahangtime.files.wordpress.com/2015/11/official-nba-rule-book-2015-16.pdf`.

National Football League 2015. *2015 NFL Rulebook*. Retrieved from the World Wide Web, December 11, 2015 at `http://operations.nfl.com/the-rules/2015-nfl-rulebook`. 193

Neilson, P. J. 2003. The Dynamic Testing of Soccer Balls. Ph.D. thesis, © Paul Neilson.

Nelson, D. M. 1994. *The Anatomy of a Game: Football, the Rules, and the Men Who Made the Game*. University of Delaware Press.

Nemec, D. 1994. *The Rules of Baseball: An Anecdotal Look at the Rules of Baseball and How They Came to Be*. Lyons Press.

Nesser, T. W., R. W. Latin, K. Berg, and E. Prentice 1996. Physiological determinants of 40-meter sprint performance in young male athletes. *Journal of Strength Conditioning Research* 10(4):263–267.

Neuhauser, M. 2011. *Nonparametric Statistical Tests: A Computational Approach*. Boca Raton, Fla.: Chapman and Hall/CRC. 67

Nevill, A., R. Holder, and A. Watts 2009. The changing shape of "successful" professional footballers. *Journal of Sports Sciences* 27(5):419–426.

Nevill, A. M., G. Atkinson, M. D. Hughes, and S.-M. Cooper 2002. Statistical methods for analyzing discrete and categorical data recorded in performance analysis. *Journal of Sports Sciences* 20(10):829–844.

Nevill, A., R. Holder, and A. Watts 2009. The changing shape of "successful" professional footballers. *Journal of Sports Sciences* 27(5):419–426.

Newton, R. R. and K. E. Rudestam 2012. *Your Statistical Consultant: Answers to Your Data Analysis Questions*. SAGE Publications.

Ngonyama, P. 2010. The 2010 FIFA World Cup: Critical voices from below. *Soccer & Society* 11(1-2):168–180.

Nicks, D. C. and E. A. Fleishman 1960. What do physical fitness tests measure? A review of factor analytic studies. Technical Report, DTIC Document.

Nimphius, S., M. R. McGuigan, and R. U. Newton 2010. Relationship between strength, power, speed, and change of direction performance of female softball players. *Journal of Strength & Conditioning Research* 24(4):885–895. 35

Noakes, T. 2003. *Lore of running*. Human Kinetics.

Noor, M. A. M., N. Kumaraswamy, R. Singh, and M. R. Abdullah 2008. Personality trait as one of psychological predictors of injuries among Malaysian professional football players.

Oberg, B., J. Ekstrand, M. Möller, and J. Gillquist 1984. Muscle strength and flexibility in different positions of soccer players. *International Journal of Sports Medicine* 5(4): 213–216.

O'Donoghue, P. G. 2001. The most important points in Grand Slam singles tennis. *Research Quarterly for Exercise and Sport* 72(2):125–131.

Ogilvie, B. C. 1967. What is an athlete? *Journal of Health, Physical Education, Recreation* 38 (6):46–48.

Okrent, D. 2000. *Nine Innings: The Anatomy of a Baseball Game*. Houghton Mifflin Harcourt.

Okubo, H. and M. Hubbard 2015. Rebounds of basketball field shots. *Sports Engineering* 18(1):43–54.

Olejnik, S. F. and J. Algina 1987. Type I error rates and power estimates of selected parametric and nonparametric tests of scale. *Journal of Educational and Behavioral Statistics* 12(1):45–61.

Oliver, D. 2004a. *Basketball on Paper: Rules and Tools of Performance Analysis*. Dulles, Va.: Brassey's Press.

Oliver, J. A. 2004b. *Basketball Fundamentals*. Human Kinetics.

Onate, J. A., B. C. Beck, and B. L. Van Lunen 2007. On-field testing environment and Balance Error Scoring System performance during preseason screening of healthy collegiate baseball players. *Journal of Athletic Training* 42(4):446.

O'Reilly, N. J. and J. P. Nadeau 2006. Revenue generation in professional sport: A diagnostic analysis. *International Journal of Sport Management and Marketing* 1(4):311–330.

Orejan, J. 2011. *Football/Soccer: History and Tactics*. McFarland.

Orlick, T. 1989. Reflections on sportpsych consulting with individual and team sport athletes at summer and Winter Olympic Games. *Sport Psychologist* 3:358–365.

Ortega, E., D. Cárdenas, P. Sainz de Baranda, and J. Palao 2006a. Analysis of the final actions used in basketball during formative years according to player's position. *Journal of Human Movement Studies* 50(6):421–437.

Ortega, E., D. Cárdenas, P. Sainz de Baranda, and J. Palao 2006b. Differences in competitive participation according to player's position in formative basketball. *Journal of Human Movement Studies* 50(2):103–122.

Osborne, J. W. and E. Waters 2002. Multiple Regression Assumptions. ERIC digest.

Ostojic, S. M., S. Mazic, and N. Dikic 2006. Profiling in basketball: Physical and physiological characteristics of elite players. *Journal of Strength & Conditioning Research* 20 (4):740–744.

Otis, C., M. Crespo, C. Flygare, P. Johnston, A. Keber, D. Lloyd-Kolkin, J. Loehr, K. Martin, B. Pluim, A. Quinn, and others 2006. The Sony Ericsson WTA Tour 10 year age eligibility and professional development review. *British Journal of Sports Medicine* 40 (5):464–468.

Ovadia, S. 2004. Ratings and rankings: Reconsidering the structure of values and their measurement. *International Journal of Social Research Methodology* 7(5):403–414.

Oxendine, J. B. 1988. *American Indian sports heritage*. U of Nebraska Press.

Palacios-Huerta, I. 2004. Structural changes during a century of the world's most popular sport. *Statistical Methods and Applications* 13(2):241–258.

Palmer, M. L., M. E. Epler, and M. F. Epler 1998. *Fundamentals of Musculoskeletal Assessment Techniques*. Lippincott Williams & Wilkins.

Panait, C. and V. Cojocaru 2013. The new e-registration and analysis methods support for objectification of the training in performance football game. In *Conference Proceedings of eLearning and Software for Education (eLSE)*, Number 03, pp. 49–54. 37

Pargman, D. 1999. *Psychological Bases of Sport Injuries*. Fitness Information Technology.

Parker, S. 1994. *The Human Body*. Shining Star Press.

Parsons, John, W. H. and T. Henman 2008. *The Tennis Book: The Illustrated Encyclopedia of World Tennis*. Carlton Books.

Paruolo, P., M. Saisana, and A. Saltelli 2013. Ratings and rankings: Voodoo or science? *Journal of the Royal Statistical Society: Series A (Statistics in Society)* 176(3):609–634.

Pate, R. R., M. L. Burgess, J. A. Woods, J. G. Ross, and T. Baumgartner 1993. Validity of field tests of upper body muscular strength. *Research Quarterly for Exercise and Sport* 64(1):17–24.

Paternoster, R., R. Brame, P. Mazerolle, and A. Piquero 1998. Using the correct statistical test for the equality of regression coefficients. *Criminology* 36:859.

Pauole, K., K. Madole, J. Garhammer, M. Lacourse, and R. Rozenek 2000. Reliability and validity of the *t*-test as a measure of agility, leg power, and leg speed in college-aged men and women. *Journal of Strength Conditioning Research* 14(4):443–450.

Pawson, T. 1972. *100 years of the FA Cup: the official centenary history*. Pan.

Payne, K. A., K. Berg, and R. W. Latin 1997. Ankle injuries and ankle strength, flexibility, and proprioception in college basketball players. *Journal of Athletic Training* 32(3): 221.

Pelletier, L. G., M. S. Fortier, R. J. Vallerand, K. M. Tuson, N. M. Briere, and M. R. Blais 1995. Toward a new measure of intrinsic motivation, extrinsic motivation, and motivation in sports: The Sport Motivation Scale (SMS). *Journal of Sport and Exercise Psychology* 17:35–35.

Pellman, E. J., D. C. Viano, A. M. Tucker, I. R. Casson, and J. F. Waeckerle 2003. Concussion in professional football: Reconstruction of game impacts and injuries. *Neurosurgery* 53(4):799–814.

Peng, C.Y. J., K. L. Lee, and G. M. Ingersoll 2002. An introduction to logistic regression analysis and reporting. *Journal of Educational Research* 96(1):3–14.

Peng, Y., K. Lo, H. Lin, and L. Wang 2009. EMG analysis of the lower extremity between varying stance squat widths in baseball catcher throwing. In *ISBS-Conference Proceedings Archive*, Volume 1.

Perkin, H. 1989. Teaching the nations how to play: Sport and society in the British Empire and Commonwealth. *The International Journal of the History of Sport* 6(2):145–155.

Perlini, A. H. and T. R. Halverson 2006. Emotional intelligence in the National Hockey League. *Canadian Journal of Behavioural Science/Revue Canadienne des Sciences du Comportement* 38(2):109.

Perneger, T. V. 1998. What's wrong with Bonferroni adjustments. *BMJ: British Medical Journal* 316(7139):1236.

Perrin, D. 1995. *Athletic Taping and Bracing*. Human Kinetics.

Peterson, M. D., M. R. Rhea, and B. A. Alvar 2004, May. Maximizing strength development in athletes: A meta-analysis to determine the dose-response relationship. *Journal of strength and conditioning research* 18(2):377–382.

Peterson, R. 1970. *Only the Ball Was White*. Prentice Hall.

Peterson, R. W. 1996. *Pigskin: The Early Years of Pro Football*. Oxford University Press.

Peterson, S. L., J. C. Weber, and W. W. Trousdale 1967. Personality traits of women in team sports vs. women in individual sports. *Research Quarterly.American Association for Health, Physical Education and Recreation* 38(4):686–690.

Pette, D. and R. S. Staron 1990. *Cellular and Molecular Diversities of Mammalian Skeletal Muscle Fibers*. Springer.

Pette, D. and R. S. Staron 1997. Mammalian skeletal muscle fiber type transitions. *International Review of Cytology* 170:143–223.

Pette, D. and R. S. Staron 2000. Myosin isoforms, muscle fiber types, and transitions. *Microscopy Research and Technique* 50(6):500–509.

Pierman, C. J. 2005. Baseball, conduct, and true womanhood. *Women's Studies Quarterly*: 68–85.

Pinheiro, J., D. Bates, S. DebRoy, D. Sarkar, and others 2007. Linear and Nonlinear Mixed Effects Models. *R Package Version* 3:57. 67

Plackett, R. L. 1983. Karl Pearson and the chi-squared test. *International Statistical Review/Revue Internationale de Statistique*:59–72.

Plisky, P. J., M. J. Rauh, T. W. Kaminski, and F. B. Underwood 2006. Star Excursion Balance Test as a predictor of lower extremity injury in high school basketball players. *Journal of Orthopaedic & Sports Physical Therapy* 36(12):911–919. 29

Pluim, B. M. 2014. The evolution and impact of science in tennis: Eight advances for performance and health. *British Journal of Sports Medicine* 48(Suppl 1):i3–i5. 39

Plumley, D. and S. W. Flint 2015. The UEFA Champions League: Maintaining the status quo? *Team Performance Management* 21(5/6):247–258.

Podlog, L. and R. C. Eklund 2005. Return to sport after serious injury: A retrospective examination of motivation and psychological outcomes. *Journal of Sport Rehabilitation* 14(1):20–34.

Pollard, R. and C. Reep 1997. Measuring the effectiveness of playing strategies at soccer. *The Statistician*:541–550.

Pomrenke, J. 2012. "Call the game!" *Base Ball: A Journal of the Early Game* 6(1).

Pope, S. W. 1995. An army of athletes: Playing fields, battlefields, and the American military sporting experience, 1890–1920. *The Journal of Military History* 59(3):435.

Potteiger, J. A. and G. D. Wilson 1989. Bridging the gap research: Training the pitcher: A physiological perspective. *Strength & Conditioning Journal* 11(3):24–26.

Powers, D. A. and Y. Xie 2008. *Statistical Methods for Categorical Data Analysis*. Emerald Group Publishing.

Proctor, D. N., W. E. Sinning, J. Walro, G. C. Sieck, and P. Lemon 1995. Oxidative capacity of human muscle fiber types: Effects of age and training status. *Journal of Applied Physiology* 78(6):2033–2038.

Puerzer, R. J. 2002. From scientific baseball to Sabermetrics: Professional baseball as a reflection of engineering and management in society. *NINE: A Journal of Baseball History and Culture* 11(1):34–48.

Qizhi, Z. 1999. The origin and development of the rules for basketball matches. *Sport Science and Technology*:Z1.

Quackenbush, N. and J. Crossman 1994. Injured athletes: A study of emotional responses. *Journal of Sport Behavior* 17(3):178.

Quinn, A. and M. Reid 2005. Traditional vs functional core training for tennis. In *14th ITF Worldwide Coaches Workshop. London, United Kingdom: The International Tennis Federation*, pp. 1–4.

Quinn, A. M. and B. J. Fallon 1999. The changes in psychological characteristics and reactions of elite athletes from injury onset until full recovery. *Journal of Applied Sport Psychology* 11(2):210–229.

Raab, M. 2003. Decision making in sports:İnfluence of complexity on implicit and explicit learning. *International Journal of Sport and Exercise Psychology* 1(4):406–433.

Rabinowitz, B. 1989. Baseball and the Great Depression. *Baseball History*:49–59.

Rader, B. G. and D. A. Sullivan 1997. *Early Innings: A Documentary History of Baseball, 1825–1908*. University of Nebraska Press.

Raglin, J. S. 1991. Anxiety and sport performance. *Exercise and Sport Sciences Reviews* 20: 243–274.

Raglin, J. S. 2001. Psychological factors in sport performance. *Sports Medicine* 31(12):875–890.

Rains, R. 2011. *James Naismith: The man who invented basketball*. Temple University Press.

Rampinini, E., D. Bishop, S. Marcora, D. Ferrari Bravo, R. Sassi, and F. Impellizzeri 2007. Validity of simple field tests as indicators of match-related physical performance in top-level professional soccer players. *International Journal of Sports Medicine* 28(3): 228.

Ramzaninezhad, R., M. H. Keshtan, M. D. Shahamat, and S. S. Kordshooli 2009. The relationship between collective efficacy, group cohesion and team performance in professional volleyball teams. *Brazilian Journal of Biomotricity* 3(1):31–39.

Randle, S., R. Weinberg, and others 1997. Multidimensional anxiety and performance: An exploratory examination of the zone of optimal functioning hypothesis. *Sport Psychologist* 11:160–174.

Rankin, W. L. and J. W. Grube 1980. A comparison of ranking and rating procedures for value system measurement. *European Journal of Social Psychology* 10(3):233–246. 174

Rao, C. R. and H. Toutenburg 1995. *Linear models*. Springer.

Raskin, R. and J. Novacek 1989. An MMPI description of the narcissistic personality. *Journal of Personality Assessment* 53(1):66–80.

Raskin, R. N. and C. S. Hall 1979. A Narcissistic Personality Inventory. *Psychological Reports* 45(2):590–590.

Real, M. R. and L. Wenner 1989. Super Bowl football versus World Cup soccer: A cultural-structural comparison. *Media, Sports, and Society*:180–203.

Reid, M., M. Crespo, F. Atienza, and J. Dimmock 2007. Tournament structure and nations' success in women's professional tennis. *Journal of Sports Sciences* 25(11):1221–1228.

Reid, M., D. McMurtrie, and M. Crespo 2010. The relationship between match statistics and top 100 ranking in professional men's tennis. *International Journal of Performance Analysis in Sport* 10(2):131–138.

Reid, M. and K. Schneiker 2008. Strength and conditioning in tennis: Current research and practice. *Journal of Science and Medicine in Sport* 11(3):248–256.

Reider, B. 2014. Moneyball. *American Journal of Sports Medicine* 42(3):533–535.

Requena, B., J. J. González-Badillo, E. S. S. de Villareal, J. Ereline, I. García, H. Gapeyeva, and M. Pääsuke 2009. Functional performance, maximal strength, and power characteristics in isometric and dynamic actions of lower extremities in soccer players. *Journal of Strength & Conditioning Research* 23(5):1391–1401.

Reynolds, J. M., T. J. Gordon, and R. A. Robergs 2006. Prediction of One Repetition Maximum strength from multiple repetition maximum testing and anthropometry. *Journal of Strength & Conditioning Research* 20(3):584–592.

Rheinheimer, D. C. and D. A. Penfield 2001. The effects of type I error rate and power of the ANCOVA *F*-test and selected alternatives under nonnormality and variance heterogeneity. *Journal of Experimental Education* 69(4):373–391.

Ribowsky, M. 1995. *A Complete History of the Negro Leagues, 1884 to 1955*. Carol Publishing Corporation.

Ridder, G., J. Cramer, and P. Hopstaken 1994. Down to ten: Estimating the effect of a red card in soccer. *Journal of the American Statistical Association* 89(427):1124–1127.

Riley, J. A. 2002. *The Biographical Encyclopedia of the Negro Baseball Leagues*. Carroll & Graf Publishers.

Ripken, C. and B. Ripken 2004. *Play Baseball the Ripken Way: The Complete Illustrated Guide to the Fundamentals*. New York: Ballantine Books.

Ripken, C. and B. Ripken 2007. *Coaching Youth Baseball the Ripken Way*. Champaign, Ill.: Human Kinetics.

Robbins, D. W. 2010. The National Football League (NFL) Combine: does normalized data better predict performance in the NFL draft? *Journal of Strength & Conditioning Research* 24(11):2888–2899.

Robbins, D. W. 2011. Positional physical characteristics of players drafted into the National Football League. *Journal of Strength & Conditioning Research* 25(10):2661–2667.

Robbins, D. W. 2012. Relationships between National Football League Combine performance measures. *Journal of Strength & Conditioning Research* 26(1):226–231.

Robbins, D. W. and W. B. Young 2012, Feb. Positional relationships between various sprint and jump abilities in elite American football players. *Journal of Strength & Conditioning Research* 26(2):388–397.

Robert, C. P. 2007. *The Bayesian Choice: From Decision Theoretic Foundations to Computational Implementation* (second ed.). New York: Springer. 67

Roberts, H. 1953. *The Story of Pro Football*. Rand McNally.

Robineau, J., T. Jouaux, M. Lacroix, and N. Babault 2012. Neuromuscular fatigue induced by a 90-minute soccer game modeling. *Journal of Strength & Conditioning Research* 26 (2):555–562.

Roetert, P. and T. S. Ellenbecker 2007. *Complete Conditioning for Tennis*. Human Kinetics.

Roetert, P. and M. Kovacs 2011. *Tennis anatomy*. Human Kinetics.

Rosenberg, M. 1965. Rosenberg Self-Esteem Scale (RSES). *Acceptance and Commitment Therapy. Measures Package* 61. 48, 52

Rowley, A. J., D. M. Landers, L. B. Kyllo, and J. L. Etnier 1995. Does the iceberg profile discriminate between successful and less successful athletes? A meta-analysis. *Journal of Sport and Exercise Psychology* 17:185–185.

Rubin, E. 1958. Questions and answers: An analysis of baseball scores by innings. *The American Statistician* 12(2):21–22.

Ruff, C. B. 2000. Body size, body shape, and long bone strength in modern humans. *Journal of Human Evolution* 38(2):269–290.

Ruggiero, J. 2011. The hall of fame. In *Frontiers in Major League Baseball*, pp. 77–92. Springer.

Rupinski, M. T. and W. P. Dunlap 1996. Approximating Pearson product-moment correlations from Kendall's tau and Spearman's rho. *Educational and Psychological Measurement* 56(3):419–429.

Russell, D. 1997. *Football and the English: A Social History of Association Football in England, 1863–1995*. Carnegie Publishing Ltd.

Rutherford, A. 2011. *ANOVA and ANCOVA: A GLM approach*. John Wiley & Sons.

Ruxton, G. D. 2006. The unequal variance *t*-test is an underused alternative to Student's *t*-test and the Mann–Whitney U test. *Behavioral Ecology* 17(4):688–690.

Ruxton, G. D. and G. Beauchamp 2008. Time for some a priori thinking about post hoc testing. *Behavioral Ecology* 19(3):690–693.

Saccoman, J. T. 1996. Sabermetrics: The team teaching approach. *Education* 117(2):200.

Safir, J. 2015. How analytics, big data, and technology have impacted basketball's quest to maximize efficiency and optimization. 37

Sagal, M.-S., P. T. Sagal, and G. E. Miller 2004. Assessment in sport psychology. *Encyclopedia of Applied Psychology, vol* 1:177–190.

Sallet, P., D. Perrier, J. M. Ferret, V. Vitelli, and G. Baverel 2005. Physiological differences in professional basketball players as a function of playing position and level of play. *Journal of Sports Medicine and Physical Fitness* 45(3):291.

Sampaio, J., S. J. Ibañez Godoy, M. Á. Gómez Ruano, A. Lorenzo Calvo, and E. Ortega Toro 2008. Game location influences basketball players performance across playing positions. *International Journal of Sport Psychology* 39(3):43–50.

Sampaio, J., M. Janeira, S. Ibáñez, and A. Lorenzo 2006. Discriminant analysis of game-related statistics between basketball guards, forwards and centres in three professional leagues. *European Journal of Sport Science* 6(3):173–178.

Santo, C. 2005. The economic impact of sports stadiums: Recasting the analysis in context. *Journal of Urban Affairs* 27(2):177–192.

Satorra, A. and P. M. Bentler 2001. A scaled difference chi-square test statistic for moment structure analysis. *Psychometrika* 66(4):507–514.

Scanlon, V. C. and T. Sanders 2014. *Essentials of Anatomy and Physiology*. FA Davis.

Schaerlaeckens, L. 2015. An Inside Look at How MLS Teams Are Using Analytics. `http://fusion.net/story/173133/major-league-soccer-analytics/`. 144

Schell, M. J. 2005. *Baseball's All-time Best Sluggers: Adjusted Batting Performance from Strikeouts to Home Runs*. Princeton University Press.

Schumacker, R. and S. Tomek 2013. Chi-square test. In *Understanding Statistics Using R*, pp. 169–175. Springer.

Scully, G. W. 2004. Player salary share and the distribution of player earnings. *Managerial and Decision Economics* 25(2):77–86. 177

Seifriz, J. J., J. L. Duda, and L. Chi 1992. The relationship of perceived motivational climate to intrinsic motivation and beliefs about success in basketball. *Journal of Sport and Exercise Psychology* 14:375–375.

Sekulic, D., B. Males, and D. Miletic 2006. Navy recruits: Fitness measuring, validation, and norming. *Military Medicine* 171(8):749–752.

Semenick, D. 1984. Anaerobic testing: Practical appliations. *Strength & Conditioning Journal* 6(5):45.

Senaux, B. 2008. A stakeholder approach to football club governance. *International Journal of Sport Management and Marketing* 4(1):4–17.

Seroyer, S. T., S. J. Nho, B. R. Bach, C. A. Bush-Joseph, G. P. Nicholson, and A. A. Romeo 2010. The kinetic chain in overhand pitching: Its potential role for performance enhancement and injury prevention. *Sports Health: A Multidisciplinary Approach* 2(2): 135–146.

Shamus, E. and J. Shamus 2001. *Sports Injury: Prevention & Rehabilitation*. New York: McGraw-Hill Medical. 26

Shapiro, S. S. and M. B. Wilk 1965. An analysis of variance test for normality (complete samples). *Biometrika*:591–611.

Shapiro, S. S., M. B. Wilk, and H. J. Chen 1968. A comparative study of various tests for normality. *Journal of the American Statistical Association* 63(324):1343–1372.

Shea, S. M. 2014. *Basketball Analytics: Spatial Tracking*. CreateSpace.

Shea, S. M. and C. E. Baker 2013. *Basketball Analytics: Objective and Efficient Strategies for Understanding How Teams Win*. Lake St. Louis, Mo.: Advanced Metrics, LLC.

Sheldon, J. P. and J. S. Eccles 2005. Physical and psychological predictors of perceived ability in adult male and female tennis players. *Journal of Applied Sport Psychology* 17 (1):48–63.

Sherwood, L. 2015. *Human Physiology: From Cells to Systems*. Cengage Learning.

Sheskin, D. J. 2003. *Handbook of Parametric and Nonparametric Statistical Procedures*. CRC Press.

Shiner, D. 2001. *Baseball's Greatest Players: The Saga Continues*. Superiorbooks. Com Incorporated.

Siegel, J. A., R. M. Gilders, R. S. Staron, and F. C. HaGerman 2002. Human muscle power output during upper-and lower-body exercises. *Journal of Strength & Conditioning Research* 16(2):173–178.

Siegel, S. 1957. Nonparametric statistics. *The American Statistician* 11(3):13–19.

Siegfried, J. and A. Zimbalist 2000. The economics of sports facilities and their communities. *Journal of Economic Perspectives*:95–114.

Sierer, S. P., C. L. Battaglini, J. P. Mihalik, E. W. Shields, and N. T. Tomasini 2008, Jan. The National Football League Combine: Performance differences between drafted and nondrafted players entering the 2004 and 2005 drafts. *Journal of Strength and Conditioning Research* 22(1):6–12.

Simenz, C. J., C. A. Dugan, and W. P. Ebben 2005. Strength and conditioning practices of National Basketball Association strength and conditioning coaches. *Journal of Strength & Conditioning Research* 19(3):495–504.

Simmons, B. 2009. *The Book of Basketball: The NBA According to the Sports Guy*. ESPN.

Simmons, R. 2007. Overpaid athletes? Comparing American and European football. *WorkingUSA* 10(4):457–471. 177

Sinclair, R. J. 1985. Baseball's Rising Sun: American Interwar Baseball Diplomacy and Japan. *Canadian Journal of the History of the Sport*:44–53.

Sindik, J. and others 2011. Differences between top senior basketball players from different team positions in big five personality traits. *Acta kinesiologica* 5(2):31–35.

Singer, J. D. and J. B. Willett 2003. *Applied Longitudinal Data Analysis: Modeling Change and Event Occurrence*. Oxford, UK: Oxford University Press. 67

Siri, W. E. 1961. Body composition from fluid spaces and density: Analysis of methods. *Techniques for measuring body composition* 61:223–244.

Skipper, J. C. 2000. *A Biographical Dictionary of the Baseball Hall of Fame*. McFarland.

Slack, T. and M. M. Parent 2006. *Understanding Sport Organizations: The Application of Organization Theory*. Human Kinetics.

Slobounov, S. 2008. Fitness assessment in athletes. *Injuries in Athletics: Causes and Consequences*:217–239.

Smekal, G., S. P. von Duvillard, C. Rihacek, R. Pokan, P. Hofmann, R. Baron, H. Tschan, and N. Bachl 2001. A physiological profile of tennis match play. *Medicine and Science in Sports and Exercise* 33(6):999–1005.

Smith, A. M., S. G. Scott, W. M. O'Fallon, and M. L. Young 1990. Emotional responses of athletes to injury. In *Mayo Clinic Proceedings*, Volume 65, pp. 38–50. Elsevier.

Smith, A. M., S. G. Scott, and D. M. Wiese 1990. The psychological effects of sports injuries coping. *Sports Medicine* 9(6):352–369.

Smith, A. M., M. J. Stuart, D. M. Wiese-Bjornstal, E. K. Milliner, W. M. O'Fallon, and C. S. Crowson 1993. Competitive athletes: Preinjury and postinjury mood state and self-esteem. In *Mayo Clinic Proceedings*, Volume 68, pp. 939–947. Elsevier.

Smith, D., S. Driver, M. Lafferty, C. Burrell, and T. Devonport 2002. Social desirability bias and direction: Modified Competitive State Anxiety Inventory–2. *Perceptual and Motor Skills* 95(3):945–952.

Smith, D. and B. Spear 1981. *Basketball, Multiple Offense and Defense*. Prentice Hall.

Smith, R. E., F. L. Smoll, S. P. Cumming, J. R. Grossbard, and others 2006. Measurement of multidimensional sport performance anxiety in children and adults: The Sport Anxiety Scale-2. *Journal of Sport and Exercise Psychology* 28(4):479.

Smith, R. E., F. L. Smoll, and R. W. Schutz 1990. Measurement and correlates of sport-specific cognitive and somatic trait anxiety: The Sport Anxiety Scale. *Anxiety Research* 2(4):263–280.

Smoll, F. L., R. E. Smith, B. Curtis, and E. Hunt 1978. Toward a mediational model of coach-player relationships. *Research Quarterly. American Alliance for Health, Physical Education and Recreation* 49(4):528–541.

Snedecor, G. W. and W. G. Cochran 1989. *Statistical Methods* (eighth ed.). Ames, Iowa: Iowa State University Press. First edition published by Snedecor in 1937.

Sohrabi, F., S. Atashak, and M. Aliloo 2011. Psychological profile of athletes in contact and non-contact sports. *Middle-East Journal of Scientific Research* 9(5):638–644.

Sparkes, A. C. 1998. Athletic identity: An Achilles' heel to the survival of self. *Qualitative Health Research* 8(5):644–664.

Spielberger, C. D., I. G. Sarason, and P. B. Defares 1985. *Stress and Anxiety*, Volume 9. Taylor & Francis.

Sporis, G., I. Jukic, S. M. Ostojic, and D. Milanovic 2009. Fitness profiling in soccer: Physical and physiologic characteristics of elite players. *Journal of Strength & Conditioning Research* 23(7):1947–1953.

Sports Reference LLC 2015. 2014 Major League Baseball team statistics and standings: team & league standard batting. Retrieved from the World Wide Web on September 7, 2015 at `http://www.baseball-reference.com/leagues/MLB/2014-standings.shtml/`. 210, 218, 223

Sprent, P. and N. C. Smeeton 2007. *Applied Nonparametric Statistical Methods* (fourth ed.). Boca Raton, Fla.: Chapman and Hall/CRC. 67

Staffo, D. F. 1998. The development of professional basketball in the United States, with an emphasis on the history of the NBA to its 50th anniversary season in 1996-97. *Physical Educator* 55(1):9.

Staron, R., E. Malicky, M. Leonardi, J. Falkel, F. HaGerman, and G. Dudley 1990. Muscle hypertrophy and fast fiber type conversions in heavy resistance-trained women. *European Journal of Applied Physiology and Occupational Physiology* 60(1):71–79.

Staudohar, P. D. 1997. The baseball strike of 1994–95. *Monthly Lab. Rev.* 120:21.

Stefani, R. T. 1987. Applications of statistical methods to American football. *Journal of Applied Statistics* 14(1):61–73.

Stefani, R. T. 1997. Survey of the major world sports rating systems. *Journal of Applied Statistics* 24(6):635–646.

Stefani, R. T. and R. Pollard 2007. Football rating systems for top-level competition: A critical survey. *Journal of Quantitative Analysis in Sports* 3(3). 175

Stewart, W. 2006. *Babe Ruth: A Biography*. Greenwood Publishing Group.

Stølen, T., K. Chamari, C. Castagna, and U. Wisløff 2005. Physiology of soccer. *Sports Medicine* 35(6):501–536.

Stoltz III, J. F. 2012. Turbulent seasons: Baseball in 1890–1891, and: Under pallor, under shadow: The 1920 American League pennant race that rattled and rebuilt baseball, and: Wins, losses, and empty seats: How baseball outlasted the Great Depression (review). *Journal of Sport History* 39(2):335–339.

Sugden, J., A. Tomlinson, and others 1998. *FIFA and the contest for world football: Who rules the people's game?* Polity Press.

Sullivan, G. 1985. *Football Rules Illustrated*. Simon and Schuster.

Sullivan, G. 1990. *All about Football*. Penguin.

Surdam, D. G. 2011. *Wins, Losses, and Empty Seats: How Baseball Outlasted the Great Depression*. U of Nebraska Press.

Sutton, L., M. Scott, J. Wallace, and T. Reilly 2009. Body composition of English Premier League soccer players: Influence of playing position, international status, and ethnicity. *Journal of Sports Sciences* 27(10):1019–1026.

Svensson, M. and B. Drust 2005. Testing soccer players. *Journal of Sports Sciences* 23(6): 601–618.

Swain, P. and A. Harvey 2012. On Bosworth field or the playing fields of Eton and Rugby? Who really invented modern football? *International Journal of the History of Sport* 29 (10):1425–1445.

Szto, C. 2015. Serving up change? Gender mainstreaming and the UNESCO–WTA partnership for global gender equality. *Sport in Society* 18(8):895–908.

Szymanski, S. and others 2010. The market for soccer players in England after Bosman: winners and losers. *Football Economics and Policy*:27–51.

Szymanski, S. and A. S. Zimbalist 2006. *National pastime: How Americans Play Baseball and the Rest of the World Plays Soccer*. Brookings Institution Press.

Tabachnick, B. G., L. S. Fidell, and others 2001. Using Multivariate Statistics.

Taimela, S., U. M. Kujala, and K. Osterman 1990. Intrinsic risk factors and athletic injuries. *Sports Medicine* 9(4):205–215.

Takahashi, J. and K. Suzuki 1993. Scoring big with soccer. *Japan Quarterly* 40(4):418.

Talsma, G. 1999. Data analysis and baseball. *The Mathematics Teacher* 92(8):738.

Tamborra, S. 2007. *Complete Conditioning for Baseball*. Human Kinetics.

Tang, M.C. 2015. Contract length, expected surplus, and specific investments empirical evidence from the National Football League. *Journal of Sports Economics* 16(3):295–311.

Tanner, R., C. Gore, and others 2013. *Physiological Tests for Elite Athletes*. Champaign, Ill.: Human Kinetics. 20, 40

Taskin, H. 2008. Evaluating sprinting ability, density of acceleration, and speed dribbling ability of professional soccer players with respect to their positions. *Journal of Strength & Conditioning Research* 22(5):1481–1486.

Taylor, J. and B. A. Schneider 1992. The Sport-Clinical Intake Protocol: A comprehensive interviewing instrument for applied sport psychology. *Professional Psychology: Research and Practice* 23(4):318.

Taylor, M. 2013. *The Association Game: A History of British Football*. Routledge.

Tazegül, Ü. 2011. Comparison of narcissims in some branches of athletes. *Journal of Sports and Performance Researches* 3:13–22.

Teichner, W. H. 1954. Recent studies of simple reaction time. *Psychological Bulletin* 51(2): 128.

Teichner, W. H. and J. L. Kobrick 1956. Effects of viewing distance with the Howard-Dolman apparatus. *Journal of the Optical Society of America* 46:837–840.

Tenenbaum, G., D. Furst, and G. Weingarten 1985. A statistical reevaluation of the STAI anxiety questionnaire. *Journal of Clinical Psychology* 41(2):239–244.

Terjung, R., K. Baldwin, W. Winder, and J. Holloszy 1974. Glycogen repletion in different types of muscle and in liver after exhausting exercise. *American Journal of Physiology–Legacy Content* 226(6):1387–1391.

Terkel, S. 1997. *The Good War: An Oral history of World War II*. New Press, The.

Thierer, A. D. 2015. The Internet of things and wearable technology: Addressing privacy and security concerns without derailing innovation. *Richmond Journal of Law & Technology* 21:6–15.

Thompson, M. 1975. On any given Sunday: Fair competitor orderings with maximum likelihood methods. *Journal of the American Statistical Association* 70(351):536–541.

Thorn, J., P. Palmer, and D. Reuther 2015. *The Hidden Game of Baseball: A Revolutionary Approach to Baseball and Its Statistics*. University of Chicago Press.

Tomarken, A. J. and R. C. Serlin 1986. Comparison of ANOVA alternatives under variance heterogeneity and specific noncentrality structures. *Psychological Bulletin* 99(1): 90.

Topend Sports 2015. Topend Sports: The Sport & Science Resource. http://www.topendsports.com/.

Torres, E. M., W. J. Kraemer, J. L. Vingren, J. S. Volek, D. L. Hatfield, B. A. Spiering, J. Y. Ho, M. S. Fragala, G. A. Thomas, J. M. Anderson, and others 2008. Effects of stretching on upper-body muscular performance. *Journal of Strength & Conditioning Research* 22(4):1279–1285.

Tracey, J. 2003. The emotional response to the injury and rehabilitation process. *Journal of Applied Sport Psychology* 15(4):279–293.

Triola, M. F. 2014. *Elementary Statistics*. Upper Saddle River, N.J.: Pearson.

Trninić, S. and D. Dizdar 2000. System of the performance evaluation criteria weighted per positions in the basketball game. *Collegium Antropologicum* 24(1):217–234.

Trninić, S., D. Dizdar, and B. Dežman 2000. Empirical verification of the weighted system of criteria for the elite basketball players quality evaluation. *Collegium Antropologicum* 24(2):443–465.

Trninić, S., D. Dizdar, and E. Lukšić 2002. Differences between winning and defeated top quality basketball teams in final tournaments of European club championship. *Collegium Antropologicum* 26(2):521–531.

Truth, S., A. P. Kennedy, and J. Press 1992. Ain't I a Woman?

Tucker, W. J., B. J. Sawyer, C. L. Jarrett, D. M. Bhammar, and G. A. Gaesser 2015. Physiological responses to high-intensity interval exercise differing in interval duration. *Journal of Strength and Conditioning Research*.

Tumilty, D. 1993. Physiological characteristics of elite soccer players. *Sports Medicine* 16 (2):80–96.

Turkin, H. 1976. *The Official Encyclopedia of Baseball*. Barnes.

Vallerand, R. J. 2004. Intrinsic and extrinsic motivation in sport. *Encyclopedia of Applied Psychology* 2(10). 52

Vallerand, R. J. 2007a. A hierarchical model of intrinsic and extrinsic motivation for sport and physical activity. In M. Hagger N. Chatzisarantis (eds.), *Intrinsic Motivation and Self-Determination in Exercise and Sport*. pp. 255–280. Champaign, Ill.: Human Kinetics.

Vallerand, R. J. 2007b. Intrinsic and extrinsic motivation in sport and physical activity. *Handbook of Sport Psychology* 3:59–83.

Vallerand, R. J. and G. F. Losier 1999. An integrative analysis of intrinsic and extrinsic motivation in sport. *Journal of Applied Sport Psychology* 11(1):142–169.

Van Pelt, D. 2014. *An Insider's Guide to Football*. The Rosen Publishing Group.

Vancil, M. 1995. *NBA Basketball Basics*. Sterling Publishing Company.

Vealey, R. and M. Chase 2008. Self-confidence in sport. *Advances in Sport Psychology* 3: 65–98.

Vealey, R. S. 1990. Advancements in competitive anxiety research: Use of the sport competition anxiety test and the Competitive State Anxiety Inventory-2. *Anxiety Research* 2(4):243–261.

Vealey, R. S. and B. Brewer 2009. Confidence in sport. *Sport Psychology*:43–52.

Vescovi, J. D. and M. R. Mcguigan 2008. Relationships between sprinting, agility, and jump ability in female athletes. *Journal of Sports Sciences* 26(1):97–107. 35

Viano, D. C. and E. J. Pellman 2005. Concussion in professional football: Biomechanics of the striking player—part 8. *Neurosurgery* 56(2):266–280.

Viano, D. C., E. J. Pellman, C. Withnall, and N. Shewchenko 2006. Concussion in professional football: performance of newer helmets in reconstructed game impacts—part 13. *Neurosurgery* 59(3):591–606.

Vickers, A. J. 2005. Parametric versus non-parametric statistics in the analysis of randomized trials with non-normally distributed data. *BMC Medical Research Methodology* 5 (1):35.

Vøllestad, M. K., I. Tabata, and J. Medbø 1992. Glycogen breakdown in different human muscle fibre types during exhaustive exercise of short duration. *Acta Physiologica Scandinavica* 144(2):135–141.

Vøllestad, M. K., O. Vaage, and L. Hermansen 1984. Muscle glycogen depletion patterns in type I and subgroups of type II fibres during prolonged severe exercise in man. *Acta Physiologica Scandinavica* 122(4):433–441.

Volpi, P. and E. Taioli 2012, Dec. The health profile of professional soccer players: Future opportunities for injury prevention. *Journal of Strength and Conditioning Research* 26 (12):3473–3479.

Waddington, I. and M. Roderick 1996. American exceptionalism: Soccer and American football. *Sports Historian* 16(1):42–63.

Wasserman, L. 2010. *All of Statistics: A Concise Course in Statistical Inference*. New York: Springer.

Wataru, O. 2009. Analytic study on the position and height of rebound balls in basketball. *Human Performance* 6:17–24.

Watkinson, J. 1998. Performance testing for baseball. *Strength & Conditioning Journal* 20 (4):16–20.

Wegener, F. 2014. *The History of Basketball and Volleyball*. GRIN Verlag.

Wegner, M. 2012. *Implicit vs. explicit processes of motivation and affect regulation in unconsciously and consciously critical situations in sports.*

Wells, K. F. and E. K. Dillon 1952. The sit and reach—A test of back and leg flexibility. *Research Quarterly. American Association for Health, Physical Education and Recreation* 23(1):115–118. 23

Welter, J. C. 2013. The Wonderlic Classic Cognitive Ability Test as a Measure of Player Selection and Success for Quarterbacks in the National Football League. Ph.D. thesis, Capella University.

West, B. T. 2006. A simple and flexible rating method for predicting success in the NCAA basketball tournament. *Journal of Quantitative Analysis in Sports* 2(3):1–14.

White, T. D., M. T. Black, and P. A. Folkens 2011. *Human Osteology*. Academic press.

Widmeyer, W. N., L. R. Brawley, and A. V. Carron 1985. *The measurement of cohesion in sport teams: The Group Environment Questionnaire*. Sports Dynamics.

Wierike, S., A. Sluis, I. Akker-Scheek, M. Elferink-Gemser, and C. Visscher 2013. Psychosocial factors influencing the recovery of athletes with anterior cruciate ligament injury: A systematic review. *Scandinavian Journal of Medicine Science in Sports* 23(5): 527–540.

Wikipedia 2015. Glossary of baseball. Retrieved from the World Wide Web on August 29, 2015 at https://en.m.wikipedia.org/wiki/Glossary_of_baseball.

Wilk, K. E., J. R. Andrews, C. A. Arrigo, M. A. Keirns, and D. J. Erber 1993. The strength characteristics of internal and external rotator muscles in professional baseball pitchers. *American Journal of Sports Medicine* 21(1):61–66.

Wilk, K. E., K. Meister, and J. R. Andrews 2002. Current concepts in the rehabilitation of the overhead throwing athlete. *American Journal of Sports Medicine* 30(1):136–151.

Wilk, K. E., P. Obma, C. D. Simpson, E. L. Cain, J. Dugas, and J. R. Andrews 2009. Shoulder injuries in the overhead athlete. *Journal of Orthopaedic & Sports Physical Therapy* 39(2):38–54.

Wilk, K. E. and M. M. Reimold 2004. Specific exercises for the throwing shoulder. *The Shoulder and the Overhead Athlete*:95.

Willardson, J. M. 2007. Core stability training: Applications to sports conditioning programs. *Journal of Strength & Conditioning Research* 21(3):979–985.

Williams, J. D., G. Abt, and A. E. Kilding 2010. Ball-Sport Endurance and Sprint Test (BEAST90): validity and reliability of a 90-minute soccer performance test. *Journal of Strength & Conditioning Research* 24(12):3209–3218.

Williams, C. and C. Wragg 2004. *Data Analysis and Research for Sport and Exercise Science: A Student Guide*. Routledge.

Winkler, P. A. and B. Esses 2011. Platform tilt perturbation as an intervention for people with chronic vestibular dysfunction. *Journal of Neurologic Physical Therapy* 35(3):105–115.

Winston, W. L. 2009. *Mathletics: How Gamblers, Managers, and Sports Enthusiasts Use Mathematics in Baseball, Basketball, and Football*. Princeton, N.J.: Princeton University Press.

Winter, E. M., A. M. Jones, R. C. R. Davison, P. D. Bromley, and T. H. Mercer 2006. *Sport and Exercise Physiology Testing Guidelines: Volume I–Sport Testing: The British Association of Sport and Exercise Sciences Guide*. Routledge.

Wisloeff, U., J. Helgerud, and J. Hoff 1998. Strength and endurance of elite soccer players. *Medicine and Science in Sports and Exercise* 30:462–467.

Wong, P., I. Mujika, C. Castagna, K. Chamari, P. Lau, and U. Wisloff 2008. Characteristics of World Cup Soccer Players.

Woodman, T. and L. Hardy 2003. The relative impact of cognitive anxiety and self-confidence upon sport performance: A meta-analysis. *Journal of Sports Sciences* 21 (6):443–457.

Woods, M. 2009. *Basketball Legends*, Volume 13. Crabtree Publishing Company.

Woods, C., R. Hawkins, M. Hulse, and A. Hodson 2003. The Football Association Medical Research Programme: An audit of injuries in professional football—an analysis of ankle sprains. *British Journal of Sports Medicine* 37(3):233–238.

Woodson, M. 2011. Comparison of bioelectrical impedance analysis instruments and skinfold calipers in the determination of percent body fat in Division I tennis players. *Celebration of Undergraduate Scholarship, Valparaison University* Retrieved from the World Wide Web, December 2015 at `https://mail.google.com/mail/u/0/#inbox/1525425b80d99057?projector=1`.

Wooten, E. P. 1965. The structural base of human movement. *Journal of Health, Physical Education, Recreation* 36(8):59–60.

Worthy, D. A., A. B. Markman, and W. T. Maddox 2009. Choking and excelling at the free throw line. *International Journal of Creativity & Problem Solving* 19(1):53–58.

Wright, A. G., A. L. Pincus, K. M. Thomas, C. J. Hopwood, K. E. Markon, and R. F. Krueger 2013. Conceptions of narcissism and the DSM-5 pathological personality traits. *Assessment*:1073191113486692.

Wright, M. J. and R. C. Jackson 2007. Brain regions concerned with perceptual skills in tennis: An fMRI study. *International Journal of Psychophysiology* 63(2):214–220.

Wughalter, E. H. and J. C. Gondola 1991. Mood states of professional female tennis players. *Perceptual and Motor Skills* 73(1):187–190.

Xiao-an, W. 2009. Analysis on the competitive strength of the offense and defense of Chinese men's basketball team in the 29th Olympics. *Journal of Chengdu Sport University* 9:019.

Xu, S.-X. and X.-P. Liu 2004. Summary of the research on basketball awareness. *Shandong Sports Science Technology* 3:6.

Yaffee, R. A. and M. McGee 2000. *An Introduction to Time Series Analysis and Forecasting: With Applications of SAS® and SPSS®*. Academic Press.

Young, W. and D. Farrow 2006. A review of agility: Practical applications for strength and conditioning. *Strength & Conditioning Journal* 28(5):24–29. 35

Young, W. B., M. H. McDowell, and B. J. Scarlett 2001. Specificity of sprint and agility training methods. *Journal of Strength & Conditioning Research* 15(3):315–319. 35

Zeng, H. Z. 2003. The differences between anxiety and self-confidence between team and individual sports college varsity athletes. *International Sports Journal* 7(1):28.

Zhang, B. 1999. A chi-squared goodness-of-fit test for logistic regression models based on case-control data. *Biometrika* 86(3):531–539.

Zhuina, D. V., V. G. Zazykin, and L. G. Maydokina 2015. Empirical study of the psychology of the winner (on the example of the Republic of Mordovia Athletes). *Modern Applied Science* 9(5):211.

Zupan, M. F., A. W. Arata, L. H. Dawson, A. L. Wile, T. L. Payn, and M. E. Hannon 2009. Wingate anaerobic test peak power and anaerobic capacity classifications for men and women intercollegiate athletes. *Journal of Strength & Conditioning Research* 23(9): 2598–2604.

Index